*There is a legend the Buddha was once
handed a flower and asked to preach on the law.
The story says he received the blossom
without a sound and silently wheeled it in his
hand. Amid the hush his most perceptive follower,
Kashyapa, suddenly burst into a smile . . .
and thus was born the wordless wisdom of Zen.*

This book does not pretend to offer
the gift of Zen. No book could do that. Rather
its purpose is to direct the reader's attention to
where the spirit of Zen has been, to the
path it has followed through history, and to the
extraordinary figures who embodied it. In so doing,
THE ZEN EXPERIENCE does all that a book can do
to offer aid on a search that is as old
as human striving toward enlightenment and as new
as each dawning moment of our lives.

THOMAS HOOVER is the author of *Zen Culture*
and a longtime student of Zen thought. He
lives in New York's Greenwich Village
and has traveled widely in China, Japan, and
India. To trace the *real* story of Zen's
tumultuous creation, he spent several years
researching the lives and original ideas
of its most dynamic masters.

THE ZEN EXPERIENCE

by Thomas Hoover

A PLUME BOOK

NEW AMERICAN LIBRARY

TIMES MIRROR

NEW YORK AND SCARBOROUGH, ONTARIO

Copyright ©1980 by Thomas Hoover

ACKNOWLEDGMENTS

Selections from *Zen and Zen Classics*, Vols. I and II, by R. H. Blyth (Tokyo: The
Hokuseido Press, copyright © 1960, 1964 by R. H. Blyth, copyright © 1978
by Frederick Franck), reprinted by permission of Joan Daves.

Selections from *Cold Mountain* by Han-shan, Burton Watson, trans. (New York:
Columbia University Press, 1970), reprinted by permission of publisher.

Selections from *The Recorded Sayings of Layman Pang*, Ruth Fuller Sasaki et al.,
trans. (New York: John Weatherhill), reprinted by permission of publisher.

Selections from *Anthology of Chinese Literature*, Cyril Birch, ed., Gary Snyder,
trans. (New York: Grove Press, copyright © 1965 by Grove Press), reprinted
by permission of publisher.

Selections from *Tao: A New Way of Thinking* by Chang Chung-yuan, (New York:
Harper & Row, Perennial Library, copyright © 1975 by Chang Chung-yuan),
reprinted by permission of publisher.

Selection from *A History of Zen Buddhism* by Heinrich S. J. Dumoulin, Paul
Peachey, trans. (New York: Pantheon Books, 1962), reprinted by permission
of publisher.

Selection by Ikkyu from *Some Japanese Portraits* by Donald Keene (Tokyo:
Kodansha International, 1979), reprinted by permission of author.

Selections from *Essays in Zen Buddhism* by D. T. Suzuki (New York: Grove
Press), reprinted by permission of publisher.

Selection from *The Sutra of Hui-neng*, Price and Wong, trans. (Boulder:
Shambala Publications), reprinted by permission of publisher.

Selections from *The Platform Sutra of the Sixth Patriarch*, Philip Yamplosky,
trans. (New York: Columbia University Press), reprinted by permission of
publisher.

Selections from *The Zen Master Hakuin* by Philip Yamplosky (New York:
Columbia University Press, 1971), reprinted by permission of publisher.

Selections from *The Golden Age of Zen* by John C. H. Wu (Taipei, Taiwan:
Hwakang Book Store), reprinted by permission of author.

Selections from *The Zen Teaching of the Hui Hai on Sudden Illumination* by
John Blofeld (New York: Samuel Weiser, 1972), reprinted by permission of
publisher.

Selections from *Zen Master Dogen* by Yoho Yukoi (New York: John Weatherhill),
reprinted by permission of publisher.

Selections from *Original Teachings of Ch'an Buddhism* by Chang Chung-yuan
(New York: Vintage, 1969), reprinted by permission of publisher.

Selections from *Swampland Flowers* by Christopher Cleary (New York: Grove
Press, copyright © 1977 by Christopher Cleary), reprinted by permission of
publisher.

(The following page is an extension of this copyright page.)

PLUME TRADEMARK REG. U.S. PAT. OFF. AND FOREIGN COUNTRIES
REGISTERED TRADEMARK—MARCA REGISTRADA
HECHO EN FORGE VILLAGE, MASS., U.S.A.

SIGNET, SIGNET CLASSICS, MENTOR, PLUME, MERIDIAN AND NAL BOOKS
are published in the United States by The New American Library, Inc.,
1633 Broadway, New York, New York 10019,
in Canada by The New American Library of Canada Limited,
81 Mack Avenue, Scarborough, Ontario M1L 1M8

First Printing, March, 1980

1 2 3 4 5 6 7 8 9

PRINTED IN THE UNITED STATES OF AMERICA

Library of Congress Cataloging in Publication Data
Hoover, Thomas, 1941-
   The Zen Experience.

   Bibliography: p.
   Includes index.
   1. Zen Buddhism—History. 2. Priests, Zen—Biography. I. Title.
BQ9262.3.H66   294.3'927'09   79-24119
ISBN 0-452-25228-8

ACKNOWLEDGMENTS

Heartfelt thanks go to Julie Hoover, who critically edited the manuscript at all stages; to Lynne Grifo, for thoughtful advice on Zen practice; and to Marylou Rinelli, for assistance in all seasons of production. Special thanks are also due Dr. Philip Yampolsky of Columbia University, who reviewed the manuscript in draft and clarified many points of fact and interpretation. I also am indebted to the works of a number of Zen interpreters for the West, including D. T. Suzuki, John Blofeld, Chang Chung-yuan, and Charles Luk. In cases where this finger pointing at the moon mistakenly aims astray, I alone am responsible.

The sole aim of Zen is to enable one to understand, realize, and perfect his own mind.

—Garma C. C. Chang

CONTENTS

THE ZEN
EXPERIENCE

Lao Tzu, Buddha, and Confucius. Kano Mitsuyori
(active ca. 1750–1800). Private collection.

PREFACE TO ZEN

Some call it "seeing," some call it "knowing," and some describe it in religious terms. Whatever the name, it is our reach for a new level of consciousness. Of the many forms this search has taken, perhaps the most intriguing is Zen. Growing out of the wisdom of China, India, and Japan, Zen became a powerful movement to explore the lesser-known reaches of the human mind. Today Zen has come westward, where we are rediscovering modern significance in its ancient insights. This book is an attempt to encounter Zen in its purest form, by returning to the greatest Zen masters.

Zen teachings often appear deceptively simple. This misconception is compounded by the Zen claim that explanations are meaningless. They *are*, of course, but merely because genuine Zen insights can arise only from individual experience. And although our experience can be described and even analyzed, it cannot be transmitted or shared. At most, the "teachings" of Zen can only clear the way to our deeper consciousness. The rest is up to us.

Zen is based on the recognition of two incompatible types of thought: rational and intuitive. Rationality employs language, logic, reason. Its precepts can be taught. Intuitive knowledge, however, is different. It lurks embedded in our consciousness, beyond words. Unlike rational thought, intuition cannot be "taught" or even turned on. In fact, it is impossible to find or manipulate this intuitive consciousness using our rational mind—any more than we can grasp our own hand or see our own eye.

The Zen masters devised ways to reach this repressed area of human consciousness. Some of their techniques—like meditation—were borrowed from Indian Buddhism, and some—like their antirational paradoxes—may have been learned from Chinese Taoists. But other inventions, like their jarring shouts and blows, emerged from their own experience. Throughout it all, however, their words and actions were only a means, never an end.

That end is an intuitive realization of a single great insight—that we and the world around are one, both part of a larger encompassing absolute. Our rational intellect merely obscures this truth, and consequently we must shut it off, if only for a moment. Rationality constrains our mind; intuition releases it.

The irony is that the person glimpsing this moment of higher consciousness, this Oneness, encounters the ultimate realization that there is nothing to realize. The world is still there, unchanged. But the difference is that it is now an extension of our consciousness, seen directly and not analytically. And since it is redundant to be attached to something already a part of you, there is a sudden sense of freedom from our agonizing bondage to things.

Along with this also comes release from the constraints of artificial values. Creating systems and categories is not unlike counting the colors of a rainbow—both merely detract from our experience of reality, while at the same time limiting our appreciation of the world's richness. And to declare something right or wrong is similarly nearsighted. As Alan Watts once observed, "Zen unveils behind the urgent realm of good and evil a vast region of oneself about which there need be no guilt or recrimination, where at last the self is indistinguishable from God." And, we might add, where God is also one with our consciousness, our self. In Zen all dualities dissolve, absorbed in the larger reality that simply is.

None of these things are taught explicitly in Zen. Instead they are discovered waiting in our consciousness after all else has been swept away. A scornful twelfth-century Chinese scholar summarized the Zen method as follows: "Since the Zen masters never run the risk of explaining anything in plain language, their followers must do their own pondering and puzzling—from which a real threshing-out results." In these pages we will watch the threshing-out of Zen itself—as its masters unfold a new realm of consciousness, the Zen experience.

TAOISM: THE WAY TO ZEN

Taoism is the original religion of ancient China. It is founded on the idea that a fundamental principle, the Tao, underlies all nature.

Long before the appearance of Zen, Taoists were teaching the superiority of intuitive thought, using an anti-intellectualism that often ridiculed the logic-bound limitations of conventional Chinese life and letters. However, Taoism was always upbeat and positive in its acceptance of reality, a quality that also rubbed off on Zen over the centuries. Furthermore, many Taoist philosophers left writings whose world view seems almost Zenlike. The early Chinese teachers of meditation (called *dhyana* in Sanskrit and Ch'an in Chinese) absorbed the Taoist tradition of intuitive wisdom, and later Zen masters often used Taoist expressions. It is fitting, therefore, that we briefly meet some of the most famous teachers of Chinese Taoism.

LAO TZU

One of the most influential figures in ancient Chinese lore is remembered today merely as Lao Tzu (Venerable Master). Taoist legends report he once disputed (and bettered) the scholarly Confucius, but that he finally despaired of the world and rode an oxcart off into the west, pausing at the Han-ku Pass—on the insistence of its keeper—to set down his insights in a five-thousand-character poem. This work, the *Tao Te Ching* (The Way and the Power), was an eloquent, organized, and lyrical statement of an important point of view in China of the sixth century B.C., an understanding later to become an essential element of Ch'an Buddhism.

The word "Tao" means many, many things—including the *élan vital* or life force of the universe, the harmonious structuring of human affairs, and—perhaps most important—a reality transcending words. Taoists declared there is a knowledge not accessible by language. As the *Tao Te Ching* announces in its opening line, "The Tao that can be put into words is not the real Tao."

Also fundamental to the Tao is the unity of mind and matter, of the one who knows and the thing known. The understanding of a truth and the truth itself cannot be separated. The Tao includes and unifies these into a larger "reality" encompassing both. The notion that our knowledge is distinguishable from that known is an illusion.

Another teaching of the *Tao Te Ching* is that intuitive insight surpasses rational analysis. When we act on our spontaneous judgment, we are almost always better off. Chapter 19 declares, "Let the people be free from discernment and relinquish intellection . . . Hold to one's original nature . . . Eliminate artificial learning and one will be free from anxieties."[1] The wise defer to a realm of insight floating in our mind beyond its conscious state.

Taoists also questioned the value of social organization, holding that the best government is the one governing least and that "the wise deal with things through non-interference and teach through no-words."[2] Taoists typically refused to draw value judgments on others' behavior. Lao Tzu asks, "What is the difference between good and bad?"[3] and concludes, "Goodness often turns out to be evil."[4] There is complete acceptance of what is, with no desire to make things "better." Lao Tzu believed "good" and "bad" were both part of Tao and therefore, "Even if a man is unworthy, Tao will never exclude him."[5] If all things are one, there can be no critical differentiation of any part. This concentration on inner perception, to the exclusion of practical concerns, evoked a criticism from the third-century-B.C. Confucian philosopher Hsun Tzu that has a curiously modern ring of social consciousness. "Lao Tzu understood looking inward, but knew nothing of looking outward. . . . If there is merely inward-looking and never outward-looking, there can be no distinction between what has value and what has not, between what is precious and what is vile, between what is noble and what is vulgar."[6] But the refusal of Lao Tzu to intellectualize what is natural or to sit in judgment over the world was the perfect Chinese precedent for Ch'an.

CHUANG TZU

The second important figure in Taoism is the almost equally legendary teacher remembered as Chuang Tzu, who is usually placed in the fourth century B.C., some two centuries after Lao Tzu. An early historian tells that once Chuang Tzu was invited to the court to serve as a minister, an invitation he declined with a typical story: An ox is selected for a festival and fattened up for several years, living the life of wealth and indulgence—until the day he is led away for sacrifice. At that reckoning what would he give to return to the simple life, where there was poverty but also freedom?

In Chuang Tzu's own book of wisdom, he also derided the faith in rationality common to Chinese scholars. To emphasize his point he devised a vehicle for assaulting the apparatus of logic—that being a "nonsense" story whose point could only be understood intuitively., There has yet to be found a more deadly weapon against pompous intellectualizing, as the Ch'an Buddhists later proved with the koan. Chuang Tzu also knew how quickly comedy could deflate, and he used it with consummate skill, again paving the way for the absurdist Zen masters. In fact, his dialogues often anticipate the Zen mondo, the exchanges between master and pupil that have comic/straight-man overtones.

In this regard, Chuang Tzu also sometimes anticipates twentieth-century writers for the Theater of the Absurd, such as Beckett or Ionesco. Significantly, the Columbia scholar Burton Watson suggests that the most fruitful path to Chuang Tzu "is not to attempt to subject his thoughts to rational and systematic analysis, but to read and reread his words until one has ceased to think of what he is saying and instead has developed an intuitive sense of the mind moving beyond the words, and of the world in which it moves."[7] This is undoubtedly true. The effect of comic parody on logic is so telling that the only way to really understand the message is to stop trying to "understand" it.

Concerning the limitations of verbal transmission, Chuang Tzu tells a story of a wheelmaker who once advised his duke that the book of ancient thought the man was reading was "nothing but the lees and scum of bygone men." The duke angrily demanded an explanation—and received a classic defense of the superiority of intuitive understanding over language and logic.

I look at the matter in this way; when I am making a wheel, if my stroke is too slow, then it bites deep but is not steady; if my stroke is too fast, then it is steady, but does not go deep. The right pace, neither slow nor fast, cannot get into the hand unless it comes from the heart. It is a thing that cannot be put into words; there is an art in it that I cannot explain to my son. That is why it is impossible for me to let him take over my work, and here I am at the age of seventy, still making wheels. In my opinion, it must have been the same with the men of old. All that was worth handing on died with them; the rest, they put into their books.[8]

Chuang Tzu's parable that perhaps best illustrates the Taoist ideal concerns a cook who had discovered one lives best by following nature's rhythms. The cook explained that his naturalness was easy after he learned to let intuition guide his actions. This approach he called practicing the Tao, but it is in fact the objective of Zen practice as well.

Prince Wen Hui remarked, "How wonderfully you have mastered your art." The cook laid down his knife and said,

"What your servant really cares for is Tao, which goes beyond mere art. When I first began to cut up oxen, I saw nothing but oxen. After three years of practicing, I no longer saw the ox as a whole. I now work with my spirit, not with my eyes. My senses stop functioning and my spirit takes over."[9]

What he described is the elimination of the rational mind, which he refers to as the senses, and the reliance upon the intuitive part of his mind, here called the spirit. He explained how this intuitive approach allowed him to work naturally.

A good cook changes his knife once a year because he cuts, while a mediocre cook has to change his every month because he hacks. I've had this knife of mine for nineteen years and have cut up thousands of oxen with it, and yet the edge is as if it were fresh from the grindstone. There are spaces between the joints. The blade of the knife has no thickness. That which has no thickness has plenty of room to pass through these spaces. Therefore, after nineteen years, my blade is as sharp as ever.[10]

Lao Tzu and Chuang Tzu did not see themselves as founders of any formal religion. They merely described the obvious, encouraging others to be a part of nature and not its antagonist. Their movement, now called Philosophical Taoism, was eclipsed during the Han Dynasty (206 B.C.–A.D. 220) in official circles by various other systems of thought, most particularly Confucianism (which stressed obedience to authority—both that of elders and of superiors—and reverence for formalized learning, not to mention the acceptance of a structured hierarchy as part of one's larger social responsibility). However, toward the end of the Han era there arose two new types of Taoism: an Esoteric Taoism that used physical disciplines to manipulate consciousness, and a Popular Taoism that came close to being a religion in the traditional mold. The first was mystical Esoteric Taoism, which pursued the prolonging of life and vigor, but this gave way during later times to Popular Taoism, a metaphysical alternative to the comfortless, arid Confucianism of the scholarly establishment.

The post-Han era saw the Philosophical Taoism of Lao Tzu and Chuang Tzu emerge anew among Chinese intellectuals, actually coming to vie with Confucianism. This whole era witnessed a turning away from the accepted values of society, as the well-organized government of the Han era dissolved into political and intellectual confusion. Government was unstable and corrupt, and the Confucianism which had been its philosophical under-pinning was stilted and unsatisfying. Whenever a society breaks down, the belief system supporting it naturally comes under question. This happened in China in the third and fourth centuries of the Christian era, and from it emerged a natural opposition to Confucianism. One form of this opposition was the imported religion of Buddhism, which provided a spiritual solace missing in the teachings of Confucius, while the other was a revival among intellectuals of Philosophical Taoism.

KUO HSIANG: A NEO-TAOIST

In this disruptive environment, certain intellectuals returned again to the insights of Lao Tzu and Chuang Tzu, creating a movement today known as Neo-Taoism. One of the thinkers who tried to reinterpret original Taoist ideas for the new times was Kuo Hsiang (d. ca. 312), who co-authored a major document of Neo-Taoism entitled *Commentary on the Chuang Tzu*. It focused on the important Taoist idea of *wu-wei*, once explained as follows: " . . . to them the key concept of Taoism, *wu* (literally, nonexistence), is not nothingness, but pure being, which transcends forms and names, and precisely because it is absolute and complete, can accomplish everything. The sage is not one who withdraws into the life of a hermit, but a man of social and political achievements, although these achievements must be brought about through *wu-wei*, 'nonaction' or 'taking no [unnatural] action.' "[11]

This concept of *wu-wei* has also been described as abstaining from activity contrary to nature and acting in a spontaneous rather than calculated fashion. In Kuo Hsiang's words:

> Being natural means to exist spontaneously without having to take any action. . . . By taking no action is not meant folding one's arms and closing one's mouth. If we simply let everything act by itself, it will be contented with its nature and destiny.[12]

Kuo Hsiang's commentary expanded on almost all the major ideas of Chuang Tzu, drawing out with logic what originally had been set in absurdism. Criticizing this, a later Ch'an monk observed, "People say Kuo Hsiang wrote a commentary on Chuang Tzu. I would say it was Chuang Tzu who wrote a commentary on Kuo Hsiang."[13] Nonetheless, the idea of *wu-wei*, processed through Buddhism, emerged in different guise in later Ch'an, influencing the concept of "no-mind."

THE SEVEN SAGES OF THE BAMBOO GROVE

Other Chinese were content merely to live the ideas of Neo-Taoism. Among these were the Seven Sages of the Bamboo Grove, men part of a larger movement known as the School of Pure Conversation. Their favorite pastime was to gather north of Loyang on the estate of one of their members, where they engaged in refined conversation, wrote poetry and music, and (not incidentally) drank wine. To some extent they reflected the recluse ideal of old, except that they found the satisfaction of the senses no impediment to introspection. What they did forswear, however, was the world of getting and spending. Although men of distinction, they rejected fame, ambition, and worldly station.

There is a story that one of the Seven Sages, a man named Liu Ling (ca. 221–330), habitually received guests while completely naked. His response to adverse comment was to declare, "I take the whole universe as my house and my own room as my clothing. Why, then, do you enter here into my trousers."[14]

It is also told that two of the sages (Juan Chi, 210–63, and his nephew Juan Hsien) often sat drinking with their family in such conviviality that they skipped the nuisance of cups and just drank directly from a wine bowl on the ground. When pigs wandered by, these too were invited to sip from the same chalice. If one exempts all nature—including pigs—from distinction, discrimination, and duality, why exclude them as drinking companions?

But perhaps the most significant insight of the Seven Sages of the Bamboo Grove was their recognition of the limited uses of language. We are told, "They engaged in conversation 'til, as they put it, they reached the Unnameable, and 'stopped talking and silently understood each other with a smile.' "[15]

THE BUDDHIST ROOTS OF ZEN

There is a legend the Buddha was once handed a flower and asked to preach on the law. The story says he received the blossom without a sound and silently wheeled it in his hand. Then amid the hush his most perceptive follower, Kashyapa, suddenly burst into a smile . . . and thus was born the wordless wisdom of Zen.

The understanding of this silent insight was passed down

through the centuries, independent of the scriptures, finally emerging as the Chinese school of Ch'an, later called Zen by the Japanese. It is said the absence of early writings about the school is nothing more than would be expected of a teaching which was, by definition, beyond words. The master Wen-yu summed it up when he answered a demand for the First Principle of Ch'an with, "If words could tell you, it would become the Second Principle."

This version of Zen's origin is satisfying, and for all we know it may even be true. But there are other, considerably more substantive, sources for the ideas that came to flower as Ch'an. Taoism, of course, had plowed away at the Confucianist clutter restraining the Chinese mind, but it was Buddhism that gave China the necessary new philosophical structure—this being the metaphysical speculations of India. Pure Chinese naturalism met Indian abstraction, and the result was Ch'an. The school of Ch'an was in part the grafting of fragile foreign ideas (Buddhism) onto a sturdy native species of understanding (Taoism). But its simplicity was in many ways a reexpression of the Buddha's original insights.

THE BUDDHA

The historic Buddha was born to the high-caste family Gautama during the sixth century B.C. in the region that is today northeast India and Nepal. After a childhood and youth of indulgence he turned to asceticism and for over half a decade rigorously followed the traditional Indian practices of fasting and meditation, only finally to reject these in despair. However, an auspicious dream and one final meditation at last brought total enlightenment. Gautama the seeker had become Buddha the Enlightened, and he set out to preach.

It was not gods that concerned him, but the mind of man and its sorrowing. We are unhappy, he explained, because we are slaves to our desires. Extinguish desire and suffering goes with it. If people could be taught that the physical or phenomenal world is illusion, then they would cease their attachment to it, thereby finding release from their self-destructive mental bondage.

The Buddha neglected to set down these ideas in written form however, perhaps unwisely leaving this task to later generations. His teachings subsequently were recreated in the form of sermons or sutras. In later years, the Buddhist movement split into two separate philosophical camps, known today as Theravada and Mahayana. The Theravada Buddhists—found primarily in southeast Asia, Sri Lanka, and Burma—venerate the early writings of Buddhism (known today as the Pali Canon) and tend to content themselves with practicing the philosophy of the Buddha rather than enlarging upon it with speculative commentaries. By contrast, the followers of Mahayana—who include the bulk of all Buddhists in China, Japan, and Tibet—left the simple prescriptions of the Buddha far behind in their creation of a vast new literature (in Sanskrit, Tibetan, and Chinese) of complex theologies. Chinese Ch'an grew out of Mahayana, as of course did Japanese Zen.

NAGARJUNA

After the Buddha, perhaps the most important Buddhist figure is the second-century A.D. Indian philosopher Nagarjuna. Some call him the most important thinker Asia has produced. According to Tibetan legends his parents sent him away from home at seven because an astrologer had predicted his early death and they wished to be spared the sight. But he broke the spell by entering Buddhist orders, and went on to become the faith's foremost philosopher.

Today Nagarjuna is famous for his analysis of the so-called Wisdom Books of Mahayana, a set of Sanskrit sutras composed between 100 B.C. and A.D. 100. (Included in this category are *The Perfection of Wisdom in 8,000 Lines,* as well as the Diamond Sutra and Heart Sutra, both essential scriptures of Zen.) Nagarjuna was the originator of the Middle Path, so named because it strove to define a middle ground between affirmation of the world and complete negation of existence.

Reality, said Nagarjuna, cannot be realized through conceptual constructions, since concepts are contained inside reality, not vice versa. Consequently, only through the intuitive mind can reality be approached. His name for this "reality" beyond the mind's analysis was *sunyata,* usually translated as "emptiness" but sometimes as "the Void." (Sunyata is perhaps an unprovable concept, but so too are the ego and the unconscious, both hypothetical constructs useful in explaining reality but impossible to locate on the operating table.) Nagarjuna's most-quoted manifesto has the logic-defying ring of a Zen koan: "Nothing comes into existence nor does anything disappear. Nothing is eternal, nor has anything any end. Nothing is identical or differentiated. Nothing moves hither and thither."

As the Ch'an teachers interpreted the teaching of *sunyata,* the things of this world are all a mental creation, since external phenomena are transient and only exist for us because of our perception. Consequently they are actually "created" by our mind (or, if you will, a more universal entity called Mind). Consequently they do not exist outside our mind and hence are a void. Yet the mind itself, which is the only thing real, is also a void since its thoughts cannot be located by the five senses. The Void is therefore everything, since it includes both the world and the mind. Hence, *sunyata*.

As a modern Nagarjuna scholar has described *sunyata*, or emptiness, it is a positive sense of freedom, not a deprivation. "This awareness of 'emptiness' is not a blank loss of consciousness, an inanimate space; rather it is the cognition of daily life without the attachment to it. It is an awareness of distinct entities, of the self, of 'good' and 'bad' and other practical determinations; but it is aware of these as empty structures."[16] The Zen masters found ways to achieve the cognition without attachment postulated by Nagarjuna, and they paid him homage by making him one of the legendary twenty-eight Indian Patriarchs of Zen by posthumous decree.

KUMARAJIVA

The Indian missionary who transmitted the idea of Emptiness to China was Kumarajiva (344–413), a swashbuckling guru who, more than any other individual, was responsible for planting sophisticated Mahayana Buddhist ideas in Chinese soil. Before telling his story, however, it may be well to reflect briefly on how Buddhism got to China in the first place.

Although there are records of a Buddhist missionary in China as early as A.D. 148, historians are hard pressed to find the name of an out-and-out native Chinese Buddhist before sometime in the third century. Buddhism, which at first apparently was confused with Taoism, seems to have come into fashion after the Neo-Taoists ran out of creative steam. Shortly thereafter, around A.D. 209, intelligible Chinese translations of Indian Mahayana sutras finally began to become available.

There were many things about Buddhism, however, that rubbed Chinese the wrong way. First there were the practical matters: Buddhism allowed, if not encouraged, begging, celibacy, and neglect of ancestors—all practices to rankle any traditional Chinese. Then there were fundamental philosophical differences: Buddhism offered to break one out of the Hindu cycle of rebirth, something the Chinese had not realized they needed; and Indian thought was naturally geared to cosmic time, with its endless cycles of eons, whereas the Chinese saw time as a line leading back to identifiable ancestors. Early missionaries tried to gain acceptability for Buddhism by explaining it in Taoist terms, including stretching the two enough to find "matching concepts" or ideas with superficial similarity, and they also let out the myth that the Buddha was actually Lao Tzu, who had gone on to India after leaving China.

When barbarians sacked the Northern Chinese center of Loyang in the year 313 and took over North China's government, many of its influential Confucianist scholars fled to the south. These émigrés were disillusioned with the social ideas of Confucianism and ready for a solace of the spirit. Thus they turned for comfort to Buddhist ideas, but using Neo-Taoist terminology and often treating Buddhism more as a subject for salon speculations than as a religion. By translating Buddhism into a Neo-Taoist framework, these southern intellectuals effectively avoided having to grapple with the new ideas in Buddhist metaphysics.

In North China, the Buddhists took advantage of the new absence of competing Confucianists to move into ruling circles and assume the role of the literate class. They preached a simple form of Buddhism, often shamelessly dwelling on magic and incantations to arouse interest among the greatest number of followers. The common people were drawn to Buddhism, since it provided for the first time in China a religion that seemed to care for people's suffering, their personal growth, their salvation in an afterlife. Thus Buddhism took hold in North China mainly because it provided hope and magic for the masses and a political firewall against Confucianism for the new rulers. As late as the beginning of the fifth century, therefore, Buddhism was misunderstood and encouraged for the wrong reasons in both north and south.

Kumarajiva, who would change all this, was born in Kucha to an Indian father of the Brahmin caste and a mother of noble blood. When he was seven he and his mother traveled to Kashmir to enter Buddhist orders together. After several years of studying the Theravada sutras, he moved on to Kashgar, where he turned his attention to Mahayana philosophy. At age twenty we find him back in Kucha, being ordained in the king's palace and sharpening his understanding of the Mahayana scriptures. He also, we are told, sharpened his non-Buddhist amorous skills, perhaps finding consolation in the illusory world of the senses for the hollow emptiness of *sunyata*.

In the year 382 or 383, he was taken captive and removed to a remote area in northeastern China, where he was held prisoner for almost two decades, much to the dismay of the rulers in Ch'ang-an, who wanted nothing more than to have this teacher (who was by then a famous Buddhist scholar) for their own. After seventeen years their patience ran out and they sent an army to defeat his recalcitrant captors and bring him back. He arrived in Ch'ang-an in the year 401 and immediately began a project crucial to the future of Chinese Buddhism. A modern scholar of Chinese religion tells what happened next. ". . . Chinese monks were assembled from far and near to work with him in translating the sacred texts. This was a 'highly structured project,' suggestive of the cooperative enterprises of scientists today. There were corps of specialists at all levels: those who discussed doctrinal questions with Kumarajiva, those who checked the new translations against the old and imperfect ones, hundreds of editors, subeditors, and copyists. The quality and quantity of the translations produced by these men in the space of eight years is truly astounding. Thanks to their efforts the ideas of Mahayana Buddhism were presented in Chinese with far greater clarity and precision than ever before. Sunyata—Nagarjuna's concept of the Void—was disentangled from the Taoist terminology that had obscured and distorted it, and this and other key doctrines of Buddhism were made comprehensible enough to lay the intellectual foundations of the great age of independent Chinese Buddhism that was to follow."[17]

The Chinese rulers contrived to put Kumarajiva's other devotion to use as well, installing a harem of ten beautiful young Chinese girls for him, through whom he was encouraged to perpetuate a lineage of his own. This genetic experiment apparently came to nothing, but two native Chinese studying under him, Seng-chao (384–414) and Tao-sheng (ca. 360–434), would carry his contribution through the final steps needed to open the way for the development of Ch'an.

SENG-CHAO

The short-lived Seng-chao was born to a humble family in the Ch'ang-an region, where he reportedly got his indispensable grounding in the Chinese classics by working as a copyist. He originally was a confirmed Taoist, but after reading the sutra of Vimalakirti (which described a pious nobleman who combined the secular life of a bon vivant businessman with an inner existence of Buddhist enlightenment, a combination instantly attractive to the practical Chinese), Seng-chao turned Buddhist. In the year 398, at age fifteen, he traveled to the northwest to study personally under the famous Kumarajiva, and he later returned to Ch'ang-an with the master.

Conversant first in the Taoist and then in the Buddhist classics, Seng-chao began the real synthesis of the two that would eventually evolve into Ch'an. The China scholar Walter Liebenthal has written that the doctrine of Nagarjuna's Middle Path, sinicized by Seng-chao, emerged in the later Ch'an thinkers cleansed of the traces of Indian origin. He declares, "Seng-chao interpreted Mahayana, [the Ch'an founders] Hui-neng and Shen-hui re-thought it."[18]

Three of Seng-chao's treatises exist today as the Book of Chao (or Chao Lun), and they give an idea of how Chuang Tzu might have written had he been a Buddhist. There is the distrust of words, the unmistakable preference for immediate, intuitive knowledge, and the masterful use of wordplay and paradox that leaves his meaning ambiguous. Most important of all, he believed that truth had to be experienced, not reasoned out. Truth was what lay behind words; it should never be confused with the words themselves:

> A thing called up by a name may not appear as what it is expected to appear; a name calling up a thing may not lead to the real thing. Therefore the sphere of Truth is beyond the noise of verbal teaching. How then can it be made the subject of discussion? Still I cannot remain silent.[19]

The dean of Zen scholars, Heinrich Dumoulin, declares, "The relationship of Seng-chao to Zen is to be found in his orientation toward the immediate and experiential perception of absolute truth, and reveals itself in his preference for the paradox as the means of expressing the inexpressible."[20] Dumoulin also notes that the Book of Chao regards the way to enlightenment as one of gradual progress. However, the idea that truth can be approached gradually was disputed by the other major pupil of Kumarajiva, whose insistence that enlightenment must arrive instantaneously has caused some to declare him the ideological founder of Zen.

TAO-SHENG

The famous Tao-sheng was the first Chinese Buddhist to advance the idea of "sudden" enlightenment, and as a result he earned the enmity of his immediate colleagues—and lasting fame as having anticipated one of the fundamental innovations of Zen thought. He first studied Buddhism at Lu-shan, but in 405 he moved to Ch'ang-an, becoming for a while a part of the coterie surrounding Kumarajiva. None of his writings survive, but the work of a colleague, Hui-yuan, is usually taken as representative of his ideas.

Tao-sheng is known today for two theories. The first was that good deeds do not automatically bring reward, a repudiation of the Indian Buddhist concept of merit. The other, and perhaps more important, deviation he preached was that enlightenment was instantaneous. The reason, he said, was simple: since Buddhists say the world is one, nothing is divisible, even truth, and therefore the subjective understanding of truth must come all at once or not at all. Preparatory work and progress toward the goal of enlightenment, including study and meditation, could proceed step-by-step and are wholesome and worthwhile, but to "reach the other shore," as the phrase in the Heart Sutra describes enlightenment, requires a leap over a gulf, a realization that must hit you with all its force the first time.

What exactly is it that you understand on the other shore? First you come to realize—as you can only realize intuitively and directly—that enlightenment was within you all along. You become enlightened when you finally recognize that you already had it. The next realization is that there actually is no "other shore," since reaching it means realizing that there was nothing to reach. As his thoughts have been quoted: "As to reaching the other shore, if one reaches it, one is not reaching the other shore. Both not-reaching and not-not-reaching are really reaching. . . . If one sees Buddha, one is not seeing Buddha. When one sees there is no Buddha, one is really seeing Buddha."[21]

Little wonder Tao-sheng is sometimes credited as the spiritual father of Zen. He championed the idea of sudden enlightenment, something inimical to much of the Buddhism that had gone before, and he distrusted words (comparing them to a net which, after it has caught the fish of truth, should be discarded). He identified the Taoist idea of *wu-wei* or "nonaction" with the intuitive, spontaneous apprehension of truth without logic, opening the door for the Ch'an mainstay of "no-mind" as a way to ultimate truth.

THE SYNTHESIS

Buddhism has always maintained a skeptical attitude toward reality and appearances, something obviously at odds with the wholehearted celebration of nature that characterizes Taoism. Whereas Buddhism believes it would be best if we could simply ignore the world, the source of our psychic pain, the Taoists wanted nothing so much as to have complete union with this same world. Buddhism teaches union with the Void, while Taoism teaches union with the Tao. At first they seem opposite directions. But the synthesis of these doctrines appeared in Zen, which taught that the oneness of the Void, wherein all reality is subsumed, could be understood as an encompassing whole or continuum, as in the Tao. Both are merely expressions of the Absolute. The Buddhists unite with the Void; the Taoists yearn to merge with the Tao. In Zen the two ideas reconcile.

With this philosophical prelude in place, we may now turn to the masters who created the world of Zen.

PART I

THE EARLY MASTERS

. . . in which a sixth-century Indian teacher
of meditation, Bodhidharma, arrives in China to initiate what
would become a Buddhist school of meditation called Ch'an.
After several generations as wanderers, these Ch'an
teachers settle into a form of monastic life and gradually
grow in prominence and recognition. Out of this prosperity
emerges a split in the eighth-century Ch'an movement,
between scholarly urban teachers who believe enlightenment
is "gradual" and requires preparation in traditional
Buddhism, and rural Ch'anists who scorn society and insist
enlightenment is experiential and "sudden," owing little to the
prosperous Buddhist establishment. Then a popular teacher
of rural Ch'an, capitalizing on a civil disruption
that momentarily weakens the urban elite, gains the upper
hand and emasculates urban Ch'an through his preaching that the
authentic line of teaching must be traced to an obscure
teacher in the rural south, now remembered as the
Sixth Patriarch, Hui-neng.

Bodhidharma. Bokkei (fifteenth century).
Courtesy of Daitoku-ji, Kyoto.

1
BODHIDHARMA:
FIRST PATRIARCH
OF ZEN

There is a Zen legend that a bearded Indian monk named Bodhidharma (ca. 470–532), son of a South Indian Brahmin king, appeared one day at the southern Chinese port city of Canton, sometime around the year 520. From there he traveled northeast to Nanking, near the mouth of the Yangtze River, to honor an invitation from China's most devout Buddhist, Emperor Wu of the Liang Dynasty. After a famous interview in which his irreverence left the emperor dismayed, Bodhidharma pressed onward to the Buddhist centers of the north, finally settling in at the Shao-lin monastery on Mt. Sung for nine years of meditation staring at a wall. He then transmitted his insights and a copy of the Lankavatara sutra to a successor and passed on—either physically, spiritually, or both. His devotion to meditation and to the aforementioned sutra were his legacies to China. He was later honored as father of the Chinese Dhyana, or "Meditation," school of Buddhism, called Ch'an.

Bodhidharma attracted little notice during his years in China, and the first historical account of his life is a brief mention in a chronicle compiled well over a hundred years after the fact, identifying him merely as a practitioner of meditation. However, later stories of his life became increasingly embellished, as he was slowly elevated to the office of First Patriarch of Chinese Ch'an. His life was made to fulfill admirably the requirements of a legend, as it was slowly enveloped in symbolic anecdotes illustrating the truth more richly than did mere fact.

However, most scholars do agree that there actually was a Bodhidharma, that he was a South Indian who came to China, that he practiced an intensive form of meditation, and that a short treatise ascribed to him is probably more or less authentic. Although the legend attached to this unshaven Indian Buddhist tells us fully as much about early Ch'an as it does about the man himself, it is nonetheless the first page in the book of Zen.

> [Bodhidharma], the Teacher of the Law, was the third son of a great Brahmin king in South India, of the Western Lands. He was a man of wonderful intelligence, bright and far-reaching; he thoroughly understood everything that he had ever learned. As his ambition was to master the doctrine of the Mahayana, he abandoned the white dress of a layman and put on the black robe of monkhood, wishing to cultivate the seeds of holiness. He practised contemplation and tranquillization; he knew well what was the true significance of worldly affairs. Inside and outside he was transpicuous; his virtues were more than a model to the world. He was grieved very much over the decline of the orthodox teaching of the Buddha in the remoter parts of the earth. He finally made up his mind to cross over land and sea and come to China and preach his doctrine in the kingdom of Wei.[1]

China at the time of Bodhidharma's arrival was a politically divided land, with the new faith of Buddhism often supplying a spiritual common denominator. Bodhidharma happened to appear at a moment when an emperor in the northwest, the aforementioned Wu (reigned 502–49), had become a fanatic Buddhist. Shortly after taking power, Wu actually ordered his imperial household and all associated with the court to take up Buddhism and abandon Taoism. Buddhist monks became court advisers, opening the imperial coffers to build many lavish and subsequently famous temples.

Emperor Wu led Buddhist assemblies, wrote learned commentaries on various sutras, and actually donated menial work at temples as a lay devotee. He also arranged to have all the Chinese commentaries on the sutras assembled and catalogued. Concerned about the sanctity of life, he banished meat (and wine) from the imperial table and became so lax about enforcing criminal statutes, particularly capital punishment, that critics credited his good nature with an increase in corruption and lawlessness. While the Taoists understandably hated him and the Confucianists branded him a distracted ineffectual sovereign, the Buddhists saw in him a model emperor. Quite simply, Emperor Wu was to southern Chinese Buddhism what Emperor Constantine was to Christianity.

The emperor was known for his hospitality to visiting Indian monks, and it is entirely possible he did invite Bodhidharma for an audience.[2] According to the legend, Emperor Wu began almost immediately to regale his visiting dignitary with a checklist of his own dedication to the faith, mentioning temples built, clergy invested, sutras promulgated. The list was long, but at last he paused, no doubt puzzled by his guest's indifference. Probing for a response, he asked, "Given all I have done, what Merit have I earned?" Bodhidharma scowled, "None whatsoever, your majesty." The emperor was stunned by this reply, but he pressed on, trying another popular question. "What is the most important principle of Buddhism?" This second point Bodhidharma reportedly answered with the abrupt "Vast emptiness."[3] The emperor was equally puzzled by this answer and in desperation finally inquired who, exactly, was the bearded visitor standing before him—to which Bodhidharma cheerfully admitted he had no idea. The interview ended as abruptly as it began, with Bodhidharma excusing himself and pressing on. For his first miracle, he crossed the Yangtze just outside Nanking on a reed and headed north.

The legend of Bodhidharma picks up again in North China, near the city of Loyang. The stories differ, but the most enduring ones link his name with the famous Shao-lin monastery on Mt. Sung. There, we are told, he meditated for nine years facing a wall (thereby inventing "wall gazing") until at last, a pious version reports, his legs fell off. At one time, relates another Zen story, he caught himself dozing and in a fit of rage tore off his eyelids and cast them contemptuously to the ground, whereupon bushes of the tea plant—Zen's sacramental drink—sprang forth. Another story has him inventing a Chinese style of boxing as physical education for the weakling monks at Shao-lin, thereby founding a classic Chinese discipline. But the most famous episode surrounding his stay at the Shao-lin concerns the monk Hui-k'o, who was to be his successor. The story tells that Hui-k'o waited in the snows outside Shao-lin for days on end, hoping in vain to attract Bodhidharma's notice, until finally in desperation he cut off his own arm to attract the master's attention.

Bodhidharma advocated meditation, sutras, and the trappings of traditional Buddhism as a way to see into one's own nature. His legends represent Zen in its formative period, before the more unorthodox methods for shaking disciples into a new mode of consciousness had been devised. However, one of the stories attributed to him by later writers sounds suspiciously like a Zen mondo (the traditional consciousness-testing exchange between master and monk). According to this story, the disciple Hui-k'o entreated Bodhidharma, saying, "Master, I have not found peace of mind. I beg you to pacify my mind for me." Bodhidharma replied, "Bring me your mind and I will pacify it for you." Hui-k'o was silent for a time, finally conceding he could not actually find his mind. "There," said Bodhidharma, "I have pacified it for you." This symbolic story illustrates eloquently the concept of the mind as a perceiver, something that cannot itself be subject to analysis. Logical introspection is impossible. The mind cannot examine itself any more than the eye can see itself. Since the mind cannot become the object of its own perception, its existence can only be understood intuitively, as Hui-k'o realized when he tried to plumb its whereabouts objectively.

The actual teachings of Bodhidharma are not fully known. The first notice of the "blue-eyed barbarian" (as later Chinese called him) is in the Chinese Buddhist history entitled *Further Biographies of Eminent Priests,* usually dated around the year 645, more than a century after he came to China. This biography also contains the brief text of an essay attributed to Bodhidharma. At the time it was compiled, Bodhidharma had not yet been anointed the First Patriarch of Zen: rather he was merely one of a number of priests teaching meditation. Accordingly there would have been no incentive to embellish his story with an apocryphal essay, and for this reason most authorities think it is authentic.[4] A later, more detailed version of the essay by Bodhidharma is contained in the *Records of the Transmission of the Lamp* (A.D. 1004). This latter text is usually the one quoted, and it is agreed to be the superior literary document.[5] We are in good company if we accept this essay as a more or less accurate record of the thoughts of the First Patriarch.

The text that Bodhidharma left was meant to show others the several ways to enlightenment.

> There are many ways to enter the Path, but briefly speaking, they are two sorts only. The one is "Entrance by Reason" and the other "Entrance by Conduct."[6]

The first of these paths, the Entrance by Reason, might more properly be called entrance by pure insight. The path advocated seems a blending of Buddhism and Taoism, by which the sutras are used as a vehicle for leading the seeker first to meditation, and then to a nonliterary state of consciousness in which all dualities, all sense of oneself as apart from the world, are erased. This is an early and eloquent summary of Zen's objectives.

> By "Entrance by Reason" we mean the realization of the spirit of Buddhism by the aid of scriptural teaching. We then come to

have a deep faith in the True Nature which is one and the same in all sentient beings. The reason that it does not manifest itself is due to the overwrapping of external objects and false thoughts. When one, abandoning the false and embracing the true, and in simpleness of thought, abides in pi-kuan [pure meditation or "wall-gazing"], one finds that there is neither selfhood nor otherness, that the masses and the worthies are of one essence, and firmly holds on to this belief and never moves away therefrom. He will not then be guided by any literary instructions, for he is in silent communication with the principle itself, free from conceptual discrimination, for he is serene and not-acting.[7]

Bodhidharma is given credit for inventing the term pi-kuan, whose literal translation is "wall-gazing," but whose actual meaning is anyone's guess. Pi-kuan is sometimes called a metaphor for the mind's confrontation with the barrier of intellect—which must eventually be hurdled if one is to reach enlightenment. In any case, this text is an unmistakable endorsement of meditation as a means for tranquilizing the mind while simultaneously dissolving our impulse to discriminate between ourselves and the world around us. It points out that literary instructions can go only so far, and at last they must be abandoned in favor of reliance on the intuitive mind.[8]

The other Path (or Tao) he described was called the "Entrance by Conduct" and invokes his Indian Buddhist origins. The description of "conduct" was divided into four sections which, taken together, were intended to subsume or include all the possible types of Buddhist practice.

By "Entrance by Conduct" is meant the Four Acts in which all other acts are included. What are the four? 1. How to requite hatred; 2. To be obedient to karma; 3. Not to seek after anything; and 4. To be in accord with the Dharma.[9]

The first Act of Conduct counseled the believer to endure all hardships, since they are payment for evil deeds committed in past existences.

What is meant by "How to requite hatred"? Those who discipline themselves in the Path should think thus when they have to struggle with adverse conditions: During the innumerable past ages I have wandered through multiplicity of existences, all the while giving myself to unimportant details of life at the expense of essentials, and thus creating infinite occasions for hate, ill-will, and wrong-doing. While no violations have been committed in this life, the fruits of evil deeds in the past are to be gathered now. Neither gods nor men can foretell what is coming upon me. I will submit myself willingly and patiently to all the ills that befall me, and I will never bemoan or complain. In the Sutra it is said not to worry over ills that may happen to you. Why? Because through intelligence one can survey [the whole chain of causation]. When this thought arises, one is in concord with the principle because he makes the best use of hatred and turns it into the service of his advance towards the Path. This is called the "way to requite hatred."[10]

The second Rule of Conduct is to be reconciled to whatever comes, good or evil. It seems to reflect the Taoist attitude that everything is what it is and consequently value judgments are irrelevant. If good comes, it is the result of meritorious deeds in a past existence and will vanish when the store of causative karma is exhausted. The important thing to realize is that none of it matters anyway.

We should know that all sentient beings are produced by the interplay of karmic conditions, and as such there can be no real self in them. The mingled yarns of pleasure and pain are all woven of the threads of conditioning causes. . . . Therefore, let gains and losses run their natural courses according to the everchanging conditions and circumstances of life, for the Mind itself does not increase with the gains nor decrease with the losses. In this way, no gales of self-complacency will arise, and your mind will remain in hidden harmony with the Tao. It is in this sense that we must understand the rule of adaptation to the variable conditions and circumstances of life.[11]

The third Rule of Conduct was the teaching of the Buddha that a cessation of seeking and a turning toward nonattachment brings peace.

Men of the world remain unawakened for life; everywhere we find them bound by their craving and clinging. This is called "attachment." The wise, however, understand the truth, and their reason tells them to turn from the worldly ways. They enjoy peace of mind and perfect detachment. They adjust their bodily movements to the vicissitudes of fortune, always aware of the emptiness of the phenomenal world, in which they find nothing to covet, nothing to delight in. . . . Everyone who has a body is an heir to suffering and a stranger to peace. Having comprehended this point, the wise are detached from all things of the phenomenal world, with their minds free of desires and craving. As the scripture has it, "All sufferings spring from attachment; true joy arises from detachment." To know clearly the bliss of detachment is truly to walk on the path of the Tao.[12]

The fourth Rule of Conduct was to dissolve our perception of object-subject dualities and view life as a unified whole. This merging of self and exterior world Bodhidharma calls pure mind or pure reason.

The Dharma is nothing else than Reason which is pure in its essence. This pure Reason is the formless Form of all Forms; it is free of all defilements and attachments, and it knows of neither "self" nor "other."[13]

Having set forth this rather elegant statement of Zen and Buddhist ideals, as ascribed to Bodhidharma, it unfortunately is necessary to add that it appears to have been taken directly from the Vajrasamadhi Sutra (attributing quotations from the sutras to Patriarchs was common), with the sole exception of the term pi-kuan.[14] At the very least, the legend at this time does not portray Bodhidharma as a despiser of the sutras. He was, in fact, using a sutra as a vehicle to promote his practice of intensive meditation. It is not known what role meditation played in Buddhism at this time. However, the scholar Hu Shih questions how well it was understood. "[An early Buddhist historian's] Biographies, which covered the whole period of early Buddhism in China from the first century to the year 519, contained only 21 names of 'practitioners of dhyana (meditation)' out of a total of about 450. And practically all of the 21 dhyana monks were recorded because of their remarkable asceticism and miraculous powers. This shows that in spite of the numerous yoga manuals in translation, and in spite of the high respect paid by intellectual Buddhists to the doctrine and practice of dhyana, there were, as late as 500, practically no Chinese Buddhists who really understood or seriously practiced dhyana or Zen."[15]

Perhaps Bodhidharma, arriving in 520, felt his praise of meditation, using the words of an existing sutra, could rouse Chinese interest in this form of Buddhism. As it turned out, he was successful beyond anything he could have imagined, although his success took several centuries. As D. T. Suzuki sums it up, "While there was nothing specifically Zen in his doctrine of 'Two Entrances and Four Acts,' the teaching of pi-kuan, wall-contemplation, was what made Bodhidharma the first patriarch of Zen Buddhism in China."[16] Suzuki interprets pi-kuan as referring to the mind in a thoughtless state, in which meditation has permitted the rational mind to be suppressed entirely. The use of meditation for this goal instead of for developing magical powers, as had been the goal of earlier dhyana masters, seems to have been the profound new idea introduced to China by Bodhidharma.[17]

The passage of Bodhidharma is also swathed in legend. What eventually happened to this traveling Indian guru? Did he die of poison, as one legend says; or did he wander off to Central Asia, as another reports; or did he go to Japan, as still another story would have it? The story that has been the most enduring (recorded in a Sung work, Ching-te ch'uan-teng-lu) tells that after nine years at the Shao-lin monastery decided to return to India and called together his disciples to test their attainment. The first disciple reportedly said, "As I view it, to realize the truth we should neither rely entirely on words and letters nor dispense with them entirely, but rather we should use them as an instrument of the Way." To this, Bodhidharma replied, "You have got my skin."

Next a nun came forward and said, "As I view it, the Truth is like an auspicious sighting of the Buddhist Paradise; it is seen once and never again." To this Bodhidharma replied, "You have attained my flesh."

The third disciple said, "The four great elements are empty and the five skandhas [constituents of the personality: body, feelings, perception, will, and consciousness] are nonexistent. There is, in fact, nothing that can be grasped." To this Bodhidharma replied, "You have attained my bones."

Finally, it was Hui-k'o's turn. But he only bowed to the master and stood silent at his place. To him Bodhidharma said, "You have attained my marrow."[18]

According to a competing story, Bodhidharma died of poisoning at the age of 150 and was buried in the mountains of Honan.[19] Not too long thereafter a lay Buddhist named Sung Yun, who was returning to China after a trip to India to gather sutras, met Bodhidharma in the mountains of Turkestan. The First Patriarch, who was walking barefoot carrying a single shoe, announced he was returning to India and that a native Chinese would arise to continue his teaching. Sung Yun reported this to Bodhidharma's disciples on his return and they opened the master's grave, only to find it empty save for the other shoe.

How much of the story of Bodhidharma is legend? The answer does not really matter all that much. As with Moses, if Bodhidharma had not existed it would have been necessary to invent him. Although his first full biography (ca. 645) makes no particular fuss over him, less than a century after this, he was declared the founder of Zen, provided with a lineage stretching directly back through Nagarjuna to the Buddha, and furnished an exciting anecdotal history. Yet as founders go, he was a worthy enough individual. He does seem to have devised a strain of Buddhist thought that could successfully be grafted onto the hardy native Chinese Taoist organism. He also left an active disciple, later to be known as the Second Patriarch, Hui-k'o, so he must have had either a charismatic personality or a philosophical position that distinguished him from the general run of meditation masters.

It is important to keep in mind that Bodhidharma, man and myth, was the product of an early form of Zen. The later masters needed a lineage, and he was tapped for the role of First Patriarch. The major problem with Bodhidharma was that many of his ideas were in direct contradiction to the position adopted by later Zen teachings. For instance, recall that he promoted the reliance on a sutra (the Lankavatara); and he heavily stressed meditation (something later Zen masters would partially circumvent). The Jesuit scholar Heinrich Dumoulin has declared that Bodhidharma's attributed teaching in no way deviates from the great Mahayana sutras.[20] It is, in fact, a far cry from later Zen ideas, says John Wu, the Chinese authority.[21] Finally, he left no claim to patriarchy, nor did his first biographer offer to do this for him.

Perhaps the evolution of Zen is best demonstrated by the slow change in the paintings of Bodhidharma, culminating in the latter-day portrayals of him as a scowling grump. His image became successively more misanthropic through the centuries, perhaps as a way of underscoring the later Zen practice of establishing a rather dehumanized relationship between the Zen master and pupil, as the master shouts, beats a monk, and destroys his ego through merciless question-and-answer sessions. For all we know, the "wall-gazing Brahmin" of ancient China may have had a wry smile to go along with his droll sense of humor. Perhaps it is fitting to close with the most lasting apocrypha associated with his name, to wit the stanza that later masters attributed to him as an alleged summary of his teaching, but which he, promulgator of the Lankavatara Sutra, would undoubtedly have disowned:

A special transmission outside the sutras;
No reliance upon words and letters;
Direct pointing to the very mind;
Seeing into one's own nature.

*Hui-k'o, The Second Patriarch Harmonizing
His Mind.* In the style of Shih K'o (d. 975). Courtesy
of the Tokyo National Museum.

2
HUI-K'O:
SECOND PATRIARCH
OF ZEN

Hui-k'o (487–593) first enters the history of Zen as an eager Chinese scholar devoted to meditation. Wishing to become a disciple of the famous Indian monk who had recently installed himself at the Shao-lin monastery, Hui-k'o set up a vigil outside the gate. Time passed and the snows began to fall, but still Bodhidharma ignored him, declaring, "The incomparable doctrine of Buddhism can only be comprehended after a long hard discipline, by enduring what is most difficult to endure and by practicing what is most difficult to practice. Men of inferior virtue are not allowed to understand anything about it."[1] Finally Hui-k'o despaired and resorted to an extreme measure to demonstrate his sincerity: he cut off his own arm and offered it to the master. (This act reportedly has been repeated since by an occasional overenthusiastic Zen novice.) Even a singleminded master of meditation like Bodhidharma could not ignore such a gesture, and he agreed to accept Hui-k'o as his first Chinese disciple.

Unlike Bodhidharma, Hui-k'o is not a mysterious, legendary figure, but rather is remembered by a detailed history that interacts periodically with known events in Chinese history.[2] He came from the Chi family and was originally named Seng-k'o, only later becoming known as Hui-k'o. The most reliable report has him coming from Wu-lao, with a reputation as a scholarly intellectual preceding him. Indeed he seems to have been a Chinese scholar in the finest sense, with a deep appreciation of all three major philosophies: Confucianism, Taoism, and Buddhism. It was toward the last, however, that he slowly gravitated, finally abandoning his scholarly secular life and becoming a Buddhist monk. He was around age forty, in the prime of what was to be a very long life, when he first encountered Bodhidharma at the Shao-lin monastery. Whether he lost his arm by self-mutilation, as the later Zen chronicles say, or whether it was severed in a fight with bandits, as the earliest history reports, may never be determined.[3] The later story is certainly more pious, but the earlier would seem more plausible.

For six years he studied meditation with Bodhidharma, gradually retreating from the life of the scholar as he turned away from intellectualism and toward pure experience. When Bodhidharma finally decided to depart, he called in all his disciples for the famous testing of their attainment recounted in Chapter 1.[4] Hui-k'o, by simply bowing in silence when asked what he had attained, proved that his understanding of the master's wordless teaching was superior, and it was he who received the Lankavatara Sutra. The event reportedly was sealed by a short refrain, now universally declared to be spurious, in which Bodhidharma predicted the later division of Ch'an into five schools:

> Originally I came to this land
> To transmit the Dharma and to save all from error
> A flower with five petals opens;
> Of itself the fruit will ripen.[5]

As the story goes, Hui-k'o remained at the Shao-lin for a while longer and then went underground, supporting himself through menial work and learning about Chinese peasant life firsthand. Reportedly, he wanted to tranquilize his mind, to acquire the humility necessary in a great teacher, and not incidentally to absorb the Lankavatara Sutra. When asked why he, an enlightened teacher, chose to live among menial laborers, he would reply tartly that this life was best for his mind and in any case what he did was his own affair. It was a hard existence, but one he believed proper. Perhaps it was in this formative period that the inner strength of Ch'an's first Chinese master was forged.

Hui-k'o's major concern during this period must inevitably have been the study of the Lankavatara Sutra entrusted him by Bodhidharma. The Lankavatara was not written by a Zen master, nor did it come out of the Zen tradition, but it was the primary scripture of the first two hundred years of Ch'an. As

D. T. Suzuki has noted, there were at least three Chinese translations of this Sanskrit sutra by the time Bodhidharma came to China.[6] However, he is usually given credit, at least in Zen records, for originating the movement later known as the Lankavatara school. As the sutra was described by a non-Ch'an Chinese scholar in the year 645, "The entire emphasis of its teaching is placed on Prajna (highest intuitive knowledge), which transcends literary expression. Bodhidharma, the Zen master, propagated this doctrine in the south as well as in the north, the gist of which teaching consists in attaining the unattainable, which is to have right insight into the truth itself by forgetting word and thought. Later it grew and flourished in the middle part of the country. Hui-k'o was the first who attained to the essential understanding of it. Those addicted to the literary teaching of Buddhism in Wei were averse to becoming associated with these spiritual seers."[7]

The Lankavatara purportedly relays the thoughts of the Buddha while ensconced on a mountain peak in Sri Lanka. Although the work is notoriously disorganized, vague, and obscure, it was to be the stone on which Hui-k'o sharpened his penetrating enlightenment. The major concept it advances is that of Mind, characterized by D. T. Suzuki as "absolute mind, to be distinguished from an empirical mind which is the subject of psychological study. When it begins with a capital letter, it is the ultimate reality on which the entire world of individual objects depends for its value."[8] On the question of Mind, the Lankavatara has the following to say:

> . . . the ignorant and the simple minded, not knowing that the world is what is seen of Mind itself, cling to the multitudinousness of external objects, cling to the notions of being and non-being, oneness and otherness, bothness and not-bothness, existence and non-existence, eternity and non-eternity. . . .[9]

According to the Lankavatara, the world and our perception of it are both part of a larger conceptual entity. The teachings of the Lankavatara cast the gravest doubt on the actual existence of the things we think we see. Discrimination between oneself and the rest of the world can only be false, since both are merely manifestations of the same encompassing essence, Mind. Our perception is too easily deceived, and this is the reason we must not implicitly trust the images that reach our consciousness.

> . . . [I]t is like those water bubbles in a rainfall which have the appearance of crystal gems, and the ignorant taking them for real crystal gems run after them. . . . [T]hey are no more than water bubbles, they are not gems, nor are they not-gems, because of their being so comprehended [by one party] and not being so comprehended [by another].[10]

Reality lies beyond these petty discriminations. The intellect, too, is powerless to distinguish the real from the illusory, since all things are both and neither at the same time. This conviction of the Lankavatara remained at the core of Zen, even after the sutra itself was supplanted by simpler, more easily approached literary works.

As Hui-k'o studied the Lankavatara and preached, he gradually acquired a reputation for insight that transcended his deliberately unpretentious appearance. Throughout it all, he led an itinerant life, traveling about North China. It is reported that he found his way to the capital of the eastern half of the Wei kingdom after its division in the year 534. Here, in the city of Yeh-tu, he taught his version of *dhyana* and opened the way to enlightenment for many people. Though unassuming in manner and dress, he nonetheless aroused antagonism from established Buddhist circles because of his success, encountering particular opposition from a conventional *dhyana* teacher named Tao-huan. According to *Further Biographies of the Eminent Priests* (645), Tao-huan was a jealous teacher who had his own following of as many as a thousand, and who resented deeply the nonscriptural approach Hui-k'o advocated. This spiteful priest sent various of his followers to monitor Hui-k'o's teaching, perhaps with an eye to accusing him of heresy, but all those sent were so impressed that none ever returned. Then one day the antagonistic *dhyana* master met one of those former pupils who had been won over by Hui-k'o's teachings. D. T. Suzuki translates the encounter as follows:

> When Tao-huan happened to meet his first messenger, he asked: "How was it that I had to send for you so many times? Did I not open your eye after taking pains so much on my part?" The former disciple, however, mystically answered: "My eye has been right from the first, and it was through you that it came to squint."[11]

The message would seem to be that Hui-k'o taught a return to one's original nature, to the primal man without artificial learning or doctrinal pretense. Out of resentment the jealous *dhyana* master reportedly caused Hui-k'o to undergo official persecution.

In later years, beginning around 574, there was a temporary but thorough persecution of Buddhism in the capital city of Ch'ang-an. Sometime earlier, an ambitious sorcerer and apostate Buddhist named Wei had decided to gain a bit of notoriety for himself by attacking Buddhism, then a powerful force in Ch'ang-an. In the year 567 he presented a document to the emperor claiming that Buddhism had allowed unsavory social types to enter the monasteries. He also attacked worship of the Buddha image on the ground that it was un-Chinese idolatry. Instead, he proposed a secularized church that would include all citizens, with the gullible emperor suggested for the role of "pope." The emperor was taken with the idea and after several years of complex political maneuvering, he proscribed Buddhism in North China.

As a result, Hui-k'o was forced to flee to the south, where he took up temporary residence in the mountainous regions of the Yangtze River. The persecution was short-lived, since the emperor responsible died soon after his decree, whereupon Hui-k'o returned to Ch'ang-an. However, these persecutions may have actually contributed to the spread of his teaching, by forcing him to travel into the countryside.

The only authentic fragment of Hui-k'o's thought that has survived records his answer to an inquiry sent by a lay devotee named Hsiang, who reportedly was seeking spiritual attainment alone in the jungle. The inquiry, which seems more a statement than a question, went as follows:

> ... he who aspires to Buddhahood thinking it to be independent of the nature of sentient beings is to be likened to one who tries to listen to an echo by deadening its original sound. Therefore the ignorant and the enlightened are walking in one passageway; the vulgar and the wise are not to be differentiated from each other. Where there are no names, we create names, and because of these names, judgments are formed. Where there is no theorizing, we theorize, and because of this theorizing, disputes arise. They are all phantom creations and not realities, and who knows who is right and who is wrong? They are all empty, no substantialities have they, and who knows what is and

what is not? So we realize that our gain is not real gain and our loss not real loss. This is my view and may I be enlightened if I am at fault?[12]

This "question," if such it is, sounds suspiciously like a sermon and stands, in fact, as an eloquent statement of Zen concerns. Hui-k'o reportedly answered as follows, in a fragment of a letter that is his only known extant work.

You have truly comprehended the Dharma as it is; the deepest truth lies in the principle of identity. It is due to one's ignorance that the mani-jewel is taken for a piece of brick, but lo! when one is suddenly awakened to self-enlightenment it is realized that one is in possession of the real jewel. The ignorant and the enlightened are of one essence, they are not really to be separated. We should know that all things are such as they are. Those who entertain a dualistic view of the world are to be pitied, and I write this letter for them. When we know that between this body and the Buddha, there is nothing to separate one from the other, what is the use of seeking after Nirvana [as something external to ourselves]?[13]

Hui-k'o insists that all things spring from the one Mind, and consequently the ideas of duality, of attachment to this or that phenomenon, or even the possibility of choice, are equally absurd. Although he knew all too well that enlightenment could not be obtained from teaching, he still did not advocate a radical break with the traditional methods of the Buddhist *dhyana* masters. His style was unorthodox, but his teaching methods were still confined to lectures and meditation. This low-key approach was still closer to the tradition of the Buddha than to the jarring techniques of "sudden enlightenment" destined to erupt out of Chinese Ch'an.

Toward the end of his life, Hui-k'o was back in Ch'ang-an, living and teaching in the same unassuming manner. His free-lance style seems to have continued to outrage the more conventional teachers, and a later story records a martyr's death for him.[14] One day, while a learned master was preaching inside the K'uang-chou Temple, Hui-k'o chanced by and started to chat with the passersby outside. Gradually a crowd started to collect, until eventually the lecture hall of the revered priest was emptied. This famous priest, remembered as Pien-ho, accused the ragged Hui-k'o to the magistrate Che Ch'ung-j'an as a teacher of false doctrine. As a result he was arrested and subsequently executed, an impious 106-year-old revolutionary.

*The Second Coming of the Fifth Patriarch,
Hung-jen.* Yin-t'o-lo (active ca. mid-14th century).
Courtesy of the Cleveland Museum of Art.

3
SENG-TS'AN, TAO-HSIN, FA-JUNG, AND HUNG-JEN:
FOUR EARLY MASTERS

The master succeeding Hui-k'o was Seng-ts'an (d. 606), who then taught Fa-jung (594–657) and Tao-hsin (580–651), the latter in turn passing the robe of the patriarchy to Hung-jen (601–74). The masters Seng-ts'an, Tao-hsin, and Hung-jen are honored today as the Third, Fourth, and Fifth Patriarchs, respectively, and revered as the torchbearers of Ch'an's formative years. Yet when we look for information about their lives, we find the sources thin and diffuse. One reason probably is that before 700 nobody realized that these men would one day be elevated to founding fathers, and consequently no one bothered recording details of their lives.

During the seventh century the scattered teachers of *dhyana* seem to have gradually coalesced into a sort of *ad hoc* movement—with sizable followings growing up around the better-known figures. A certain amount of respectability also emerged, if we can believe the references to imperial notice that start appearing in the chronicles. It would seem that the *dhyana* or Ch'an movement became a more or less coherent sect, a recognizable if loosely defined school of Buddhism. However, what the movement apparently was striving to become was not so much a branch of Buddhism in China as a Chinese *version* of Buddhism. The men later remembered as the Third, Fourth, and Fifth Patriarchs have in common a struggle to bend Buddhist thought to Chinese intellectual requirements, to sinicize Buddhism. Whereas they succeeded only in setting the stage for this transformation (whose realization would await other hands), they did establish a personality pattern that would set apart all later masters: a blithe irreverence that owed as much to Chuang Tzu as to Bodhidharma.

When reading the biographies that follow, it is useful to keep in mind that the explicit details may well have been cooked up in later years to satisfy a natural Chinese yearning for anecdotes, with or without supporting information. Yet the fact that the *dhyana* practitioners eventually became a movement in need of a history is itself proof that these men and their stories were not complete inventions. In any case, they were remembered, honored, and quoted in later years as the legendary founders of Ch'an.

SENG-TS'AN, THE THIRD PATRIARCH (d. 606)

The question of the Second Patriarch Hui-k'o's successor was troublesome even for the ancient Ch'an historians. The earliest version of his biography (written in 645, before the sect of Ch'an and its need for a history existed) declares, "Before [Hui-k'o] had established a lineage he died, leaving no worthy heirs." When it later became necessary for Ch'an to have an uninterrupted patriarchy, a revised history was prepared which supplied him an heir named Seng-ts'an, to whom he is said to have transmitted the doctrine.[1] The story of their meeting recalls Hui-k'o's first exchange with Bodhidharma, save that the roles are reversed. The text implies that Seng-ts'an was suffering from leprosy when he first encountered Hui-k'o, and that he implored the Master for relief in a most un-Zenlike way, saying: "I am in great suffering from this disease; please take away my sins."

Hui-k'o responded with, "Bring me your sins, and I will take them away."

After a long silence, Seng-ts'an confessed, "I've looked, but I cannot find them."

To which Hui-k'o replied, echoing Bodhidharma's classic rejoinder, "Behold, you have just been cleansed."

Another version of the story says Hui-k'o greeted Seng-ts'an with the words, "You are suffering from leprosy; why should you want to see me?"

To this Seng-ts'an responded, "Although my body is sick, the mind of a sick man and your own mind are no different."

Whatever actually happened, it was enough to convince Hui-k'o that he had found an enlightened being, one who perceived the unity of all things, and he forthwith transmitted to Seng-ts'an the symbols of the patriarchy—the robe and begging bowl of Bodhidharma—telling him that he should take refuge in the Buddha, the Dharma (the universal truth proclaimed by Buddha), and the Sangha (the Buddhist organization or priesthood). Seng-ts'an replied that he knew of the Sangha, but what was meant by the Buddha and the Dharma? The answer was that all three were expressions of Mind.[2]

This exchange seems to have taken place while Hui-k'o was in the northern Wei capital of Yeh-tu.[3] In later years Seng-ts'an found it necessary to feign madness (to escape persecution during the anti-Buddhist movement of 574), and finally he went to hide on Huan-kung mountain for ten years, where his mere presence reportedly was enough to tame the wild tigers who had terrorized the people there. The only surviving work that purportedly relays his teaching is a poem, said to be one of the earliest Ch'an treatises, which is called the *Hsin-hsin-ming*, or "On the Believing Mind."[4] It starts off in a lyrical, almost Taoist, voice worthy of Chuang Tzu, as it celebrates man's original nature and the folly of striving.

There is nothing difficult about the Great Way
But, avoid choosing!
Only when you neither love nor hate,
Does it appear in all clarity.

. . .

Do not be anti- or pro- anything.
The conflict of longing and loathing,
This is the disease of the mind.
Not knowing the profound meaning of things,
We disturb our (original) peace of mind to no purpose.[5]

Next, the poem turns to an acknowledgment of the Mahayanist concept of the all-encompassing Mind, the greatest single truth of the universe, and of Nagarjuna's Void, the cosmic emptiness of *sunyata*.

Things are things because of the Mind.
The Mind is the Mind because of things.
If you wish to know what these two are,
They are originally one Emptiness.
In this Void both (Mind and things) are one,
All the myriad phenomena contained in both.[6]

The poem closes with an affirmation of the Ch'an credo of unity and the absence of duality as a sign of enlightenment.

In the World of Reality
There is no self, no other-than-self.
. . .
All that can be said is "No Duality!"
When there is no duality, all things are one,
There is nothing that is not included.
. . .
The believing mind is not dual;
What is dual is not the believing mind.
Beyond all language,
For it there is no past, no present, no future.[7]

Since the earliest historical sources maintain that Seng-ts'an left no writings, some have questioned the attribution of this lilting work to the Third Patriarch. Whatever its authorship, the real importance of the poem lies in its subtle merging of Taoism and Buddhism. We can watch as the voices of ancient China and ancient India are blended together into a perfect harmony until the parts are inseparable. It was a noble attempt to reconcile Buddhist metaphysics with Chinese philosophical concepts, and it was successful in a limited way. As for Seng-ts'an, the legends tell that he finally was overcome by his longing for the south and, handing down the symbols of the patriarchy to a priest named Tao-hsin, he vanished.

TAO-HSIN, THE FOURTH PATRIARCH (580–651)

China, whose political turmoil had sent the early Patriarchs scurrying from one small kingdom to another, found unity and the beginnings of stability under a dynasty known as the Sui (581–618), the first in three and a half centuries (since the end of the Han in 220) able to unify the land.[8] This brief dynasty (which soon was replaced by the resplendent T'ang) came to be dominated by the Emperor Yang, a crafty politician who maneuvered the throne away from an elder brother—partially, it is said, by demonstrating to his parents his independence of mind by abandoning all the children he begat in the ladies' quarters. Whereas his father had undertaken the renovation of the North Chinese capital of Ch'ang-an—not incidentally creating one of the glories of the ancient world and the site of the finest moments of the later T'ang Dynasty—Emperor Yang decided to reconstruct the city of Loyang, some two hundred miles to the east. The result was a "Western Capital" at Ch'ang-an and an "Eastern Capital" at Loyang, the latter city soon to be the location of some pivotal episodes in Ch'an history.

For the construction of Loyang, a fairyland of palaces and gardens, millions of citizens were conscripted and tens of thousands died under forced labor. Emperor Yang's other monument was a grand canal, linking the Yellow River in the north with the rich agricultural deltas of the Yangtze in the south, near Nanking. The emperor loved to be barged down this vast waterway—journeys that unsympathetic historians have claimed were merely excuses to seek sexual diversions away from the capital. In any case, his extravagances bankrupted the country and brought about his overthrow by the man who would become the founder of the T'ang Dynasty, later to reign under the name of Emperor T'ai-tsung (ruled 626–49).

The T'ang is universally regarded as one of the great ages of man, and it is also considered the Golden Age of Ch'an. The founding emperor, T'ai-tsung, was a wise and beneficent "Son of Heaven," as Chinese rulers were styled.[9] Under his influence, the capital city of Ch'ang-an became the most cosmopolitan metropolis in the ancient world, with such widespread influence that when the first visiting Japanese came upon it, they were so dazzled they returned home and built a replica for their own capital city. The city was laid out as a grid, with lavish vermilion imperial palaces and gardens clustered regally at one end. Its inhabitants numbered upward of two million, while its international markets and fleshpots were crowded with traders from the farthest reaches of Asia and Europe, echoing with a truly astounding cacophony of tongues: Indian, Japanese, Turkish, Persian, Roman Latin, and Arabic, not to mention the many dialects of Chinese. Christians moved among the Buddhists, as did Muslims and Jews. Artisans worked with silver, gold, jewels, silks, and porcelains, even as poets gathered in wine shops to nibble fruits and relax with round-eyed foreign serving girls. Such were the worldly attractions of Ch'ang-an during the early seventh century. This new sophistication and urbanization, as well as the political stability that made it all possible, was also reflected in the change in Ch'an—from a concern chiefly of nomadic *dhyana* teachers hiding in the mountains to the focus of settled agricultural communities centered in monasteries.

The growth in Ch'an toward an established place in Chinese life began to consolidate under the Fourth Patriarch, Tao-hsin, the man whose life spanned the Sui and the early T'ang dynasties. He is best remembered today for two things: First, he was particularly dedicated to meditation, practicing it more avidly than had any dhyana master since Bodhidharma; and second, he is credited with beginning the true monastic tradition for Ch'an. His formation of a self-supporting monastic community with its own agricultural base undoubtedly brought Ch'an a long way toward respectability in Chinese eyes, since it reduced the dependence on begging. Itinerant mendicants, even if teachers of dhyana, had never elicited the admiration in China they traditionally enjoyed in the Indian homeland of the Buddha. Begging was believed to fashion character, however, and it never disappeared from Ch'an discipline. Indeed, Ch'an is said to have encouraged begging more than did any of the other Chinese Buddhist sects, but as a closely regulated form of moral training.

Tao-hsin, whose family name was Ssu-ma, came from Honan, but he left home at seven to study Buddhism and met the Third Patriarch, Seng-ts'an, while still in his teens. When Seng-ts'an decided to drop out of sight, he asked this brilliant pupil to take up the teaching of dhyana and Bodhidharma's Lankavatara Sutra at a monastery on Mt. Lu. Tao-hsin agreed and remained for a number of years, attracting followers and reportedly performing at least one notable miracle. The story says that he saved a walled city from being starved out by bandits by organizing a program of public sutra chanting among its people. We are told that the robbers retired of their own accord while, as though by magic, previously dry wells in the city flowed again. One day not too long thereafter Tao-hsin noticed an unusual purple cloud hanging over a nearby mountain. Taking this as a sign, he proceeded to settle there (the mountain later became known as Shuang-feng or "Twin Peaks") and found the first Ch'an community, presiding over a virtual army of some five hundred followers for the next thirty years.

He is remembered today as a charismatic teacher who finally stabilized dhyana teaching. In an age of political turmoil, many intellectuals flocked to the new school of Ch'an, with its promise of tranquil meditation in uneasy times. Tao-hsin apparently encouraged his disciples to operate a form of commune, in which agriculture and its administration were merged with the practice of meditation.[10] In so doing, he seems not only to have revolutionized the respectability of dhyana practice, but also to have become something of a national figure himself. This, at any rate, is what we may surmise from one of the more durable legends, which has him defying an imperial decree to appear before the emperor, T'ai-tsung.

This legend concerns an episode which allegedly took place around the year 645. As the story goes, an imperial messenger arrived one day at the mountain retreat to summon him to the palace, but Tao-hsin turned him down cold. When the messenger reported this to the emperor, the response was to send back a renewed invitation. Again the messenger was met with a refusal, along with a challenge.

"If you wish my head, cut it off and take it with you. It may go but my mind will never go."

When this reply reached the emperor, he again dispatched the messenger, this time bearing a sealed sword and a summons for the master's head. But he also included a contradictory decree requiring that Tao-hsin not be harmed. When the master refused a third time to come to the palace, the messenger read the decree that his head should be severed. Tao-hsin obligingly bent over, with the command "Cut it off." But the messenger hesitated, admitting that the imperial orders also forbade harming him. On hearing this Tao-hsin reportedly roared with laughter, saying, "You must know that you possess human qualities."[11]

The Fourth Patriarch's teachings are not well known, other than for the fact that he supposedly devised and promoted new techniques to help novices achieve intensive meditation. The following excerpt of his teaching illustrates his fervor for *dhyana*.

Sit earnestly in meditation! The sitting in meditation is basic to all else. By the time you have done this for three to five years, you will be able to ward off starvation with a bit of meal. Close the door and sit! Do not read the sutras, and speak to no man! If you will so exercise yourself and persist in it for a long time, the fruit will be sweet like the meat which a monkey takes from the nutshell. But such people are very rare.[12]

The de-emphasis on the sutras points the way to later Ch'an. Interestingly, however, the usefulness of sitting in meditation would also come under review in only a few short years, when the new style of Ch'an appeared.

The reports of Tao-hsin say that Hung-jen, who was to become the Fifth Patriarch, was one of his followers and grasped the inner meaning of his teaching. It was Hung-jen whom he asked to construct a mausoleum in the mountainside, the site of his final repose, and when it was finished he retired there for his last meditation. After he passed away, his body was wrapped in lacquered cloth, presenting a vision so magnificent that no one could bear to close the mausoleum.

Aside from his historical place as the founder of the first real community for Ch'an, there is little that can be said with assurance about Tao-hsin. However, a manuscript discovered early in this century in the Buddhist caves at Tun-huang purportedly contains a sermon by the Fourth Patriarch entitled "Abandoning the Body."

> The method of abandoning the body consists first in meditating on Emptiness, whereby the [conscious] mind is emptied. Let the mind together with its world be quieted down to a perfect state of tranquility; let thought be cast in the mystery of quietude, so that the mind is kept from wandering from one thing to another. When the mind is tranquilized in its deepest abode, its entanglements are cut asunder. . . . The mind in its absolute purity is like the Void itself.[13]

The text goes on to quote both Lao Tzu and Chuang Tzu, as well as some of the older sutras, and there is a considerable reference to Nagarjuna's Emptiness. This text, real or spurious, is one more element in the merging of Taoism and Buddhism that was early Ch'an, even as its analysis of the mind state achieved in meditation anticipates later Ch'an teachings.

FA-JUNG, THE ST. FRANCIS OF ZEN (594–657)

In the parade of Patriarchs, we should not overlook the maverick Fa-jung, a master who was never officially crowned a Patriarch, but whose humanity made him a legend.[14] Fa-jung (594–657), whose family name was Wei, was born in a province on the south bank of the Yangtze River and in his early years was a student of Confucian thought. But before long his yearning for spiritual challenge led him to Buddhism. He finally settled in a rock cave in the side of a cliff near a famous monastery on Mt. Niu-t'ou, where his sanctity reportedly caused birds to appear with offerings of flowers.

According to the Zen chronicle *Transmission of the Lamp* (1004), sometime between 627 and 649 the Fourth Patriarch, Tao-hsin, sensed that a famous Buddhist was living on Mt. Niu-t'ou and went there to search out the man. After many days of seeking, he finally came upon a holy figure seated atop a rock. As the two meditation masters were becoming acquainted, there suddenly came the roar of a tiger from the bramble farther up the mountain. Tao-hsin was visibly startled, causing Fa-jung—friend of the animals—to observe wryly, "I see it is still with you." His meaning, of course, was that Tao-hsin was still enslaved by the phenomenal world, was not yet wholly detached from his fears and perceptions.

After they had chatted a while longer, Fa-jung found occasion to leave his seat and attend nature at a detached location. During his absence Tao-hsin wrote the Chinese character for the Buddha's name on the very rock where he had been sitting. When Fa-jung returned to resume his place, he was momentarily brought up short by the prospect of sitting on the Buddha's name. Expecting this, Tao-hsin smiled and said, "I see it is still with you."

He had shown that Fa-jung was still intimidated by the trappings of classical Buddhism and had not yet become a completely detached master of the pure Mind. The story says that Fa-jung failed to understand his comment and implored Tao-hsin to teach him Ch'an, which the Fourth Patriarch proceeded to do.

Tao-hsin's message, once again, was to counsel nondistinction, nonattachment, nondiscrimination; he said to abjure emotions, values, striving. Just be natural and be what you are, for that is the part of you that is closest to the Buddhist ideal of mental freedom.

> There is nothing lacking in you, and you yourself are no different from the Buddha. There is no way of achieving Buddhahood other than letting your mind be free to be itself. You should not contemplate nor should you purify your mind. Let there be no craving and hatred, and have no anxiety or fear. Be boundless and absolutely free from all conditions. Be free to go in any direction you like. Do not act to do good, nor to pursue evil. Whether you walk or stay, sit or lie down, and whatever you see happen to you, all are the wonderful activity of the Great Enlightened One. It is all joy, free from anxiety—it is called Buddha.[15]

After Tao-hsin's visit, the birds offering flowers no longer appeared: evidence, said the later Ch'an teachers, that Fa-jung's physical being had entirely vanished. His school on Mt. Niu-t'ou flourished for a time, teaching that the goals of Ch'an practice could be realized by contemplating the Void of Nagarjuna. As Fa-jung interpreted the teachings of the Middle Path:

> All talk has nothing to do with one's Original Nature, which can only be reached through sunyata. No-thought is the Absolute Reality, in which the mind ceases to act. When one's mind is free from thoughts, one's nature has reached the Absolute.[16]

Although Fa-jung's teachings happened to be transmitted to Japan in later years, through the accident of a passing Japanese pilgrim, his school did not endure in either country beyond the eighth century. His was the first splinter group of Zen, and perhaps it lacked the innovation necessary to survive, because it clung too much to traditional Buddhism.

As Fa-jung's years advanced, he was encouraged to come down from his mountain and live in a monastery, which his better judgment eventually compelled him to do. It is reported that after his final farewell to his disciples he was followed down the mountain by the laments of all its birds and animals. A more ordinary teacher would have been forgotten, but this beloved St. Francis of Zen became the topic of lectures and a master remembered with reverence ever after.

HUNG-JEN, THE FIFTH PATRIARCH (601–74)

The other well-known disciple of the Fourth Patriarch, Tao-hsin, was the man history has given the title of Fifth Patriarch, Hung-jen (601–74). The chronicles say that he came from Tao-hsin's own province and impressed the master deeply when, at age fourteen, he held his own with the Fourth Patriarch in an introductory interview. As the exchange has been described, Tao-hsin asked the young would-be disciple his family name, but since the word for "family name" is pronounced the same as that for "nature," Hung-jen answered the question as though it had been, "What is your 'nature'?"—deliberately misinterpreting it in order to say, "My 'nature' is not ordinary; it is the Buddha-nature."

Tao-hsin reportedly inquired, "But don't you have a 'family name'?"

To which Hung-jen cleverly replied, "No, for the teachings say that our 'nature' is empty."[17]

Hung-jen went on to become the successor to the Fourth Patriarch, with an establishment where several hundred followers gathered. The chronicles have little to say about the actual life and teachings of the Fifth Patriarch, but no matter. His place in history is secured not so much for what he said—there is actually very little that can reliably be attributed to him—but rather for his accidental appearance at the great crossroads of Zen. Hung-jen and his monastery became the symbol of a great philosophical debate that occupied the first half of the eighth century, a conflict to be examined in detail in the two chapters to follow. Suffice it to say here that the chronicles at least agree that he was an eminent priest and well respected, a man to whom an early-eighth-century document attributes eleven disciples of note.[18] Among those listed who are particularly important to the events that follow are a monk named Shen-hsiu and another named Hui-neng, the men whose names would one day be associated with a celebrated midnight poetry contest in Hung-jen's monastery.

This contest eventually came to symbolize the conflict between the teachings of gradual enlightenment and sudden enlightenment, between intellectual and intuitive knowledge, between sophisticated urban Buddhism and unlettered rural teachers, and between promoters of the abstruse but challenging Lankavatara Sutra sanctioned by Bodhidharma and the cryptic Diamond Sutra. Quite simply, it was a battle between what would eventually be known as the Northern and Southern schools of Ch'an, and it concerned two fundamentally opposing views of the functions of the human mind. As things turned out, the gradual, Northern, Lankavatara Sutra faction went on for years thinking it had won—or perhaps not really aware that there was a battle in progress—while the anti-intellectual, Southern, Diamond Sutra faction was gathering its strength in the hinterlands for a final surge to victory. When the Southern school did strike, it won the war handily and then proceeded to recast the history of what had gone before, even going so far as to put posthumous words of praise for itself into the mouths of the once-haughty Northern masters. Thus the mighty were eventually brought low and the humble lifted up in the annals of Ch'an. It is to the two masters whose names are associated with this battle that we must turn next.

Chinese Literati Illustrating the Four
Accomplishments of Calligraphy, Painting, Chess and
Psaltry (detail). Kano Eitoku (1543–1590).
Courtesy of the Smithsonian Institution, Freer
Gallery of Art, Washington, D.C.

4

SHEN-HSIU AND SHEN-HUI:
"GRADUAL" AND "SUDDEN" MASTERS

Whereas the Ch'an Patriarchs of earlier times had been, more often than not, fractious teachers ignored by emperors and gentry alike, the T'ang Dynasty saw Ch'an masters rise to official eminence, receiving honors from the highest office in China. The first half of the eighth century witnessed what was to be the greatest battle within the school of Ch'an, but it was also the time when Ch'an was finally recognized by Chinese ruling circles. The name most often associated with this imperial recognition is the famous, or perhaps infamous, Empress Wu.[1]

Wu was not born to royalty, but in the year 638, when she was thirteen, she was placed in Emperor T'ai-tsung's harem as a concubine of relatively low rank. Disapproving historians claim that one day she managed to catch the crown prince, the heir apparent to the aging emperor, in what we today might euphemistically call the bathroom, and seduced him at a moment when he was without benefit of trousers. Thus she was already on familiar terms with the next emperor when her official husband, Emperor T'ai-tsung, went to his ancestors in the summer of 649. Although she was only twenty-four years old, custom required that she join all the deceased emperor's concubines in retirement at a monastery—which ordinarily would have been the last anyone heard of her. As it happened, however, the new emperor's first wife was childless, with the effect that he began devoting increasing attention to a favorite concubine. Knowing of the emperor's earlier acquaintance and infatuation with Wu, the barren empress recalled her from the convent, intending to divert the emperor from his current favorite. The cure, however, turned out to be far more deadly than the ailment.

Through an intrigue that apparently included murdering her own child by the emperor and then blaming the empress, Wu soon had both the empress and the competing concubine in prison. Not content with mere imprisonment for her rivals, she went on to have them both boiled alive—after first amputating their hands and feet, eliciting a dying curse from the concubine that she would return as a cat to haunt Wu. To escape this curse, Wu permanently banned cats from the imperial compound, and eventually persuaded the emperor to move the government from Ch'ang-an to Loyang, where for the next half century she tried to exorcise the memory of her deed. In late 683 Wu's husband, the emperor, died, and for a time she allowed his son, the true heir, to occupy the throne—until she could find a pretext to take over the government completely.

A couple of years after the emperor's death, when Wu was aged sixty, she became infatuated with a lusty peddler of cosmetics and aphrodisiacs, a man whose virility had made him a favorite with various serving ladies around the palace. To give him a respectable post, she appointed him abbot of the major Buddhist monastery of Loyang—enabling him to satisfy, as it were, a double office in the service of the state. His antics and those of his followers did the cause of Buddhism little good over the next few years. When in 695 his arrogance finally became too much even for Wu, she had him strangled by the court ladies and his body sent back to the monastery in a cart. Although Wu is remembered today as an ardent Buddhist, some have suggested that her devotions turned as much to the claims of fortunetelling by Buddhist nuns (some of whose organizations in Loyang reportedly ran brothels on the side) as to a pious concern with Indian philosophy.

SHEN-HSIU (605-706), THE FIRST "SIXTH PATRIARCH"

It is known that around 701 Empress Wu invited an aging Ch'an monk named Shen-hsiu, follower of the Lankavatara school of Bodhidharma, to come north to the imperial capital from his monastery in central China.[2] He was over ninety at the time and had amassed a lifelong reputation for his rigorous practice of *dhyana.* Shen-hsiu agreed reluctantly, reportedly having to be carried on a pallet into the presence of the empress. It is said that Wu curtsied to him, an unusual act for a head of state, and immediately moved him into the palace, where he seems to have become the priest-in-residence. As for why Empress Wu would have chosen to honor a lineage of Ch'an Buddhism, it has been pointed out that she was at the time attempting to supplant the established T'ang Dynasty of her late husband with one of her own. And since the T'ang emperors had honored a Buddhist lineage, it was essential that she do the same—but one of a different school. Shen-hsiu was both eminent and unclaimed, an ideal candidate to become the court Buddhist for her fledgling dynasty—which, needless to say, was never established. Nonetheless, Shen-hsiu was given the title of "Lord of the law of Ch'ang-an and Loyang," and he preached to vast crowds drawn from the entire northern regions. To solidify his eminence, Wu had monasteries built in his honor at his birthplace, at his mountain retreat, and in the capital.

Shen-hsiu, who briefly reigned as the Sixth Patriarch of Ch'an, was described in the early chronicles as a sensitive and bright child who, out of despair for the world, early on turned away from Confucianism to become a Buddhist monk. At age forty-six he finally found his way to the East Mountain retreat of the Fifth Patriarch, Hung-jen, where he studied under the master until achieving enlightenment. As noted previously he was among the eleven most prominent individuals remembered from the monastery of the Fifth Patriarch. He later left the monastery and traveled for almost two decades, during which time another of the students of Hung-jen, Fa-ju, eclipsed him in fame and followers. However, Shen-hsiu seems to have been the best known Master, eventually becoming the titular head of the Lankavatara faction, also to be known as the Northern school—possibly because Shen-hsiu brought it to the urbanized, sophisticated capitals of North China, Loyang and Ch'ang-an. This was Ch'an's most imperial moment, and no less than a state minister composed the memorial epitaph for Shen-hsiu's gravestone. Although his specific teachings are not well known, a verse survives from one of his sermons that seems to suggest that the teachings of Ch'an were really teachings of the mind and owed little to traditional Buddhism.

> The teaching of all the Buddhas
> In one's own Mind originally exists:
> To seek the Mind without one's Self,
> Is like running away from the father.[3]

After he died a pupil named P'u-chi (d. 739) carried on his organization in the capital. This was the high point of official Ch'an, signifying the moment of the Lankavatara school's greatest prestige.

Perhaps most important, the success of Shen-hsiu was also the success of Ch'an, or what appeared to be success. The sect had risen from being the passion of homeless teachers of *dhyana* to the object of imperial honors in the midst of China's finest moment, the T'ang Dynasty. The T'ang was an era to be remembered forever for its poetry, its art, its architecture, its cultural brilliance.[4] Unfortunately for Northern Ch'an, this cultural brilliance was beginning to be the province of groups other than the blueblooded gentry that traditionally had controlled China's culture. The glories of the T'ang were to some degree the creation of the nongentry, and an outcast warrior would before long bring the government to its knees, even as an obscure Ch'an master from the rural south was soon to erase Shen-hsiu's seemingly permanent place in history.

SHEN-HUI (670-762), THE "MARTIN LUTHER" OF CH'AN

The David to Shen-hsiu's Goliath was a master with a similar-sounding name: Shen-hui. This theological street fighter was a native of the province of Hupeh, some distance south of the lavish twin T'ang captials of Ch'ang-an and Loyang.[5] He began as a Taoist scholar, but later turned to Buddhism, traveling even farther south around his fortieth year to become the disciple of a priest named Hui-neng, whose temple was Ts'ao-ch'i, just north of the southern port city of Canton in Kuangtung province. It will be remembered that Hui-neng (whose legend we will explore in the next chapter) had also been a disciple of the Fifth Patriarch, Hung-jen, studying alongside Shen-hsiu. Shen-hui is thought to have studied under Hui-neng for around five years, until the latter's death in 713. After this he traveled about China, ending up at Hua-t'ai, slightly northeast of the capital of Loyang. He seems to have been a man of charismatic presence, one who inspired followers easily. Then, in the year 732, at a convocation of Ch'an worthies at the temple, he mounted the platform and, in a historic moment, declared that the great Ch'an organizations of China, heretofore beholden to Shen-hsiu as Sixth Patriarch, were following a false master.[6]

The historical significance of this convocation and Shen-hui's attack might be likened to the defiant act of Martin Luther, when he challenged church hierarchy in sixteenth-century Germany. With superb audacity, Shen-hui went on to spell out a new history of Ch'an that supported his claims. His revised chronicle culminated with the name of his old teacher Hui-neng, theretofore an obscure follower of the Fifth Patriarch, Hung-jen, whom he declared Sixth Patriarch. He insisted that Shen-hsiu, the man honored by Empress Wu, had posed falsely as the heir of Hung-jen. The Northern school of Shen-hsiu and his heir, P'u-chi, had perpetrated a historical deceit, said Shen-hui, robbing the true Sixth Patriarch, the southerner Hui-neng, of his due recognition. For Shen-hui to have challenged the hand-picked school of the ruling family was an incredibly courageous act, but perhaps one that was just audacious enough to win public sympathy.

He touted this new proposition more or less full-time between the years 732 and 745, as he traveled about North China and got to know the officials of the T'ang regime. His political standing gradually improved and he was eventually invited (in 745, at age seventy-seven) to Loyang to assume leadership of the great Ho-tse temple. Although the particular object of his criticism, Shen-hsiu's disciple P'u-chi, had died in 739, Shen-hui's attacks on the lineage continued undiminished. Politics finally caught up with him, however, when a follower of Shen-hsiu's "Northern" Ch'an named Lu I, who just happened to be chief of imperial censors, accused him of plotting against the government (citing as evidence the large crowds he routinely attracted). Finally, Emperor Hsuan-tsung (grandson of Empress Wu) himself summoned Shen-hui from Loyang to Ch'ang-an, where he questioned the master and finally sent him into exile in the deep south. This was about 753. It was at this point that Chinese political history and Ch'an collide, for the throne was soon to need Shen-hui's help.

Emperor Hsuan-tsung (reigned 712–756) has been credited by many with the wreck of the T'ang Dynasty. At the beginning of his reign the capital had been in the east at Loyang (where Empress Wu had moved it to escape her memories), but the aristocracy in the west successfully pressured him to bring it back to Ch'ang-an. In his declining years Hsuan-tsung became infatuated with the wife of his son, a lady now infamous in Chinese history as Yang Kuei-fei. She subsequently was divorced by her husband and became a member of the emperor's harem in 738, coming to enjoy enormous influence in affairs of state. She had first been brought to the emperor's attention by one of her relatives, and in typical Chinese style she procured government posts for all available members of her family. As the poet Tu Fu (712-770) described her machinations:

> So many courtiers now throng around the court
> That honest men must tremble;
> And it's said that the gold plate from the treasury
> Has gone to the kinsmen of Lady Yang.[7]

Although none of these blood relatives ever rose to the rich opportunities the situation afforded, another of her favorites compensated abundantly for their political ineptitude.

His name was An Lu-shan, a "barbarian" of Turkish extraction, born in 703, who first entered China as a slave to an officer in a northern garrison of the empire. After distinguishing himself as a soldier, he came to the attention of Yang Kuei-fei, who was so charmed by the man that she adopted him as her son. Before long he was a familiar figure at the court, reportedly very fat and possessing a flair for entertaining the bored aristocracy by his flippancy. Eventually he was made governor of a frontier province, where under pretense of a foreign threat he proceeded to recruit an army of alarming proportions and questionable allegiance.

Meanwhile, back in the capital, Lady Yang and her relatives had taken over the government, whereupon they unwisely decided that An Lu-shan should be brought under firmer control. With their hostility providing him just the pretext needed, he marched his new army toward Ch'ang-an, pausing only long enough to conquer Loyang and proclaim himself emperor. This was in January 756. By July he had also taken Ch'ang-an, from which the royal family had already fled. Conditions deteriorated sufficiently that the troops supporting the throne demanded, and got, the head of Lady Yang Kuei-fei as the price for continued support. (On imperial orders she was strangled by a eunuch.) In the meantime, the imperial T'ang forces found reinforcements, including some Arab mercenaries. After a battle outside Ch'ang-an which left An Lu-shan's forces in disarray, the rebel was murdered, some say by his own son. Soon thereafter the victorious mercenaries sacked and looted Loyang, ending forever its prominence in Chinese history. The government of the T'ang survived, but it was penniless after the many war years in which it could not enforce taxation.[8]

The time was now 757, some four years after Shen-hui's banishment. The destitute government, desperate for money, decided to set up ordination platforms in the major cities across China and raise cash by selling certificates of investiture for

Buddhist monks. (Since entry into the priesthood removed an individual from the tax rolls, it was accepted practice for the Chinese government to require an advance compensation.) Shen-hui's oratorical gifts were suddenly remembered by some of his former followers, and the old heretic was recalled to assist in the fundraising. He was such an effective fundraiser in the ruined city of Loyang that the government commissioned special quarters to be built for him on the grounds of his old temple, the Ho-tse. (He was later to be remembered as the Master of Ho-tse.)

The price for his cooperation seems to have been the official acceptance of his version of Ch'an's history. In his battle with the Northern school of Ch'an he had outlived his opponents and through a bizarre turn of events had finally won the day. Solely through his persistence, the obscure Southern Ch'an monk Hui-neng was installed as Sixth Patriarch in Ch'an histories (replacing Shen-hsiu), and one history went so far as to declare Shen-hui himself the Seventh Patriarch.

The philosophical significance of what Shen-hui's "Southern" doctrine brought to Ch'an has been described as nothing less than a revolution. A modern Zen scholar has claimed that Shen-hui's revolution produced a complete replacement of Indian Buddhism with Chinese philosophy, keeping only the name. Shen-hui, he claims, swept aside all forms of meditation or *dhyana* and replaced it with a concept called no-mind: the doctrines of "absence of thought" and "seeing into one's original nature."[9]

Perhaps this philosophical *coup d'etat* may best be understood by comparing the Northern and Southern teachings. The discredited Northern school of Shen-hsiu had preached that the road to enlightenment must be traversed "step by step," that there were in fact two stages of the mind—the first being a "false mind" which perceives the world erroneously in dualities, and the second a "true mind" which is pure and transcends all discriminations and dualities, perceiving the world simply as a unity. One proceeds from the "false mind" to the "true mind" step by step, through the suppression of erroneous thought processes by the practice of *dhyana* or meditation, in which the mind and the senses slowly reach a state of absolute quietude.

The Southern school took issue with this theory of the mind on a number of points. To begin, they said that if there really is no duality in the world, then how can the mind be divided into "false" and "true"? They argued that the answer quite simply is that there is only one mind, whose many functions are all merely expressions of single true reality. The unity of all things is the true reality; our minds are also part of this reality; and upon realizing this, you have achieved the same enlightenment experience once realized by the Buddha. There is no "false mind" and "true mind," nor is there any need for a long program of dhyana to slowly suppress false thoughts. All that is needed is to practice "absence of thought" and thereby intuitively to realize a simple truth: One unity pervades everything. This realization they called Buddha-mind, and it could only happen "all at once" (not "step by step"), at any time and without warning. This moment of primal realization they called "seeing into one's original nature."

Although Shen-hui is somewhat vague about exactly what practice should replace meditation, the scholar Walter Liebenthal has inferred the following about Shen-hui's attitude toward "sudden enlightenment" as a replacement for meditation: "He seems to have rejected meditation in the technical sense of the word. Instead of methodical endeavors designed to promote religious progress he recommends a change of point of view leading to non-attachment. . . . Non-attachment in this case means that external objects are not allowed to catch our fancy. . . . [A] thing recollected is isolated, it is singled out of the whole, and is thus an illusion; for all short of the undifferentiated continuum is illusive. The senses work as usual . . . but 'no desire is aroused.' . . . This change happens suddenly, that is, it is not dependent upon preceding exertions; it can be brought about without first passing through the stages of a career. That is why it is called 'sudden awakening.' "[10] Liebenthal interprets Shen-hui as saying that whereas the purpose of meditation should be merely to erase our attachment to physical things, it also removes our cognizance of them, which is not necessarily a requirement for nonattachment. It should be possible for us to be aware of the world without being attached to it and enslaved by it. According to Shen-hui's sermon:

When thus my friends are told to discard as useless all they have learned before, then those who have spent fifty or more, or only twenty years practicing meditation, hearing this, might be very much puzzled. . . . Friends, listen attentively, I speak to you of self-deception. What does self-deception mean? You, who have assembled in this place today, are craving for riches and pleasures of intercourse with males and females; you are thinking of gardens and houses. . . . The Nirvana Sutra says, "To get rid of your passions is not Nirvana; to look upon them as no matter of yours, that is Nirvana."[11]

So far so good; but how do we reach this state of recognition without attachment? Apparently the way is to somehow find our original state, in which we were naturally unattached to the surrounding world. The way is to mentally disassociate ourselves from the turmoil of society that surrounds us and look inward, touching our original nature. In this way, both *prajna* and *samadhi*, awareness and noninvolvement, which have been described as the active and passive sides of meditation, are achieved simultaneously.

> Now, let us penetrate to that state in which we are not attached. What do we get to know? Not being attached we are tranquil and guileless. This state underlying all motions and passions is called *samadhi*. Penetrating to this fundamental state we encounter a natural wisdom that is conscious of this original tranquility and guilelessness. This wisdom is called *prajna*. The intimate relation between *samadhi* and *prajna* is thus defined.
>
> . . . If now you penetrate to that state in which your mind is not attached, and yet remains open to impressions, and thus are conscious of the fact that your mind is not attached, then you have reached the state of original blankness and tranquility. From that state of blankness and tranquility there arises an inner knowledge through which blue, yellow, red, and white things in this world are well distinguished. That is *prajna*. Yet no desires arise from these distinctions. That is *samadhi*.
>
> . . . It follows that freedom from attachment (to external things, which replaces meditation in Ch'an Buddhism), enables you to look into the heart of all the Buddhas of the past, and yet it is nothing else than what you yourselves experience today.[12]

Perhaps the most revolutionary thing about this approach was that it seemed to eliminate the need for all the traditional apparatus of Buddhism. It had little or nothing to do with organized religion, and even less connection with the mountains of Indian philosophy that had gone before. A thousand years of Indian thought had been distilled down to a single truth: The realization of our original nature comprises enlightenment. If this were taken at face value, then there was no longer any need for the Buddhist community, the sutras, the chanting, even meditation. There was, in fact, no longer any need for Buddhism. It had been reduced, as the Chinese scholar Wing-tsit Chan has observed, to a concern for the mind alone.

By redefining meditation, Shen-hui had "laid the foundations of Chinese Zen which was no Zen at all."[13] As Shen-hui now described meditation or dhyana:

Sitting motionless is no dhyana; introspection into your own mind is no dhyana; and looking inward at your own calmness is no dhyana.[14]. . . Here in my school, to have no thoughts is sitting, and to see one's original nature is dhyana (Ch'an).[15]

What happened to Indian meditation? No wonder the scholar Hu Shih has described this new teaching as a Chinese revolt against Buddhism.

The political triumph of Shen-hui made Southern Ch'an the official sect, but it also meant that he, now one of the leading religious figures in China, had necessarily become a part of the ruling establishment. Little wonder that the actual future of Ch'an soon reverted back to rural teachers, men who could more convincingly claim to despise the ways of the world, as they meditated in their secluded mountain retreats far from imperial patronage. Shen-hui's school of "Southern" Ch'an of Ho-tse temple, which had established dominance in the north, was soon to be eclipsed by these new vigorous but unlettered rural Ch'anists.[16] Interestingly, the official recognition of the court seemed to quickly extinguish any school of Ch'an that received it. Shen-hsiu was honored by Empress Wu, and his school was then supplanted by that of Shen-hui, whose own imperial recognition and honors were soon to be dust in the history of Ch'an, as the new rural school burst on the scene and effectively took over.[17]

The disorders surrounding and following the rebellion of An Lu-shan are commonly considered today as signaling the decline of the great age of the T'ang Dynasty. They certainly signified the atrophy of the war-torn North Chinese capitals as the political power in China. Loyang and Ch'ang-an came to be replaced in economic influence by the south, a region relatively untouched by the constant struggles North China had to mount against barbarian invaders. Northern scholars retired to the pastoral south, where they lazed in peaceful gardens and recalled the great poets of the early T'ang. Thus Northern urban Ch'an followed the general demise of North Chinese political strength.

Was Shen-hui really the father of the new "meditationless" Ch'an of the mind? Some traditional scholars claim it was not really Shen-hui who revolutionized Ch'an, but rather his master, the Southern teacher Hui-neng. For example, D. T. Suzuki believed that whereas Shen-hui was correct in equating meditation with the primal knowledge of self called *prajna*, he actually taught that this knowledge came about through rational understanding rather than intuition.[18] It was Hui-neng, said Suzuki, who correctly understood that *prajna* was intuition and who knew that it could be realized only through the "sudden" path rather than through the "step-by-step" path. This may well have been true. Just as the Apostle Paul interpreted the teachings of an obscure provincial teacher, Jesus of Nazareth, and popularized them among the urban centers of the Roman Empire, so Shen-hui dispensed the ideas of Hui-neng in northern cities, possibly tempering them where necessary to gain acceptance from the more rationally inclined urban Ch'anists. To continue the analogy, Shen-hui (like Paul) never quotes his mentor directly in his writings—something he certainly would have done if there had been anything to quote—but in a few decades there would be a full autobiography of Hui-neng complete with a "sermon." Shen-hui's own contribution was to open the way for the antimeditation rural school to take over Ch'an. We may now turn to the almost legendary Hui-neng, remembered as the "Sixth Patriarch."

*Hui-neng, The Sixth Patriarch, Destroying
the Sutra (detail).* Liang K'ai (Southern Sung Dynasty).
Courtesy of Takanaru Mitsui, Tokyo.

5
HUI-NENG:
THE SIXTH PATRIARCH AND FATHER OF MODERN ZEN

The master honored today as the father of modern Zen was an impoverished country lad from South China, whose attributed autobiography, *The Platform Sutra of Hui-neng*, is the only "sutra" of Buddhism written by a Chinese.[1] In this work, Hui-neng (638–713) told the story of his rise from obscurity to fame. He described his father as a high Chinese official who, unjustly banished and reduced to a commoner, died of shame while Hui-neng was still a small child. To survive, the fatherless boy and his mother sold wood in the marketplace at Han-hai, near Canton in South China. Then one day he chanced to overhear a man reciting a passage from the Diamond Sutra. Hui-neng stopped to listen, and when he heard the phrase "Let your mind function freely, without abiding anywhere or in anything," he was suddenly awakened. Upon inquiry, he discovered that the reciter was a follower of the Fifth Patriarch, Hung-jen. This teacher, the stranger said, taught that by reciting the Diamond Sutra it was possible to see into one's own nature and to directly experience enlightenment.

The Diamond Sutra (sometimes called the Vajracchedika Sutra) became the passion of Hui-neng as well as the touchstone for the new Chinese Ch'an. An unusually brief work, it has been called the ultimate distillation of the Buddhist Wisdom Literature. The following excerpt is representative of its teaching.

All the mind's arbitrary concepts of matter, phenomena, and of all conditioning factors and all conceptions and ideas relating thereto are like a dream, a phantasm, a bubble, a shadow, the evanescent dew, the lightning's flash. Every true disciple should thus look upon all phenomena and upon all the activities of the mind, and keep his mind empty and self-less and tranquil.[2]

The Diamond Sutra does not search the philosophic heights of the Lankavatara Sutra, the treatise revered by the early *dhyana* school of Bodhidharma, and precisely for this reason it appealed to the Southern school—whose goal was the simplification of Ch'an. Hui-neng could not resist the call and immediately set out for the East Mountain monastery of the Fifth Patriarch.

When he arrived, Hung-jen opened the interview by asking the newcomer his origin. Hearing that he was from the Canton region, the old priest sighed, "If you're from the south you must be a barbarian. How do you expect to become enlightened?" To this Hui-neng shot back, "The people in the north and south may be different, but enlightenment is the same in both regions." Although this impertinence caused the master to immediately recognize Hui-neng's mental gifts, he said nothing and simply put him to work threshing and pounding rice. (This exchange, incidentally, will be recognized as the memorable first encounter between two generations of masters, an obligatory element in all the legends of the early Patriarchs.)

For the next eight months, the young novice toiled in obscurity, never so much as seeing the Fifth Patriarch. Then one day the old priest called an assembly and announced that he was ready to pass on the robe of the patriarchy to the one who could compose a verse showing an intuitive understanding of his own inner nature. The disciples talked over this challenge among themselves and decided, "The robe is certain to be handed down to Shen-hsiu, who is head monk and the natural heir. He will be a worthy successor to the master, so we will not bother composing a verse."

Shen-hsiu, the same master later exalted by the Empress Wu in Loyang, knew what was expected of him and began struggling to compose the verse. After several days' effort, he found the courage to write an unsigned *gatha* on a corridor wall in the dark of night.

Our body is the Bodhi-tree
And our mind a mirror bright.

Carefully we wipe them hour by hour,
And let no dust alight.[3]

When the Fifth Patriarch saw the verse, he convened an
assembly in the corridor, burned incense, and declared that they
all should recite the anonymous passage. Afterward, however,
he summoned Shen-hsiu to his private quarters and inquired if
he was author of the verse. Receiving an affirmative reply, the
master said, "This verse does not demonstrate that you have yet
achieved true understanding of your original nature. You have
reached the front gate, but you have not yet entered into full
understanding. Prepare your mind more fully and when you are
ready, submit another *gatha*." It is a Ch'an commonplace that
Shen-hsiu's verse stressed methodical practice and was perfectly logical—just the opposite of the sudden, antilogical leap
of intuition that is true enlightenment. Shen-hsiu departed, but
try as he might he could not produce the second *gatha*.

In the meantime, Hui-neng overheard the monks reciting
Shen-hsiu's lines. Although he recognized that its author had
yet to grasp his own original nature, Hui-neng asked to be
shown the verse and allowed to do homage to it. After he was
led to the hall, the illiterate lad from the barbarian south asked
to have a *gatha* of his own inscribed next to the one on the wall.

There is no Bodhi-tree
Nor stand of a mirror bright.
Since all is void,
Where can the dust alight?[4]

Although the assembly was electrified by the insight contained in this *gatha*, the diplomatic old Fifth Patriarch publicly
declared that its author lacked full understanding. During the
night, however, he summoned young Hui-neng to the darkened
meditation hall, where he expounded the Diamond Sutra to him
and then ceremonially passed to him the robe of Bodhidharma,
symbol of the patriarchy. He also advised him to travel
immediately to the south, to stay underground for a time in the
interest of safety, and then to preach the Dharma to all who
would listen. Hui-neng departed that very night, crossing the
Yangtze and heading south—the anointed Sixth Patriarch at age
twenty-four.

When the other monks realized what had happened, they
hastily organized a party to retrieve Hui-neng and the Ch'an

relics. Finally one of the pursuers, a burly former soldier, reached the new Sixth Patriarch in his hideaway. Suddenly overcome by the presence of Hui-neng, he found himself asking not for the return of the robe but rather for instruction. Hui-neng obliged him with, "Not thinking of good, not thinking of evil, tell me what was your original face before your mother and father were born." This celebrated question—which dramatizes the Zen concept of an original nature in every person that precedes and transcends artificial values such as good and evil—caused the pursuer to be enlightened on the spot.

For the next several years Hui-neng sought seclusion, living among hunters in the south and concealing his identity. The legends say his kindly nature caused him sometimes to secretly release animals from the hunters' traps and that he would accept only vegetables from their stewpots. But this life as an anonymous vagabond, a Patriarch while not even a priest, could not be his final calling. One day when the time felt right (in 676, as he neared forty), he renounced the life of a refugee and ventured into Canton to visit the Fa-hsing temple. One afternoon as he lingered in the guise of an anonymous guest, he overheard a group of monks arguing about a banner flapping in the breeze.

One monk declared, "The banner is moving."

Another insisted, "No, it is the wind that is moving."

Although he was only a lay observer, Hui-neng could not contain himself, and he interrupted them with his dramatic manifesto, "You are both wrong. It is your mind that moves."

The abbot of the temple, standing nearby, was dumbstruck by the profound insight of this stranger, and on the spot offered to become his pupil. Hui-neng declined the honor, however, requesting instead that his head be shaved and he be allowed to enter Buddhist orders, a priest at last. He was shortly acclaimed by one and all as the Sixth Patriarch, and after a few months in Canton he decided to move to a temple of his own at Ts'ao-ch'i, where he taught for the next four decades. From this monastery came the teachings that would define the faith.

The foregoing story, perhaps the most famous in the Zen canon, is drawn mainly from the aforementioned Platform Sutra of Hui-neng, purportedly an autobiography and sermon presented to an assembly in his later years.[5] (The setting was a temple near his monastery, where he was invited to lecture one day by the local abbot. It was transcribed by one of his disciples, since Hui-neng traditionally was said to have been illiterate.) The document has come down to us in three parts. The first part is the story just summarized: a poetry contest at the monastery of the Fifth Patriarch in which the man later to lead Northern Ch'an is humiliated by a bumpkin, who himself must then flee the wrath of the Ch'an establishment and wait for recognition in the south. The second part is a lecture that scholars believe probably represents the general outline of Hui-neng's views on man's original nature. The third part is a highly embellished account of his later years, usually dismissed as the pious invention of a more recent date.

The real life of Hui-neng is a historical puzzle that may well never be resolved. For example, it is common to note that the later Ch'an writers took great pains to render Hui-neng as illiterate and unlettered as possible, the more to emphasize his egalitarianism. (This in spite of the fact that the sermon attributed to him refers to at least seven different sutras.) The facts were adjusted to make a point: If a simple illiterate wood peddler could become Patriarch, what better proof that the faith is open to all people? Many of the traditional anecdotes surrounding his early years are similarly suspect, and in fact the most respected Hui-neng scholar has declared, "If we consider all the available material, and eliminate patiently all the inconsistencies by picking the most likely legends, we can arrive at a fairly credible biography of Hui-neng. If, on the other hand, we eliminate the legends and the undocumented references to the Sixth Patriarch, we may conclude that there is, in fact, almost nothing that we can really say about him."[6] Yet does it *really* matter whether the legend is meticulously faithful to the facts? Hui-neng is as much a symbol as a historical individual, and it was essential that his life have legendary qualities. In his case, art may have helped life along a bit, but it was for a larger purpose.

The purpose was to formalize the new philosophical ideas of Southern Ch'an. The second part of the Platform Sutra, which details his philosophical position, has been characterized as a masterpiece of Chinese thought, the work not of a scholar but of a natural sage whose wisdom flowed spontaneously from deep within. Yet it is commonly conceded that the uniqueness of his message lies not so much in its being original (which most agree it is not) but in its rendering of the basic ideas of Buddhism into Chinese terms.[7] Buddhism itself seems at times to be in question, as the Sixth Patriarch discounts traditional observances, even suggesting that the Buddhist Western Paradise, known as the Pure Land, might be merely a state of mind.

> The deluded person concentrates on Buddha and wishes to be born in the other land; the awakened person makes pure his own mind. . . . If only the mind has no impurity, the Western Land is not far. If the mind gives rise to impurities, even though you invoke the Buddha and seek to be reborn in the West, it will be difficult to reach . . . but if you practice straightforward mind, you will arrive there in an instant.[8]

Hui-neng also questioned the traditional Ch'an practice of sitting in meditation, declaring it to be more a mind-set than a physical act (if his Sutra is authentic, then he predates his pupil Shen-hui on this point). He also broke it apart into two different categories: the sitting and the meditation.

> . . . what is this teaching that we call "sitting in meditation"? In this teaching "sitting" means without any obstruction anywhere, outwardly and under all circumstances, not to activate thoughts. "Meditation" is internally to see the original nature and not become confused.[9]

Elsewhere he is quoted as declaring that protracted sitting only shackles the body without profiting the mind.[10] Although Hui-neng severely took to task those who depended on meditation, there is no evidence that he forbade it entirely. What he did reject was a *fixation* on meditation, a confusion—to use a later Zen expression—of the finger pointing at the moon with the moon itself. Even so, this was a radical move. Hui-neng presents us with the startling prospect of a *dhyana* teacher questioning the function of *dhyana*—until then the very basis of the school.

Yet the sutra is far from being all negative. It has a number of positive messages, including the following: All people are born in an enlightened state, a condition in which good and evil are not distinguished. Nor are there distracting discriminations, attachments, and perturbations of the spirit in this primal estate. (A very similar view is found throughout the poetry of William Wordsworth, to give only one example from Western thought.[11]) But if man's original nature is pure and unstained, how then does evil enter into a person's character? He faces this classic theological question head-on:

Good friends, although the nature of people in this world is from the outset pure in itself, the ten thousand things are all within their own natures. If people think of all the evil things, then they will practice evil; if they think of all the good things, then they will practice good. Thus it is clear that in this way all the dharmas (aspects of humanity) are within your own natures, yet your own natures are always pure. The sun and moon are always bright, yet if they are covered by clouds, although they are bright, below they are darkened, and the sun, moon, stars, and planets cannot be seen clearly. But if suddenly the wind of wisdom should blow and roll away the clouds and mists, all forms in the universe appear at once. . . . [I]f a single thought of good evolves, intuitive wisdom is born. As one lamp serves to dispel a thousand years of darkness, so one flash of wisdom destroys ten thousand years of ignorance.[12]

As Hui-neng viewed it, there is latent within us all the condition of enlightenment, the state that precedes our concern with good and evil. It can be reclaimed through an intuitive acquaintance with our own inner natures. This is well summarized by the Hui-neng scholar Philip Yampolsky: "The Platform Sutra maintains that the nature of man is from the outset pure, but that his purity has no form. But by self-practice, by endeavoring for himself, man can gain insight into this purity. Meditation, *prajna*, true reality, purity, the original nature, self-nature, the Buddha nature, all these terms, which are used constantly throughout the sermon, indicate the same undefined Absolute, which when seen and experienced by the individual himself, constitutes enlightenment."[13]

This condition of original innocence that is enlightenment can be reclaimed through "no-thought," a state in which the mind floats, unattached to what it encounters, moving freely through phenomena, unperturbed by the incursions and attractions of the world, liberated because it is its own master, tranquil because it is pure. This is the condition in which we were born and it is the condition to which we can return by practicing "no-thought." Although it happens to be similar to the condition that can be realized through arduous meditation, Hui-neng apparently did not believe that meditation was required. This primal condition of the mind, this glimpse into our original nature, could be realized instantaneously if our mind were receptive. But what *is* this state called "no-thought"? According to Hui-neng:

> To be unstained in all environments is called no-thought. If on the basis of your own thoughts you separate from environment, then, in regard to things, thoughts are not produced. If you stop thinking of the myriad things, and cast aside all thoughts, as soon as one instant of thought is cut off, you will be reborn in another realm. . . . Because man in his delusion has thoughts in relation to his environment, heterodox ideas stemming from these thoughts arise, and passions and false views are produced from them.[14]

Yampolsky characterizes "no-thought" as follows: "Thoughts are conceived as advancing in progression from past to present to future, in an unending chain of successive thoughts. Attachment to one instant of thought leads to attachment to a succession of thoughts, and thus to bondage. By cutting off attachment to one instant of thought, one may, by a process unexplained, cut off attachment to a succession of thoughts and thus attain to no-thought, which is the state of enlightenment."[15] Precisely how this condition of "no-thought" enlightenment is achieved is not explained in the Platform Sutra and in fact has been the major concern of Zen ever since. The one thing that all will agree is that the harder one tries to attain it, the more difficult it becomes. It is there inside, waiting to be released, but it can be reached only through the intuitive mind. And it happens suddenly, when we least expect.

The master Hui-neng stands at the watershed of Zen history. Indeed he may be the watershed, in the embodied form of a legend. There seems reason to suspect that he was canonized well after the fact, as was Bodhidharma. But whereas Bodhidharma provided an anchor for the original formation of a separate Dhyana sect in Chinese Buddhism, Hui-neng became the rallying symbol for a new type of Ch'an, one wholly Chinese, and one that seemed to discount Bodhidharma's old mainstay, meditation. He became the Chinese answer to the Indian Bodhidharma.

Hui-neng redefined the specific characteristics of the Ch'an goal and described in nontheological terms the mind state in which duality is banished. But he failed to go the next step and explain how to get there. All he did was point out (to use the terminology of logic) that meditation not only was not a *sufficient* condition for enlightenment, it might not even be a *necessary* condition. What then *was* required? The answer to this question was to be worked out during the next phase of Ch'an, the so-called Golden Age of Zen, when a new school of Southern Ch'an exploded (to use a common description) in the south and went on to take over all of Ch'an. These new teachers seem to have accepted Hui-neng as their patron, although the direct connection is not entirely clear. These masters learned how to impose a torture chamber on the logical mind, bringing to it such humiliations that it finally annihilated ego or self and surrendered to *prajna*, intuitive wisdom. They devised systematic ways to produce the state of "no-thought" that Hui-neng and Shen-hui apparently could only invoke.

PART II

THE GOLDEN
AGE OF ZEN

. . . . in which teachers of rural, Southern
Ch'an begin to experiment with new ways to precipitate
the "sudden" enlightenment experience, even bringing into
question the role of meditation. Along with the search
for new techniques goes the attempt to define precisely what
enlightenment is and to formalize the transmission process. During
this time, Ch'an monasteries become independent organizations
and Ch'an a recognized, if eccentric, Buddhist sect.
The iconoclastic, self-supporting Ch'an establishments ride
out a persecution of Buddhism in the mid-ninth century
that effectively destroys all other Buddhist schools in China.
This is the great creative era of Ch'an, in which the
sect secures its own identity and creates its own texts for
use by later generations.

Ma-tsu (right) and Layman P'ang (detail). Artist unknown,
inscription by Yu-chi Chih-hui (ca. 1215–1300). Courtesy of
Tennei-ji, Kyoto, and the Kyoto National Museum.

6

MA-TSU:
ORIGINATOR OF
"SHOCK" ENLIGHTENMENT

If Hui-neng was the Sixth Patriarch, then who was the seventh? Although several of his followers are mentioned in the Platform Sutra, the only one who seems to have made any difference in Ch'an history was Shen-hui (670–762), who successfully destroyed the Northern school of Shen-hsiu (605–706) and elevated Hui-neng. Although Shen-hui was given the accolade of Seventh Patriarch in some parts of the north, history was to be written elsewhere. Shen-hui's school of "Southern" Ch'an was soon compromising with the remaining Northern Ch'anists—conceding that the study of the sutras could go along hand in hand with sudden enlightenment—and he seems to have enjoyed a little too much his role as imperial socialite. The only member of Shen-hui's school to realize any historical prominence was Tsung-mi (780–841), whose fame attaches not to his original thought but rather to his scholarly writings describing the various sects of Ch'an.[1] A littérateur and friend of the famous poet Po Chu-i (772–846), he also tried unsuccessfully to mediate between the followers of the step-by-step sutra-reading Buddhists of the cities and the all-at-once, antiliterary proponents of sudden enlightenment in the country, but he succeeded only in bringing the history of Northern Ch'an to a dignified close.[2]

The Chinese scholar Hu Shih skillfully pinpoints why the social success of Shen-hui's new "Southern" school in the north actually contributed to its decline. As he saw it: "The explanation is simple. Zennism could not flourish as an officially patronized religion, but only as an attitude of mind, a method of thinking and a mode of living. An officially patronized teacher of Buddhism is obliged to perform all the traditional rituals and ceremonies which the true Zennist despises. Shen-hui succeeded in establishing Zennism as a state religion, but by so doing he almost killed it. All further development of Chinese Zen had to come from those great teachers who valued simple life and intellectual freedom and independence more than worldly recognition."³ And in fact just such teachers had begun springing up like mushrooms. On lonely mountaintops, teachers of sudden enlightenment were experimenting with new ways to transmit wordless insight. They seem to have despised traditional Buddhism, perhaps partly because Buddhism—by which is meant the cultural elitists and aristocrats in the capitals of Ch'ang-an and Loyang—had so long despised them. (Recall the Fifth Patriarch's greeting to Hui-neng: "If you're from the south, you must be a barbarian.") Although traditional Buddhism (including teachers of dhyana) continued to flourish, and the city of Ch'ang-an remained a model for Asian civilization, the political power of the T'ang government in the north gradually withered. And as it declined, so too did the fortunes of the traditional Ch'an establishments that had flourished under imperial patronage.

The new Ch'an teachers of the Southern school may have felt smug in their new prestige and independence, but they still were subject to the ingrained Chinese desire for a lineage. (Perhaps in the land of Confucius, spiritual ancestors were essential to dignity.) The triumph of the legend of Hui-neng in the north had not been lost on the Ch'anists elsewhere, and it effectively meant that for any Ch'an school to have respectability nationwide, it had to be able to trace its lineage back to this illiterate southerner and his temple at Ts'ao-ch'i. Unfortunately this turned out to be difficult, since by the time Hui-neng actually came to be recognized as the Sixth Patriarch, he had been dead for half a century and there were few Chinese who even knew firsthand of his existence—and none besides Shen-hui who ever claimed to have studied under him. How then could he be made the founder of the Ch'an schools blooming all over China?

The scholar Hu Shih has speculated somewhat knavishly on how Hui-neng's "lineage" may have been created after the fact: "By the last quarter of the eighth century, there began to be a great stampede of almost all the Ch'an schools to get on the bandwagon of the school of Hui-neng. . . . Hui-neng died early in the eighth century, and his disciples were mostly unknown ascetics who lived and died in their hilly retreats. One could easily have paid a visit to some of them. So in the last decades of the century, some of those unknown names were remembered or discovered. Two of the names thus exhumed from obscurity were Huai-jang of the Heng Mountains in Hunan, and Hsing-ssu of the Ch'ing-yuan Mountains of Kiangsi. Neither of these names appeared in earlier versions of Hui-neng's life story."[4]

These two masters, Nan-yueh Huai-jang (677–744) of Hunan and Ch'ing-yuan Hsing-ssu (d. 740) of Kiangsi, were made the missing links between Hui-neng and the two schools of Ch'an that would one day become Japanese Rinzai and Soto, respectively. Since the lineage most important for the early years of Ch'an's Golden Age was that which would one day be the Rinzai school, the tradition of Huai-jang will be examined here first. As noted above, although the legend says that Huai-jang once studied under the Sixth Patriarch, Hui-neng, supporting historical evidence is not readily found. However, he is thought to have studied under another follower of the Fifth Patriarch Hung-jen and to have been a part of the general scene of Southern Ch'an.[5] His actual function may have been to supply a direct line of descent between Hui-neng and the man who was to be the creator of Rinzai Zen as we know it today.

That man is the famous Ma-tsu Tao-i (709–788), who even if not a direct spiritual descendant of Hui-neng was certainly a product of the same exciting period of intellectual ferment. According to the more or less contemporary record left by the northern historian Tsung-mi, Ma-tsu (which means "Patriarch Ma") was a native of Szechuan who was ordained a monk at an early age by a Korean master in his home province.[6] Young Ma traveled on, as was common with beginning Ch'an monks, and (so say the later legends) finally came to the monastery of Huai-jang, located on Mt. Nan-yueh. The story of their first encounter became a standard among later Ch'an masters, for it is a particularly effective discrediting of that onetime Ch'an mainstay, meditation, which became anathema to the more revolutionary Southern school.

As the story goes, Huai-jang one day came upon Ma-tsu absorbed in meditation and proceeded to question the purpose of his long bouts of dhyana. Ma-tsu immediately replied, "I want to become a Buddha, an enlightened being."

Saying nothing, Huai-jang quietly picked up a brick and started rubbing it on a stone. After a time Ma-tsu's curiosity bested him and he inquired, "Why are you rubbing that brick on a stone?"

Huai-jang replied, "I am polishing it into a mirror."

Ma-tsu probably knew by this time that he had been set up, but he had to follow through: "But how can you make a mirror by polishing a brick on a stone?"

The celebrated answer was: "How can *you* become enlightened by sitting in meditation?"

The point, driven home time and again throughout the eighth century, was that enlightenment is an active, not a passive, condition. And Ma-tsu himself was to become the foremost exponent of enlightenment as a natural part of life.

Ma-tsu always made a profound impression on his contemporaries, and no small part may be attributable to his peculiar physical traits. As *The Transmission of the Lamp* describes him:

> In appearance and bearing he was most striking. He glared as a tiger does and he ambled like a cow. He could touch his nose with his tongue, and on the soles of his feet were wheel-shaped marks [physical qualities also attributed to the Buddha]. During the period [of 713–41] he studied the *dhyana* . . . under Master Huai-jang, who then had nine disciples. Of these only [Ma-tsu] received the sacred mind seal.[7]

However, his real immortality derives from his contribution to the arsenal of methods for shocking novices into enlightenment. It will be recalled that the legendary Sixth Patriarch, Hui-neng, neglected to explain exactly what a person should do to "see into one's own nature." Ma-tsu apparently was the first master who developed nonmeditative tricks for nudging a disciple into the state of "no-thought." He was an experimenter, and he pioneered a number of methods that later were perfected by his followers and the descendants of his followers. He was the first master to ask a novice an unanswerable question, and then while the person struggled for an answer, to shout in his ear (he liked the syllable "Ho!")—hoping to jolt the pupil into a nondualistic mind state. Another similar technique was to call out someone's name just as the person was leaving the room, a surprise that seemed to bring the person up short and cause him to suddenly experience his original nature. A similar device was to deliver the student a sharp blow as he pondered a point, using violence to focus his attention completely on reality and abort ratiocination. Other tricks included responding to a question with a *seemingly* irrelevant answer, causing the student to sense the irrelevancy of his question. He would also sometimes send a pupil on a "goose chase" between himself and some other enlightened individual at the monastery, perhaps in the hope that bouncing the novice from one personality to another would somehow shake his complacency. Whatever the technique, his goal was always to force a novice to uncover his original nature for himself. He did this by never giving a straight answer or a predictable response and therefore never allowing a disciple to lapse into a passive mental mode.

Ma-tsu also seems to have simplified the idea of what constitutes enlightenment. As he defined it, "seeing into one's own nature" simply meant understanding (intuitively, not rationally) who you are and what you are. This truth could be taught with whatever method seemed appropriate at a given moment. As Hu Shih so eloquently describes his teaching, ". . . any gesture or motion, or even silence, might be used to communicate a truth. [Recall the Buddha once enlightened a follower by holding up a flower.] Ma-tsu developed this idea into a pedagogical method for the new Zen. There is no need to seek any special faculty in the mind for the enlightenment. Every behavior is the mind, the manifestation of the Buddha-nature. Snapping a finger, frowning or stretching the brow, coughing, smiling, anger, sorrow, or desire . . . is the functioning of the Buddhahead: it is the Tao, the Way. There is no need to perform any special act, be it *dhyana* or worship, in order to achieve the Tao. To be natural is the Way. Walk naturally, sit naturally, sleep naturally, live naturally—that is the Way. Let the mind be free: do not purposely do evil; nor purposely do good. There is no Law to abide, no Buddhahood to attain. Maintain a free mind and cling to nothing: that is Tao."[8]

Thus it seems that the most preeminent Ch'an master of the eighth century not only repudiated all the apparatus of traditional Buddhism, he also simplified enlightenment down to a quite secular condition of acceptance of the natural state of human affairs. For instance, although he was familiar with the great Mahayana sutras, Ma-tsu never mentions Hui-neng or the Diamond Sutra. His Ch'an, expressed in simple everyday language, seems merely so many ways of finding out who you are and what you are. Furthermore, there seems to be nothing specifically that you can do to accelerate the occurrence of sudden enlightenment, other than use traditional practices to make your psyche as uncomplicated as possible and then wait for the moment to strike (he, of course, experimented to find ways to accelerate the arrival of that moment). But he has nothing encouraging to say about the effectiveness of meditation as an aid to finding the desired nonrational insight, which he sometimes described using the borrowed term "Tao":

Cultivation is of no use for the attainment of Tao. The only thing that one can do is to be free of defilement. When one's mind is stained with thoughts of life and death, or deliberate action, that is defilement. The grasping of the Truth is the function of everyday-mindedness. Everyday-mindedness is free from intentional action, free from concepts of right and wrong, taking and giving, the finite or the infinite. . . . All our daily activities—walking, standing, sitting, lying down—all response to situations, our dealings with circumstances as they arise: all this is Tao.[9]

Ma-tsu eventually left Huai-jang (if, in fact, he ever met him in the first place) and presided over a community of Ch'an disciples at K'ai-yuan temple in Kiangsi. This was to be the incubator for the greatest thinkers of the eighth century, and the setting for some of the finest Ch'an anecdotes. The anecdote, incidentally, is the perfect Ch'an teaching device, since it forces the listener to find its meaning in his own inner experience. The sermon provided the theoretical basis for an idea, but the anecdote showed the theory in action and made the listener share in a real experience, if only vicariously. But first we will begin with a sermon credited to him, in which he summarizes the *philosophical* position he held. There was nothing particularly new about his understanding; it was his method that was novel. His sermon said, in essence, that reality is merely our mind, and that enlightenment comprised the nonrational recognition of this.

All of you should realize that your own mind is Buddha, that is, this mind is Buddha's Mind. . . . Those who seek for the Truth should realize that there is nothing to seek. There is no Buddha but Mind; there is no Mind but Buddha.[10]

Again there is the counsel against discriminations between good and evil, since the original Mind transcends these:

Do not choose what is good, nor reject what is evil, but rather be free from purity and defilement. Then you will realize the emptiness of sin.[11]

This is not a preachment of values; rather it is the insight that there is a reality beyond our puny discriminations. If you can achieve this larger perspective, then good and evil become an inconsequential part of the larger flow of life.

His sermon then returns to the theme of the mind as the arbiter of reality, recalling the Void of Nagarjuna and pointing out that even the workings of the mind are ephemeral and possess no self-nature.

Thoughts perpetually change and cannot be grasped because they possess no self-nature. The Triple World [of desire, form, and beyond-form] is nothing more than one's mind. The multitudinous universe is nothing but the testimony of one Dharma [truth]. What are seen as forms are the reflections of the mind. The mind does not exist by itself; its existence is manifested through forms. . . . If you are aware of this mind, you will dress, eat, and act spontaneously in life as it transpires, and thereby cultivate your spiritual nature. There is nothing more that I can teach you.[12]

The essence of this teaching is that reality is, for us, merely what our mind says it is, and "enlightenment" or "becoming a Buddha" is merely coming to terms with ourselves and with this tricky mind that constantly devises our reality for us.

This credo is remembered most vividly in two anecdotes that were later enshrined in a famous collection of koans called the Wu-men Kuan (or Mumonkan in Japanese). In both of these anecdotes, Ma-tsu is asked, "What is Buddha?"—meaning what is the spirituality that all seek. In one he replied, "Mind is Buddha" (Mumonkan, Case 30), and in the other anecdote he said, "No mind, no Buddha" (Mumonkan, Case 33), which merely affirms that spirituality is in the mind, and for its realization one must realize the mind.[13] In either instance he is merely following the earlier idea that there is no reality and thus no enlightenment outside the mind.

These two exchanges are part of a single anecdote of Ma-tsu recorded in the chronicles.

A monk asked why the Master maintained, "The Mind is the Buddha." The Master answered, "Because I want to stop the crying of a baby." The monk persisted, "When the crying has stopped, what is it then?" "Not Mind, not Buddha," was the answer. "How do you teach a man who does not uphold either of these?" The Master said, "I would tell him, 'Not things.' " The monk again questioned, "If you met a man free from attachment to all things, what would you tell him?" The Master replied, "I would let him experience the Great Tao."[14]

As the scholar John Wu has pointed out, "This dialogue reveals an important secret about Ma-tsu's art of teaching. Sometimes he used a positive formula, sometimes he used a negative formula. On the surface they are contradictory to each other. But when we remember that he was using them in answering persons of different grades of attainments and intelligence, the contradiction disappears at once in the light of a higher unity of purpose, which was in all cases to lead the questioner to transcend his present state."[15]

Another example of a seemingly contradictory position is recorded as a koan in another famous collection, the Blue Cliff Record (Case 3). In this anecdote, Ma-tsu is asked one day about his health, and he responded with, "Sun-faced Buddhas, Moon-faced Buddhas."[16] According to a Buddhist tradition, a Sun-faced Buddha lives for eighteen hundred years, a Moon-faced Buddha lives only a day and a night. Perhaps he was proposing these two contradictory cases to demonstrate the irrelevance of an inquiry after his physical state. It would have been far better if the question had concerned his mind.

A story describing how Ma-tsu handled other teachers who wandered by depicts very well the way that he could undermine logic and categorization. In a particularly famous anecdote, a visiting teacher proposed a condition of duality, a condition equivalent to that of a switch that can be either off or on. Having permitted the teacher to adopt this very un-Zen position, Ma-tsu proceeds to demolish him. The story goes as follows:

> A monk who lectured on Buddhism came to the Master and asked, "What is the teaching advocated by the Ch'an masters?" Ma-tsu posed a counterquestion: "What teachings do you maintain?" The monk replied that he had lectured on more than twenty sutras and sastras. The Master exclaimed, "Are you not a lion?" The monk said, "I do not venture to say that." The Master puffed twice and the monk commented, "This is the way to teach Ch'an." Ma-tsu retorted, "What way do you mean?" and the monk said, "The way the lion leaves the den." The Master became silent. Immediately the monk remarked, "This is also the way of Ch'an teaching." At this the Master again asked, "What way do you mean?" "The lion remains in his den." "When there is neither going out nor remaining in, what way would you say this was?" The monk made no answer. . . .[17]

Ma-tsu had posed a seemingly unanswerable question, at least a question that logic could not answer. This provocative exchange, later to be known as a mondo, was a new teaching technique that departed significantly from the earlier methods of Hui-neng and Shen-hui, who mounted a platform, gave a sermon, and then politely received questions from the audience.

But how did Ma-tsu handle this question when it was presented to *him*? He fell back on the fact that reality is what we make it, and all things return to the mind. He once handled essentially the same question that he put to the visiting monk, showing how it can be done. His response is the essence of Zen.

A monk once drew four lines in front of Ma-tsu. The top line was long and the remaining three were short. He then demanded of the Master, "Besides saying that one line is long and the other three are short, what else could you say?" Ma-tsu drew one line on the ground and said, "This could be called either long or short. That is my answer."[18]

Language is deceptive. But if it is used to construct an antilogical question, it can equally be used to construct an antilogical reply.

Ma-tsu discovered and refined what seems to have eluded the earlier teachers such as Hui-neng and Huai-jang: namely, the trigger mechanism for sudden enlightenment. As noted earlier, he originated the use of shouting and blows to precipitate enlightenment, techniques to become celebrated in later decades in the hands of men such as Huang-po and Lin-chi, masters who shaped the Rinzai sect. As a typical example, there is the story of a monk coming to him to ask, "What was the purpose of Bodhidharma's coming from the West?" which is Ch'an parlance for "What is the basic principle of Zen?" As the monk bowed reverently before the old master waiting for the reply that would bring it all together, Ma-tsu knocked him to the ground, saying, "If I do not strike you, people all over the country will laugh at me." The hapless monk picked himself up off the ground and—suddenly realizing he had just tasted the only reality there is—was enlightened on the spot.[19]

Obviously, every boxer does not experience enlightenment when he receives a knockout punch. The blow of enlightenment is meant to rattle the questioning mind and to disrupt, if only for an instant, its clinging to abstractions and logic. It seems almost as though enlightenment were a physical phenomenon that sometimes can best be achieved by a physical process—such as a blow or a shout.

The violence seemed to work both ways, for the monks often gave him a dose of his own medicine. An example is reported in the following story:

It happened once that his disciple Yin-feng was pushing along a cart, while Ma-tsu was sitting on the road with his feet stretched out. Yin-feng requested him to draw back his feet, but Ma-tsu said, "What is stretched out is not to be drawn back again!" Yin-feng retorted, "Once advanced, there is no turning backward!" Disregarding the master, he kept pushing the cart until it ran over and injured his feet. Ma-tsu returned to the hall with an axe in his hand, saying, "Let the one who a few moments ago injured my feet with his cart come forward!" Yin-feng, not to be daunted, came forward stretching his neck in front of the master. The master [peacefully] put down his axe.[20]

The significance of this story, if it has any significance, is that it conveys the atmosphere of Ch'an monasteries around 750. It demonstrates that the leader of a monastery had to win his spurs. He had to be tougher, more audacious, and faster than anybody else.

During the T'ang it was common to use the ox as a metaphor for all that is uncontrollable in human nature. The ox was not necessarily bad; it just had to be governed. The rigor with which this control was applied at Ma-tsu's monastery is illustrated in the story concerning one of the disciples, a former hunter who Ma-tsu encountered one day working in the monastery kitchen.

"What are you doing?" asked the master—a question that never got a straight answer from an enlightened Ch'an monk.

"I am herding an ox," the man replied, a metaphorical way of saying he was trying to discipline himself.

"And how," shot back Ma-tsu, "do you go about tending it?"

The monk replied, "Whenever it starts to go to grass [i.e., self-indulgence], I yank it back by the nostrils [the tender part of the great animal]."

To which Ma-tsu admiringly replied, "If you really can do that by yourself, then I may as well retire."[21]

This story illustrates the emphasis on self-control that was a part of the Ch'an monasteries. Yet self-control was only to be practiced for what it gave in return. There were no value judgments or rules that had to be followed. The point was to do what seemed the most rewarding. For example, there is a story that a local governor asked Ma-tsu, "Master, should I eat meat and drink wine?" The master did not give him a reply that implied a value judgment, but rather outlined the rewards of the two possible paths: "To eat and drink is your natural right, to abstain from meat and wine is your chance for greater blessedness."[22]

Ma-tsu often used the structure of language, with its natural capacity for parallels, as a teaching tool in itself.

Another time a monk asked, what is the meaning of Bodhidharma coming from the West?" "What is the meaning [of your asking] at this moment?" replied the Master.[23]

The monk was interested in abstract issues (using the Ch'an metaphor for enlightenment's meaning); Ma-tsu reminded him that the only reality that mattered was his own being, his own needs. And he did it using almost identical language.

Ma-tsu was constantly testing his disciples, keeping them on their toes and reinforcing their enlightenment. There is the story that one evening while enjoying the moonlight with three of his disciples (including the two most famous, Huai-hai and Nan-ch'uan), he asked them the question "what should we do right now, this very moment?"—a typical Zen challenge. One of the monks said, "It would be best to be studying the sutras of the ancients who have achieved enlightenment." The monk Huai-hai, who was later to receive Ma-tsu's mantle, countered, "It would be good to practice meditation."

At that point Nan-ch'uan, the third monk, simply rose, shook the sleeves of his robe, and silently walked away. Ma-tsu acknowledged this as the right answer and declared, "The sutra scriptures are returnable to the Buddhist canon, and meditation to the undifferentiated ocean, but Nan-ch'uan alone leaps over and transcends these."[24] Nan-ch'uan's response was a triumph of physical action and simplicity over religiosity and abstraction.

Ma-tsu is reported in the chronicles to have had 139 enlightened disciples, many of whom went on to become Ch'an leaders in their own districts. The most outstanding were the monks Huai-hai and Nan-ch'uan and a layman named P'ang—all three of whom are today remembered in anecdotes that have become Ch'an scriptures. But others were probably just as active and enlightened. Southern Ch'an was expanding, with mountaintop retreats blossoming everywhere. Many teachers probably have been forgotten only because they had no disciples who took the pains to transcribe and preserve their teachings. Ma-tsu himself also apparently wrote nothing, but he was more fortunate in his disciples. In any case, he reportedly died in the typical Ch'an way. He predicted his death a month in advance, and when the time came, he bathed, assumed the meditation posture, and silently passed on.

*Priest Sewing Under the Morning
Sun.* Attributed to Ka'o (active ca. 1350
or slightly earlier). Courtesy of the
Cleveland Museum of Art.

7

HUAI-HAI:
FATHER OF
MONASTIC CH'AN

Among the many celebrated disciples of Ma-tsu, the man whose influence has been most pervasive throughout the succeeding centuries was Po-chang Huai-hai (720–814). He is the master credited with founding the first wholly Ch'an monastery, with devising a special set of rules for Ch'an discipline, and with writing a closely argued treatise on sudden enlightenment. Whereas Ma-tsu and others of his disciples such as Nan-ch'uan experimented with ways to help novices break through the barrier of reason, Huai-hai examined the phenomenon of enlightenment itself and described the mental state of preparedness necessary to reach the Other Shore. Huai-hai has been somewhat unjustifiably neglected by the modern Zen movement, perhaps because his expository style did not lend itself to memorable anecdotes or koan cases.

The accounts of Huai-hai's origin are contradictory, but he seems to have begun his Buddhist studies early, becoming the pupil of a master named Tao-chih in a small town in the present-day province of Chekiang.[1] (It was this master who gave him the religious name Huai-hai, or "Ocean of Wisdom.") After he came to maturity, the story goes, he heard of the great master Ma-tsu in the province of Kiangsi, and he traveled there to study.

Among the many anecdotes surrounding Huai-hai's stay with Ma-tsu, perhaps the finest is that of the auspicious first encounter. The story says that when Huai-hai arrived, the old master immediately asked what previous temple he had traveled from, followed by: "What do you come here to find?"

Huai-hai replied, "I have come to discover the truth of Buddha."

To this Ma-tsu replied, "What can you expect to learn from me? Why do you ignore the treasure in your own house and wander so far abroad?"

Understandably puzzled, Huai-hai asked, "What is this treasure that I have been ignoring?"

To which came the celebrated reply: "The one who questions me at this moment is your treasure. Everything is complete in it. It is lacking in nothing, and furthermore the things it possesses are inexhaustible. Considering that you can use this treasure freely, why then do you persist in wandering abroad?" It is said that with these words Huai-hai suddenly had an intuitive, nonrational acquaintance with his own mind.[2]

Among the other classic tales of Huai-hai's apprenticeship under Ma-tsu is the often repeated account of the day the two of them were walking together along a path when suddenly a flock of migratory geese was heard passing overhead. Ma-tsu turned to his pupil and asked, "What was that sound?" Huai-hai innocently replied, "It was the cry of wild geese." Ma-tsu paused and then demanded of his pupil, "Where have they gone?" Huai-hai said, "They have flown away."

This was an unacceptably drab, straightforward answer for a Zen man, and in disgust Ma-tsu whirled, grabbed Huai-hai's nose, and twisted it until his disciple cried out in panic, causing Ma-tsu to observe, "So you thought they had flown away. Yet they were here all the time."[3]

The legends say that this exchange, in the typical harsh style of Ma-tsu, caused Huai-hai to confront his original nature. What Ma-tsu had done was to give his pupil a vivid lesson in the concept of an indivisible unity which pervades the world; things do not come and go—they are there always, part of a permanent fabric. Huai-hai was being invited to stop viewing the world as a fragmented collection of elements and see it rather as a unified whole.

The interactions of master and novice were always dynamic. For example, another story says that one day Ma-tsu asked Huai-hai how he would teach Ch'an. Huai-hai responded by holding up a dust whisk vertically. Ma-tsu continued by asking him, "Is this all there is? Is there nothing more?" Huai-hai replied by throwing down the whisk. (One interpreter has said that raising the dust whisk revealed the mind's function, whereas throwing it down returned function to the mind's substance.)[4] According to some versions of this episode, Ma-tsu responded by shouting at the top of his lungs, rendering Huai-hai deaf for three days. This shout is said to have been the occasion of Huai-hai's final enlightenment.

Huai-hai seems to have been a kindly man, warm and personable, not given to the roughhouse methods of some of his contemporaries. Instead of flamboyance, we find a friendly type who concentrated on guiding a community of disciples (sometimes called a "Zen forest") and giving a helping hand to all. We will pass over the many other anecdotes involving his stay with Ma-tsu and turn instead to his more significant contributions to the growth of Ch'an.[5] These fall into two major categories: First, he founded the first wholly Ch'an monastery and for it formulated a set of monastic rules that are today still respected in Zen monasteries; and second, he was one of the first Southern Ch'an masters to explore the psychology of "sudden enlightenment" and to write a lucid analysis of the mental preparation it required.

Before detailing Huai-hai's contribution to monastic Ch'an, perhaps it would be well to recall briefly the character of the traditional Buddhist monastery in China during the T'ang (618-907) era. Buddhist monasteries had long been governed by a set of rules known as the *vinaya*. These rules prescribed everything from the color of the robes for the priesthood to the penalties attached to eating onions or garlic (forbidden primarily because they were thought to be stimulants, not necessarily because of their social liabilities in close quarters). There were also some specific and quite solemn commandments—for example, monks or nuns could be expelled from the community for stealing, killing, lying, or sexual congress. Originating in India, these rules had been subsequently transplanted to China, where they gradually were made even more strict, although their enforcement apparently was not always rigorous. Perhaps because of this laxity the T'ang regime established penalties even more severe than those imposed by the Buddhist authorities.[6] For example, whereas the *vinaya* indirectly countenanced the eating of meat (through the loophole that all charitable gifts must be accepted since they give the laity merit, and if a gift happened to be meat it still had to be consumed for the sake of the donor), the T'ang government prescribed thirty days of hard labor for monks caught partaking. Since citizens entering Buddhist orders were taken off the tax rolls, the government took pains to ensure that monastic life was rigorous enough to discourage simple tax dodgers.[7] Although the Chinese Buddhist schools were almost all members of the side of Buddhism known as Mahayana, they apparently followed the rules of Theravada Buddhism, since the latter were clearer and more easily understood.[8] Huai-hai decided to merge the two sets of rules and from them to devise a new set of guidelines specifically for Ch'an, thereby creating a code of monastic discipline that eventually would rule Zen behavior throughout the world.

The record concerning how the Ch'an monastic system initially was established is less detailed than we might wish. The legendary Fourth Patriarch, Tao-hsin, was said to have been the first *dhyana* master to settle down in one place and nurture a band of disciples. *Dhyana* teachers seem to have allied themselves with the conventional Buddhists in the decades that followed, living in their monasteries much as the hermit crab finds a home in the shells of other species. If their numbers were large they might have their own separate quarters, but they still had to respect the rules of their host sect, which more often than not was the Vinaya school.[9] Gradually, however, a transformation occurred, as Ch'an masters became increasingly distinguishable from the leaders of other sects and Ch'an itself grew to increasing proportions, particularly in the south.

It is not surprising that the man who made monastic Ch'an a reality was Ma-tsu's pupil Po-chang Huai-hai. In the recorded anecdotes Huai-hai is characterized as a level-headed, pragmatic man whom one can easily imagine having superior administrative ability. As John Wu characterizes his rules, "It was this rule [of Huai-hai] that instituted for the first time the Zen monastic system. In its emphasis on moral discipline and its matter of factness, it is comparable to the Holy Rule of St. Benedict. The duties of the Abbot and various functionaries under him are meticulously defined. The daily life of the monks is regulated in detail. Of particular interest are the rites of taking vows and the universal duty of working in the fields."[10]

It is difficult to say exactly what was the nature of the rules Huai-hai formulated, since his original precepts have been recast a number of times down through the years, with the earliest surviving version being that preserved in a 1282 Chinese Yuan Dynasty document called "the Holy Rule of Po-chang [Huai-hai]." If we look beyond the details, however, we see that his emphasis on the creation of a self-supporting monastic establishment was in a sense a further sinicization of Indian Buddhism, through the rejection of begging as the primary means of support. (Begging was not abandoned entirely, since it is valuable for teaching humility; instead it was retained in a regulated, symbolic form, but made a second line of economic defense.) The monasteries were intended to survive on their own, since Huai-hai insisted that meditation and worship be integrated with physical labor. Whereas the ideal Indian holy man was one who relied on begging, Huai-hai believed that in China it was holier to work for a living. This was the core of his teachings, as symbolized in his famous manifesto: "A day without work is a day without food." Nothing could have been more sympathetically received among the Chinese, and Huai-hai is probably rightly credited with inoculating Ch'an against the governmental persecution of 845 that destroyed so many other Buddhist sects. He practiced what he preached, and even when he reached old age he continued to toil in the fields. In fact, his disciples finally became so concerned for his health that they took the unprecedented step of hiding his gardening hoe. But true to his rule, he refused to eat until it was returned.

Perhaps we can infer something of Huai-hai's regulations from the routine in contemporary Zen monasteries (of the Rinzai sect).[11] Monks rise well before light (before they can see the lines in the palm of their hand), and after their morning toilet they gather in the main hall for sunrise devotions—in this case rapid chanting of scriptures, a device more for developing powers of concentration than for piety. They then return to the meditation hall, where chanting resumes. Next comes breakfast, usually plain rice with a modest vegetable garnish, and then back to the meditation hall for ceremonial tea and announcements of the day's schedule. Afterward each monk meets individually with the master in his quarters, where the monk's enlightenment is tested and a koan may be assigned. (The master, incidentally, enjoys a private room; the monks sleep together in a common hall, arranged according to rank.) After this, the monks attend to the garden and grounds of the monastery, and later in the morning there may be begging or visits to lay patrons for donations. After lunch (the main meal; its leftovers are supper) there is more work in the garden of the monastery, planting and harvesting, as well as repairing the buildings or other maintenance chores. Later on there may be more chanting, as well as cleaning and upkeep of the interior of the buildings. And in between there may be meditation. Then as nightfall descends the evening bell rings out to signify the work day's ending. During the evening the monk may meditate more or receive further instruction from the master or his brothers. Finally, late in the evening, to bed—at the end of a long day. It should be noted that there are also many special days on which meals, ceremonies, or activities may assume a different character.

It is significant that the monasteries of early Ch'an are said not to have had a Buddha hall or a place for worship; rather they had only a Dharma or lecture hall, in which the master gave a talk, followed by sharp exchanges with his disciples, who often were rowdy and sometimes left at will to demonstrate their independence of mind. These were places of irreverence and unfettered intellectual inquiry; and apparently there was no enforced study of the traditional Buddhist literature. With monasteries of their own where they could do as they pleased, the Ch'an masters found their rebellion complete. Theirs now was an unhampered search for the perennial philosophy.

With this in mind we may now turn to the psychological teachings of the lawgiver Huai-hai. Unlike the piecemeal story of his contribution to monastic life, which is preserved in spirit more than in letter, the writings on enlightenment that bear his name are rather firmly attributed. This is, in fact, a significant new aspect of Ch'an history, since his work represents one of the oldest documents actually composed by a master—as compared to a sermon transcribed and edited by some follower. According to the extant writings, after Huai-hai had studied with Ma-tsu for several years, he returned to his home temple to care for his first master, Tao-chih, who was by then aged and ill—an act of duty any Chinese would immediately understand. It was during this return visit with his old master that he composed a treatise setting forth the theoretical basis of sudden enlightenment. It is said that when this document was shown to Ma-tsu, he compared Huai-hai to a great pearl whose luster penetrated all time and space. (Curiously, Ma-tsu himself appears not to have made a great fuss about the meaning of sudden enlightenment, seemingly taking the "theory" for granted and moving along to the "practice.")

"The Zen Teaching of Huai-hai on Sudden Illumination" was

composed in the form of an imaginary question-and-answer session, in which Huai-hai effectively interviewed himself on the question of sudden enlightenment and the specific problems a person might encounter in trying to prepare for it. He stressed that one of the most important things to do was to suspend making value judgments about things, since this leads almost directly to splitting things into camps of good and bad, likes and dislikes. This opens one to the world of categories and dualities, just the opposite from oneness. According to Huai-hai, the first thing to do is strive for:

> . . . total relinquishment of ideas as to the dual nature of good and bad, being and non-being, love and aversion, void and non-void, concentration and distraction, pure and impure. By giving all of them up, we attain to a state in which all opposites are seen as void. . . . Once we attain that state, not a single form can be discerned. Why? Because our self-nature is immaterial and does not catch a single thing foreign to itself. That which contains no single thing is true Reality. . . .[12]

The desire to avoid love and aversion is inextricably tied with the freedom from distinctions, duality, judgments, or prejudices:

> Wisdom means the ability to distinguish every sort of good and evil; dhyana means that, though making these distinctions, you remain wholly unaffected by love or aversion for them.[13]

Elsewhere he describes this goal as:

> Being able to behold men, women and all the various sorts of appearances while remaining as free from love and aversion as if they were actually not seen at all. . . .[14]

In this manner we can operate on the principle of unity, even in a world where appearances have multiplicity.

But how exactly can we say that all things are one? It is not something that can be fully understood with the rational mind, and initially it must be taken partly on faith, as a holding action until we can understand it intuitively. His translator John

Blofeld uses the traditional Buddhist analogy of the sea, which is both constantly changing and yet eternally changeless: "Contemplation of the movement and shifting composition of sea-waves is a useful symbolical approach; for, not only are the waves and the sea identical in substance, but also a given wave does not preserve its individual identity for a single moment as the water composing it is never for an instant entirely the same; thus, by the time it reaches us from a distance, every drop it contains will be other than the drops composing it when we saw it first. On the other hand, sea-water is sea-water and the wave is entirely composed of that. Each wave is void—a mere fluctuating appearance identical in substance with every other wave and with the entire ocean. . . ."[15] Waves are a perfect metaphor for the idea of everything and nothing at once, since they are both ephemeral and part of a larger reality, the sea, out of which they emerge, assume a physical appearance, and then dissolve. They seem to exist, yet you cannot grasp and hold them. They are both existing and nonexistent. Thus they resemble the Void, a kind of energy that manifests itself through diverse illusory objects of the senses, but which is itself ungraspable, changeless unity. With this in mind, perhaps it is easier to understand Huai-hai when he declares:

> The nature of the Absolute is void and yet not void. How so? The marvellous "substance" of the Absolute, having neither form nor shape, is therefore undiscoverable; hence it is void. Nevertheless, that immaterial, formless "substance" contains functions as numerous as the sands of the Ganges, functions which respond unfailingly to circumstances, so it is also described as not void.[16]

By focusing on this idea of unity in an Absolute, we also interact with our own perception of time. Since it is important that the mind not dwell on anything, naturally enough this applies to time as well as space.

> If you want to understand the non-dwelling mind very clearly, while you are actually sitting in meditation, you must be cognizant only of the mind. . . . Whatever is past is past, so do not sit in judgment upon it; for when minding about the past ceases of itself, it can be said that there is no longer any past. Whatever is in the future is not here yet, so do not direct your hopes and longings towards it; for, when

minding about the future ceases of itself, it can be said that there is no future. Whatever is present is now at hand; just be conscious of your non-attachment to everything—non-attachment in the sense of not allowing any love or aversion for anything to enter your mind; for, when minding the present ceases of itself, we may say that there is no present.[17]

He has taken the idea of the "now" to an interesting new dimension. By cutting off thoughts of past and future, you not only save yourself mental anguish, you also no longer need distinguish the idea of the "present" . . . and you have just eliminated a major aspect of attachment.

Huai-hai is not blind to the difficulty of such rigorous mind control, and he offers some of the first practical advice from a Ch'an master for controlling the mind. Not surprisingly, it is an admonition to stop trying so hard, to just focus on goals rather than forcing the mind's behavior. For example, if you are meditating and your mind wants to meander and look for something to dwell on, what should you do?

Should your mind wander away, do not follow it, whereupon your wandering mind will stop wandering of its own accord. Should your mind desire to linger somewhere, do not follow it and do not dwell there, whereupon your mind's questing for a dwellingplace will cease of its own accord. Thereby, you will come to possess a non-dwelling mind—a mind which remains in the state of non-dwelling. If you are fully aware in yourself of a non-dwelling mind, you will discover that there is just the fact of dwelling, with nothing to dwell upon or not to dwell upon. This full awareness in yourself of a mind dwelling upon nothing is known as having a clear perception of your own mind or, in other words, as having a clear perception of your own nature.[18]

By way of wrapping up his treatise, he summarizes his technique for sudden illumination in a bold manifesto:

You should know that setting forth the principle of deliverance in its entirety amounts only to this—WHEN THINGS HAPPEN, MAKE NO RESPONSE: KEEP YOUR

MINDS FROM DWELLING ON ANY THING WHATSOEV-
ER: KEEP THEM FOREVER STILL AS THE VOID AND
UTTERLY PURE.[19]

Perhaps it is time we asked what exactly is the point of all
this. When we have achieved his goal, we have effectively cut
off all attachments, rationality, discernment, values, sensations.
But why would we want to do this in the first place? Huai-hai
answers that by releasing ourselves from this enslaving bondage
to our ego and its attachments, we become the masters of our
own being, free to experience the world but no longer at its
mercy. And furthermore we no longer have even to think about
being in the state of "no-thought." It is this natural state of
wisdom that is our goal.

> Concentration (dhyana) involves the stilling of your mind
> so that you remain wholly unmoved by surrounding
> phenomena. Wisdom means that your stillness of mind is
> not disturbed by your giving any thought to that stillness,
> that your purity is unmarred by your entertaining any
> thought of purity and that, in the midst of such pairs of
> opposites as good and evil, you are able to distinguish
> between them without being stained by them and, in this
> way, to reach the state of being perfectly at ease and free of
> all dependence.[20]

This is the state called enlightenment, a new way of
experiencing reality that relies entirely upon intuition. Then we
realize that all this time our rational mind has been leading us
along, telling us that appearances are real and yet keeping us
from really experiencing things firsthand, since the rational
mind believes in names, categories, duality. Consequently,
before this sudden moment of intuitive understanding, we saw
the world as through a glass darkly, with ourselves as subject
and the falsely perceived exterior world as object. After this
experience we see things clearly, but we perceive them for what
they really are—creations of mind as devoid of genuine
substance as the world we create in our dreams or the ocean's
waves that we can see but cannot hold. Knowing this, we can
regard the world dispassionately, no longer caught in the web of
ego involvement that enslaves those not yet enlightened. Since
this whole world view only can be understood intuitively, it is
not surprising that it must one day "dawn on you" when you

least expect, like a sudden inspiration that hits you after logic has failed. Huai-hai's instructions are intended to be preparations for this moment, attributes to adopt that will make you ready and receptive when your "sudden" enlightenment hits.

Huai-hai's concept of sudden enlightenment was quite straightforward, and it apparently was not absolutely necessary that meditation be employed. (In fact, he has defined *dhyana* as a state of mind, not an action.) Enlightenment is release from the ego, the primary thing standing in the way of mental peace in a world of getting and spending, of conflict and competition. The ancient Ch'an masters knew well the griefs and mental distress that haunt the heart of man, and thinkers such as Huai-hai explored its cure more fully than we realize today.

Eccentric Chinese Folk Figure.
Soga Shohaku (1730–1793). Courtesy of the
Smithsonian Institution, Freer Gallery
of Art, Washington, D.C.

8

NAN-CH'UAN
AND CHAO-CHOU:
MASTERS OF THE IRRATIONAL

The best-remembered disciple of Ma-tsu was Nan-ch'uan P'u-yuan (748–835), founder of a famous monastery and a brilliant if short-lived lineage whose finest example was his pupil Chao-chou Ts'ung-shen (778–897). *The Transmission of the Lamp* reports that Nan-ch'uan was born in the North China province of Honan.[1] He began study of meditation at age ten, and according to the *Biographies of Eminent Monks* compiled in the Sung (*Sung kao-seng chuan*) he went to study Buddhism on Mt. Sung, near Loyang, when he was thirty and became a priest of traditional Buddhism, apparently of the Vinaya school.[2] After his ordination, he traveled to various of the better-known monasteries, perfected his knowledge of Buddhist scriptures, and landed finally at the mountain establishment of the Ch'an master Ma-tsu.

The legend says that although there were eight hundred followers of Ma-tsu, the precocious Nan-ch'uan was immediately elevated to the position of the foremost disciple, and none of the others ventured to debate with him.[3] He finally achieved his complete enlightenment under the old master. It is not clear when he arrived or how long he stayed with Ma-tsu, but he reportedly left the monastery in 795—as he neared fifty—and founded his own community on Mt. Nan-ch'uan, a location in Anhwei province north of Kiangsi, building the original lodging with his own hands and attracting several hundred disciples. His most famous follower, aside from the later master Chao-chou, was the layman Lu Hsuan, the provincial governor of the Hsuan district. The story says that after residing in his mountain retreat for thirty years, without once venturing out, he finally acceded to the requests of the governor to come down and teach Ch'an to the people on the plain. He thus enjoyed a great fame as a teacher of Ch'an, although today he is remembered by anecdotes rather than by any attributed writings.

The governor seems to have been puzzled by some of the teachings of Seng-chao (384–414), the early, pre-Ch'an Buddhist. He specifically asked Nan-ch'uan the meaning of a statement in *The Book of Chao* that all things come from the same source and accordingly there can be no difference between right and wrong, which are themselves the same, by virtue of a common origin. The story says that Nan–ch'uan pointed to a patch of peonies in the garden and said, "Governor, when people of the present day see these blossoms, it is as if they see them in a dream."[4]

The point seems to be that the unenlightened cannot fully perceive the flower as it really is, cannot experience it directly and purely. Instead it is approached as an object apart from the viewer, the subject. It is not seen as an extension of his or her own reality. The ordinary mind permits this dichotomy of nature, but in the Zen mind, man and flower become one, merged into a seamless fabric of life. This is the kind of statement that in later years would be isolated from the chronicles and made into a "public case" or koan, a teaching device for novices. Its meaning is not meant to be discerned through the logical processes, and even less through the medium of language. When a later master was asked what Nan-ch'uan had meant, he answered with the equally enigmatic "Pass me a brick."[5]

The other celebrated story about the governor is perhaps easier to understand. The story says that one day Lu Hsuan posed the following problem to Nan-ch'uan: "What if I told you that a man had raised a goose in a bottle, watching it grow until one day he realized that it had grown too large to pass through the bottle's neck? Since he did not want to break the bottle or kill the goose, how would he get it out?" Nan-ch'uan began quietly, "My esteemed governor," and then he shouted, "THE GOOSE IS OUT!" The story says that Lu Hsuan suddenly was enlightened on the spot.[6] Nan-ch'uan had shown that one who posed a hypothetical question could be answered by an equally hypothetical response. There is a common Ch'an (and Taoist) reference to a truth being caught in the net of words. Here Nan-ch'uan shows how to extract truth from verbal encumbrances. Another anecdote recounts a similar incident:

A monk said to Nan-ch'uan, "There is a jewel in the sky; how can we get hold of it?" Nan-ch'uan said, "Cut down bamboos and make a ladder, put it up in the sky, and get hold of it!" The monk said, "How can the ladder be put up in the sky?" Nan-ch'uan said, "How can you doubt your getting hold of the jewel?"[7]

Many of his finest exchanges with pupils are preserved in *The Transmission of the Lamp.* For maximum impact it is perhaps best to lean back and let his wordplay wash over the rational mind like a cool, cleansing surf. As with the Taoist Chuang Tzu, the best way to comprehend this antilogical phenomenon is to forget about trying to grasp it intellectually, for only then can we understand.

The Governor said, "There is a piece of stone in my house. Sometimes it stands up and sometimes it lies down. Now, can it be carved into the image of Buddha?" "Yes, it is possible," answered the Master. "But it is impossible to do so?" countered the Governor."It is impossible! It is impossible!" exclaimed the Master.[8]

This dialogue sounds almost as though it were from an undiscovered scene from *Waiting for Godot,* as Vladimir and Estragon test the meaninglessness of language. And for pure Ionesco, it is hard to top the following incident:

Once Master Nan-ch'uan told Kuei-tsung and Ma-yu that he was going to take them with him to visit Nan-yang Hui-chung, the National Teacher. Before they began their journey, Nan-ch'uan drew a circle on the road and said, "As soon as you give a right answer we will be on our way." Thereupon Kuei-tsung sat down inside the circle and Ma-yu bowed in woman's fashion. The Master said to them, "Judging by this answer, it will not be necessary to go."[9]

The attitude of Nan-ch'uan toward conventional pieties, as well as toward the societal, rationalistic concerns of Confucianism, are perhaps best illustrated by the farewell he gave to his distinguished follower:

When Governor Lu was about to return to his office in Hsuan-cheng, he came to bid the Master good-bye. The latter asked him, "Governor, you are going back to the capital. How will you govern the people?" The Governor replied, "I will govern them through wisdom." The Master remarked, "If this is true, the people will suffer for it."[10]

Nan-ch'uan had a refreshing lack of pomposity that would have well served a good many other Zen masters, ancient and modern.

When the Master was washing his clothes, a monk said, "Master! You still are not free from 'this'?" Master Nan-ch'uan replied, lifting the clothes, "What can you do about 'this'?"[11]

This calls to mind the anecdote concerning Alexander the Great, who when asked if he was a god as had been widely reported, responded by suggesting that the question be directed to the man who carried out his chamber pot.

His attitude toward the great Ch'an teachers of the past seems similarly lacking in awe.

A monk inquired, "From patriarch to patriarch there is a transmission. What is it that they transmit to one another?" The Master said, "One, two, three, four, five." The monk asked, "What is that which was possessed by the ancients?" The Master said, "When it can be possessed, I will tell you." The monk said dubiously, "Master, why should you lie?" The Master replied, "I do not lie. [The Sixth Patriarch Hui-neng] lied."[12]

Nan-ch'uan was accustomed to the rough-and-tumble of Ma-tsu's monastery, a place of shouting, beating, harangues, insults, "mindless" interviews, misleading clues, and mind-fatiguing "irrelevancies." Yet it was all done with a high intensity and intended for the quite noble purpose of forcing a disciple to find his own first nature, his own enlightenment. The monastery as it developed under these wild men of Southern Ch'an was nothing less than a high-pressure cell for those who chose to enter. Although these new techniques for shaking nonintellectual insights into Ch'an novices were essentially the invention of Ma-tsu, they were transplanted, refined, and expanded by men like Nan-ch'uan, whose new monastery seems to have had the same deadly-serious zaniness as Ma-tsu's.

Some of the most instructive anecdotes associated with Nan-ch'uan are those involving his star pupil, Chao-chou

Ts'ung-shen (778–897), who came to be one of the major figures of the Golden Age of Ch'an and one of the best-remembered of the wild Southern masters. Although his real name was Ts'ung-shen, he is remembered in history (as are many Ch'an masters) by the name of the mountain where he held forth during his mature years. He was born in Ts'ao-chou in Shantung and early on became a novice monk at a local monastery. However, the urge to travel was irresistible and he left before being ordained, arriving at Nan-ch'uan's monastery while still a lad. The traditional first exchange typifies their long and fruitful relationship. Nan-ch'uan opened with the standard question:

"Where have you just come from?"
"I have just left Shui-hsiang [named for a famous state of Buddha]."
"Have you seen the standing image of Buddha?"
"What I see is not a standing image of Buddha but a supine Enlightened One!"
"Are you your own master or not?"
"Yes, I am. [i.e., I already have a master.]"
"Where is this master of yours?"
"In the middle of the winter the weather becomes bitterly cold. I wish all blessings on you, sir."
At this, Nan-ch'uan decided that this visitor was promising and permitted him to become his disciple.[13]

Chao-chou's strange answer seems to have been his own way of signifying he had chosen Nan-ch'uan as his future master. Nan-ch'uan, for his own part, seems to have recognized in this quizzical repartee all the makings of a great Ch'an worthy.

The exploits of Nan-ch'uan and Chao-chou form the core of the great anecdotal literature of Ch'an's Golden Age. Neither was a great innovator, a great writer, or a great organizer, but together they were able to explore the highest limits of the dialogue as a vehicle for enlightenment. And their dialogues, incidentally, did not always necessarily require words.

One day, in the monastery of Nan-chu'an, the monks of the east and west wing had a dispute over the possession of a cat. They all came to Nan-ch'uan for arbitration. Holding a knife in one hand and the cat in the other, Nan-ch'uan said, "If any one of you can say the right thing, this cat will be saved; otherwise it will be cut into two pieces." None of the monks could say anything. Nan-ch'uan then killed the cat. In the evening, when Chao-chou returned to the monastery, Nan-ch'uan asked him what he would have said had he been there at the time. Chao-chou took off his straw sandals, put them upon his head, and walked out. Whereupon Nan-ch'uan commented, "Oh, if only you had been here, the cat would have been saved."[14]

Chao-chou's response used no language and was devoid of distinctions, being neither positive nor negative. This is one of the most celebrated stories in The Transmission of the Lamp, and one that is probably richer if we avoid subjecting it to too much commentary.

The point was specifically intended to be as simple as possible, but this very simplicity is disturbing to the complicated intellectual mind. There is a particularly telling story of the exchange Chao-chou held with Nan-ch'uan concerning the Tao, meaning the way to enlightenment:

When Chao-chou asked his master, "What is the Tao?" the latter replied, "Tao is nothing else than the ordinary mind." "Is there any way to approach it?" pursued Chao-chou further. "Once you intend to approach it," said Nan-ch'uan, "you are on the wrong track." "Barring conscious intention," the disciple continued to inquire, "how can we attain to a knowledge of the Tao?" To this the master replied, "Tao belongs neither to knowledge nor to no-knowledge. For knowledge is but illusive perception, while no-knowledge is mere confusion. If you really attain true comprehension of the Tao, unshadowed by the slightest doubt, your vision will be like the infinite space, free of all limits and obstacles. Its truth or falsehood cannot be established artificially by external proofs." At these words Chao-chou came to an enlightenment. Only after this did he take his vows and become a professed monk.[15]

Nan-ch'uan's assertion that Tao is nothing else than the ordinary mind, but that it cannot be reached by deliberate searching, is the longstanding commonplace of Ch'an. However, he here adds an interesting new assertion: He claims here that although the person finding this enlightenment has no doubt of its reality, it cannot be proved or disproved by any objective tests. There is no way that the enlightened person can be shown objectively to have achieved his goal. The Ch'an masters could test enlightenment by matching the claimant's illogic against their own; if his "craziness" matched, then the disciple passed. But there is, by definition, no objective test of enlightenment. But then, how *do* you test the ultimate realization that there is nothing to realize other than what you knew all along? Quite simply, the master's intuition is the final authority.

Their dialogues frequently were full of electricity, as witness another exchange that ended quite differently:

> Chao-chou asked, "Tao is not external to things; the externality of things is not Tao. Then what is the Tao that is beyond things?" The master struck him. Thereupon Chao-chou took hold of the stick and said, "From now on, do not strike a man by mistake." The Master said, "We can easily differentiate between a dragon and a snake, but nobody can fool a Ch'an monk."[16]

Chao-chou here seems to be declaring to Nan-ch'uan that his enlightenment is genuine. And Nan-ch'uan, for his part, is asserting that the Master's judgment, not the monk's, is the final criterion. In another incident Chao-chou actually has the last word.

> Once Nan-ch'uan said to Chao-chou, "Nowadays it is best to live and work among members of a different species from us." (This recalls the Buddhist proverb: It is easier to save the beasts than to save mankind.) Chao-chou, however, thought otherwise. He said, "Leaving alone the question of 'different,' let me ask you what is 'species' anyway?" Nan-ch'uan put both of his hands on the ground, to indicate the species of the quadrupeds. Chao-chou, approaching him from behind, trampled him to the ground, and then ran into the Nirvana Hall crying, "I repent, I repent." Nan-ch'uan, who appreciated his act of trampling, did not understand the reason of his repentance. So he sent his attendant to ask the disciple what was he repenting for. Chao-chou replied, "I repent that I did not trample him twice over."[17]

In spite of such occasional bursts of exuberance, Chao-chou seems overall to have been comparatively mild-mannered for a Ch'an master. He rarely chose to berate or beat his disciples, as did

Ma-tsu or his own master, Nan-ch'uan. In many ways, Chao-chou was the finest hope for the lineage of Nan-ch'uan, but he seems not to have been overly concerned with its continuation. In fact, it is somewhat ironic that Huai-hai, who was more an organizer than a creator, ended up with a lineage perpetuating his line down to the present day, whereas Nan-ch'uan's lineage effectively ended with his disciple Chao-chou, although both men were remarkable teachers. In fact, Chao-chou almost never did settle down to run a monastery. After Nan-ch'uan died he resumed his travels and for many years roamed across China, visiting with other Ch'an masters. He seems to have gradually worked his way back north, for it was in the north that he realized his most lasting fame and influence. But his reputation was gained before he had a monastery of his own and without the aid of permanent disciples. The real acclaim seems to have been associated with a journey to a famous Buddhist pilgrimage site, Mt. Wut'ai, in the northeastern edge of Shensi province, where he preached a sermon that brought him wide recognition. Although he loved nothing more than wandering the craggy mountains of China, friends tried to convince him to settle down—as related in an incident when he was near eighty, after many years of wandering:

> Once, as he was visiting Chu-yu, the latter said, "A man of your age should try to find a place to settle down and teach." "Where is my abiding place?" Chao-chou asked back. "What?" said his host, "With so many years on your head, you have not even come to know where your permanent home is!" Chao-chou said, "For thirty years I have roamed freely on horseback. Today, for the first time I am kicked by an ass!"[18]

He finally did settle down, at eighty, accepting an invitation to come and live at the Kuan-yin monastery in Chao-chou in northeastern China, where he stayed until his death some forty years later. His lack of interest in worldly, administrative details is illustrated by the story that during his forty years as abbot of the monastery he installed no new furnishings and made no attempt to collect alms. Perhaps this tells us why Huai-hai's line won the day. Yet Chao-chou was the popular favorite. His preference for colloquial language endeared him to the people. He tried to demonstrate that enlightenment can be found and subsequently heightened through ordinary everyday activities. The following anecdote suggests his idea of Buddhism had little to do with the Buddha:

Master Chao-chou was asked by a monk,
"Who is the Buddha?"
"The one in the shrine," was the answer.
"Isn't it a clay statue that sits in the shrine?" the monk went
    on.
"Yes, that is right."
"Then who is the Buddha?" the monk repeated.
"The one in the shrine," replied the Master.
A monk asked, "What is my own self?"
"Have you finished your rice gruel?" asked the Master.
"Yes, I have finished it," replied the monk.
"Then go and wash your dishes," said the Master.
When the monk heard this, he was suddenly awakened.[19]

The thrust of this anecdote is that through the everyday doing of
what needs to be done, we can find authentic values and our
original nature. As the modern scholar Chang Chung-yuan points
out, "This simple activity of the Ch'an monk, washing the dishes
after eating gruel, is the most ordinary thing, the sort of activity that
is completely spontaneous and requires no mental effort. While
engaged in it, a man is free from assertion and negation."[20]

When we are doing manual tasks we experience them directly;
we do not have to intellectualize about them. This acting without
thought, without judgments of good or bad, is in fact a parable of
enlightenment. So it was that Chao-chou could so effectively use
rote tasks as a teaching device, for they showed a novice how he
could free his mind from its enslavement to opinions and values.
This stress on the meaningfulness of daily manual activities, as
distinct from philosophical speculation, seems to have been the
major position of Chao-chou. This attitude is particularly borne out
in another celebrated Chao-chou anecdote.

One morning, as Chao-chou was receiving new arrivals, he
asked one of them, "Have you been here before?" "Yes," the
latter replied. "Help yourself to a cup of tea," he said. Then he
asked another, "Have you been here before?" "No, Your
Reverence, this is my first visit here." Chao-chou again said,
"Help yourself to a cup of tea." The Prior of the monastery
took Chao-chou to task, saying, "The one had been here
before, and you gave him a cup of tea. The other had not been
here, and you gave him likewise a cup of tea. What is the
meaning of this?" Chao-chou called out, "Prior!" "Yes,"
responded the Prior. "Help yourself to a cup of tea!"[21]

Behind this possibly deceptive simplicity, however, there must have been a penetrating intelligence, for a very large number of his anecdotes were important enough to become enshrined in those famous collections of koans the Mumonkan and the Blue Cliff Record. One of the best known is the following:

> A monk asked, "Since all things return to One, where does this One return to?" "When I was in Tsing-chou, I had a robe made which weighed seven *chin* [pounds]" replied the Master.[22]

The answer is a perfect example of "no-thought," the antilogic condition in which rationality is disengaged. To attempt to subject it to analysis would be to miss the entire point.

An even more famous koan, and one that has become the traditional starting point for beginners, is the following:

> A monk asked Chao-chou, "Has a dog the Buddha Nature?" Chao-chou answered, "Mu."[23]

Here the word mu, meaning "nothingness" or "un," is an elegant resolution of a perplexing Zen dilemma. Had Chao-chou answered in the affirmative, he would have been tacitly instigating a dualistic view of the universe, in which a dog and a man are allowed to be discussed as separate objects. But to have responded negatively would have been to even more strongly betray the Zen teaching of the Oneness permeating all things. An answer was called for, but not an explanation. So the master responded with a nonword—a sound that has been adopted in later Zen practice as symbolic of the unity of all things.

This wisdom made Chao-chou such a legend in his own lifetime that many monks from the south came north to try to test him, but he always outwitted them, even when he was well past a hundred. Perhaps it would be well to round out his story with a garland of some of the exchanges he had with new monks:

> A new arrival said apologetically to the master, "I have come here empty-handed!" "Lay it down then!" said the master. "Since I have brought nothing with me, what can I lay down?" asked the visitor. "Then go on carrying it!" said the master.[24]

> One day Chao-chou fell down in the snow, and called out, "Help me up! Help me up!" A monk came and lay down beside him. Chao-chou got up and went away.[25]

A monk asked, "When a beggar comes, what shall we give him?" The master answered, "He is lacking in nothing."[26]

When a monk asked him, "What is the real significance of Bodhidharma's coming from the west?" his answer was, "The cypress tree in the courtyard." When the monk protested that Chao-chou was only referring to a mere object, the Abbot said, "No, I am not referring you to an object." The monk then repeated again the question. "The cypress tree in the courtyard!" said the Abbot once more.[27]

A monk besought him to tell him the most vitally important principle of Ch'an. The master excused himself by saying, "I must now go to make water. Think even such a trifling thing I have to do in person."[28]

Chao-chou was of a unique breed of "Golden Age" masters, who created Ch'an's finest moment. Even Chao-chou knew this, for he is quoted as recognizing that Ch'an had already passed through its most dynamic epoch.

"Ninety years ago," he said; "I saw more than eighty enlightened masters in the lineage of Ma-tsu; all of them were creative spirits. Of late years, the pursuit of Ch'an has become more and more trivialized and ramified. Removed ever farther from the original spirit of men of supreme wisdom, the process of degeneration will go on from generation to generation."[29]

Chao-chou died in his one hundred and twentieth year, surely one of the most venerable Ch'an masters. Fortunately his pessimistic assessment of Ch'an's future was only partly correct. Although he himself had no illustrious heirs, there were other Southern Ch'an masters who would extend the lineage of Ma-tsu into what would one day be the Rinzai school, among these a layman named P'ang and the master Huang-po.

Han-shan. Ka'o (active
ca. 1350 or slightly earlier). Courtesy
of the Smithsonian Institution, Freer Gallery
of Art, Washington, D.C.

9

P'ANG AND HAN-SHAN:
LAYMAN AND POET

Each of the better-known disciples of Ma-tsu exemplified some particular aspect of Ch'an: Whereas Po-chang Huai-hai advanced Ch'an's organizational and analytical side, Nan-ch'uan embodied the illogical, psychologically jolting approach to the teaching. But what about the Ch'an outside the monasteries? Did Ma-tsu's influence extend to the lay community? Although little has been preserved to help answer these questions, we do have the stories of two Ch'an poets who operated outside the monastic system: Layman P'ang (740?–811) and Han-shan (760?–840?). They were part of a movement called *chu-shih*, lay believers who were drawn to Buddhism but rejected the formal practices, preferring to remain outside the establishment and seek enlightenment on their own.[1] However, P'ang studied under Ma-tsu himself, and Han-shan sometimes echoed the master's teachings in his verse.

The man known to history as Layman P'ang was born in the mid-eighth century.[2] He grew to manhood in the city of Heng-yang, where his Confucianist father served as a middle-level official. Although he was educated in all the classics, he became a practicing Buddhist early and never faltered in his devotion. Sometime after marrying he became so obsessed with the classic Chinese ideal of a spiritual-poetic hermitage that he actually had a thatched cottage built adjacent to his house. Here he spent time with his wife—and now a daughter and son—meditating, composing poetry, and engaging in characteristically Chinese musings. A story relates that he was sitting in his thatched cottage one day when he became exasperated with the difficulties of his path and declared, "How difficult it is! How difficult it is! My studies are like drying the fibers of ten thousand pounds of flax by hanging them in the sun." His wife overheard this outburst and contradicted him, "Easy, easy, easy. It's like touching your feet to the ground when you get out of bed. I have found the teaching right in the tops of flowering plants." His daughter, Ling-chao, heard both outbursts and showed them the truth with her assertion, "My study is neither difficult nor easy. When I am hungry I eat. When I am tired I rest."[3]

Then one day, thought to have been sometime between the years 785 and 790, P'ang decided to go the final step and sever his ties with the materialism that weighed him down. After donating his house for a temple, he loaded his remaining possessions into a boat—which he proceeded to maneuver into the middle of a river and sink.

We do not know if his wife and son welcomed this final freedom from material enslavement, but his daughter seems to have approved, for she helped him wend his now-penurious way through the world by assisting him in making and selling bamboo household articles. Free at last, P'ang traveled about from place to place with no fixed abode, living, so the legends say, "like a leaf." The image of P'ang and his daughter as itinerant peddlers, wandering from place to place, made a searing impression on the Chinese mind, and for centuries he has been admired in China—admired, but not necessarily emulated.

Whom did P'ang go to visit? He seems to have known personally every major Ch'an figure in China. The first master visited was the famous Shih-t'ou (700–790), sometime rival of Ma-tsu. (It will be recalled that the Sixth Patriarch, Hui-neng, had among his disciples a master called Huai-jang [677–744], teacher of Ma-tsu and head of the lineage of now Japanese Rinzai. Another of the Sixth Patriarch's legendary followers was Hsing-ssu [d. 740], whose pupil Shih-t'ou is connected to the line that became Japanese Soto. Ma-tsu and Shih-t'ou headed the two major movements of Southern Ch'an in the eighth century.)[4] In 786 P'ang appeared at the retreat of Shih-t'ou on the mountain called Nan-yueh. He greeted Shih-t'ou by asking him one of the standard Ch'an questions, which Shih-t'ou answered by quietly placing a hand over P'ang's mouth—causing the Layman's first enlightenment experience. P'ang studied under Shih-t'ou—although probably in a nonmonastic capacity—for some time, until one day Shih-t'ou decided to test him.

"Tell me," began Shih-t'ou, "how have you practiced Ch'an after coming here to this mountain?"

P'ang shot back in a characteristic manner, saying, "There is really nothing words can reveal about my daily life."

Shih-t'ou continued, "It is just because I know words cannot that I ask you now."

At this, P'ang was moved to offer a verse:

> My daily activities are not unusual,
> I'm just naturally in harmony with them.
> Grasping nothing, discarding nothing,
> In every place there's no hindrance, no conflict.
>
> . . .
>
> [My] supernatural power and marvelous activity:
> Drawing water and carrying firewood.[5]

The declaration that drawing water and carrying firewood were miraculous acts demonstrated P'ang's understanding of "everyday-mindedness"—the teaching of no-teaching, the approach of no-approach.[6] The story says that Shih-t'ou acknowledged the Layman's enlightenment, and went on to inquire whether P'ang wished to exchange his pauper's robe of white for a monk's raiment of black. P'ang reputedly answered him with an abrupt "I will do what I like." Apparently concluding that he had absorbed all of Shih-t'ou's teaching, P'ang arose and absented himself, heading for Kiangsi and the master Ma-tsu.

P'ang's adventures with Ma-tsu are not particularly well recorded, given the two years he reportedly studied under the master. However, the account of their meeting has become a Ch'an standard. According to the story, P'ang asked Ma-tsu, "What kind of man is he who has no companion among all things?"

Ma-tsu answered, "After you swallow all the water in the West River in one gulp, I will tell you." It is said that when P'ang heard this, he was suddenly aware of the essence of Ch'an.[7]

If this exchange seems puzzling, with its subtle wordplay that weaves in and out between realism and symbolism, what about another recorded exchange between the two:

> One day the Layman addressed Ma-tsu, saying: "A man of unobscured original nature asks you please to look upward."
> Ma-tsu looked straight down.
> The Layman said: "You alone play marvelously on the stringless ch'in [lute]."

Ma-tsu looked straight up.

The Layman bowed low. Ma-tsu returned to his quarters.

"Just now bungled it trying to be smart," then said the Layman.[8]

The modern master Charles Luk speculates that P'ang's request to Ma-tsu to look up at an enlightened man was intended to trap the old master: "In reply Ma-tsu looked down to reveal the functioning of the enlightened mind. P'ang then praised the master for playing so well on the stringless lute. Thereat Ma-tsu looked up to return functioning to the enlightened mind. . . . In Ch'an parlance, looking down is 'function,' which means the mind wandering outside to deliver living beings, and looking up is returning function to 'substance' (the mind) after the work of salvation has been done. P'ang's act of prostrating is 'function' and Ma-tsu's return to the abbot's room means returning function to 'substance' to end the dialogue, for nothing further can be added to reveal substance and function."[9]

Although the Layman declined monastic orders, he apparently could hold his own with the best of Ma-tsu's followers, as well as with other Ch'an monks he encountered in his travels. Often monks sought him out merely to match wits. A typical exchange is reported with a follower of Shih-t'ou named P'u-chi, who once came to test P'ang:

One day P'u-chi visited the Layman.

"I recall that when I was in my mother's womb I had a certain word," said the Layman. "I'll show it to you, but you mustn't hold it as a principle."

"You're still separated from life," said P'u-chi.

"I just said you mustn't hold it as a principle," rejoined the Layman.

"How can I not be awed by a word that astounds people?" said P'u-chi.

"Understanding such as yours is enough to astonish people," replied the Layman.

"The very statement 'don't hold it as a principle' has become a principle," said P'u-chi.

"You're separated not only by one or two lives," said the Layman.

"It's all right for you to reprove a rice-gruel [-eating] monk [like me]," returned P'u-chi.

The Layman snapped his fingers three times.[10]

The precise meaning of this exchange will not be tackled here, but P'ang apparently came off on top. Now and then, however, P'ang seems to have been equaled or bested. There is a story of an exchange he had with one of the monks at Ma-tsu's monastery, named Shih-lin.

> One day Shih-lin said to the Layman: "I have a question I'd like to ask. Don't spare your words."
> "Please go on," said the Layman.
> "How you do spare words!" exclaimed Shih-lin.
> "Unwittingly by this discussion we've fallen into a snare [of words]," said the Layman.
> Shih-lin covered his ears.
> "You adept, you adept!" cried the Layman.[11]

Another time P'ang is reminiscent of Chao-chou in demonstrating that it is possible to hold one's own without the use of words.

> The Layman was once lying on his couch reading a sutra. A monk saw him and said: "Layman! You must maintain dignity when reading a sutra."
> The Layman raised up one leg.
> The monk had nothing to say.[12]

Layman P'ang studied under Ma-tsu for two years, but he finally decided to resume his life as a wandering student of Ch'an. He left Ma-tsu declaring the family his source of strength, or so it would seem from his parting verse presented to the master.

> I've a boy who has no bride,
> I've a girl who has no groom;
> Forming a happy family circle,
> We speak about Birthless.[13]

And off he went to travel, a completely enlightened man after his stay in Kiangsi. He turned increasingly to poetry during these years of wandering across the central part of China, composing some of his most sensitive verse. One poem in particular seems to capture the carefree spirit of these years of wanderings:

> The wise man, perceiving wealth and lust,
> Knows them to be empty illusion;
> Food and clothes sustain body and life—

I advise you to learn being as is.
When it's time, I move my hermitage and go,
And there's nothing to be left behind.[14]

One of Layman P'ang's most enduring companions was the monk Tan-hsia T'ien-jan, known for his irreverence. The following is typical of the exchanges recorded between the two:

> When the Layman was walking with Tan-hsia one day he saw a deep pool of clear water. Pointing to it with his hand, he said: "Being as it is we can't differentiate it."
> "Of course we can't," replied Tan-hsia.
> The Layman scooped up and threw two handfuls of water on Tan-hsia.
> "Don't do that, don't do that!" cried Tan-hsia.
> "I have to, I have to!" exclaimed the Layman.
> Whereupon Tan-hsia scooped up and threw three handfuls of water on the Layman, saying: "What can you do now?"
> "Nothing else," replied the Layman.
> "One seldom wins by a fluke," said Tan-hsia.
> "Who lost by a fluke?" returned the Layman.[15]

To attempt to explicate this exchange would be to ride the wind. They are in a completely different reality from that in which mere books are written and read.

What occupied Madam P'ang during the Layman's wanderings is not known. However, she seems well on the way to enlightenment herself. A story says that one day she went to a Buddhist temple to make an offering of food. The priest asked her the purpose of the offering so that he could post the customary notice identifying the name of a donor and the date and purpose of the gift. This was called "transferring merit," since the knowledge of her good deed would be "transferred" from herself to others. It is reported that Mrs. P'ang took her comb, stuck it in the back of her hair, and announced to the stunned priest, "Transference of merit is accomplished."[16] She seemed a part of P'ang's enlightenment, even if not a companion in his travels.

Eventually P'ang and his daughter, Ling-chao, ended up back in the north, near Hsiang-yang, the city of his birth, which he had left when a very small child. But instead of moving into the town, they lived in a cave about twenty miles to the south. And to this cave often journeyed a distinguished visitor—Prefect Yu Ti of Hsiang province, an important official who had learned of P'ang's verse and his reputation for Ch'an teaching. Originally a vicious and arrogant dictator who delighted in persecuting Buddhists, he had been converted by a Ch'an monk and had become a strong supporter of the faith. In fact, it is Yu Ti whom we must thank for our knowledge of P'ang, for it was he who collected the poetry and stories of the Layman after his death.

P'ang lived in his cave with Ling-chao for two years, and then he suddenly declared that it was time to die. In a dramatic gesture, he assumed a meditating posture and asked Ling-chao to go outside and tell him when the sun reached high noon, at which time he would pass on. She went out, but quickly returned to announce that it was already noon but that there was an eclipse. P'ang jumped up and ran out to see this event, but while he was gone Ling-chao seated herself in his place, folded her hands, and died herself. P'ang returned from her diversionary announcement, saw what had happened, and declared, "Her way was always swift. Now she has gone ahead of me." In respect he postponed his own death for a week.[17]

Hearing of this episode, Prefect Yu Ti rushed to the scene. The Layman addressed him with, "I pray you to hold all that is thought to be real as empty, and never take that which is empty as being real. Farewell. The world is merely a shadow, an echo."[18] He then laid his head on the prefect's knee and died. He left a request that his body be cremated and his ashes scattered across the waters of nearby lakes and rivers.

When P'ang's wife heard of the death of her husband and daughter, she said, "That stupid girl and ignorant old man have gone away without telling me. How unbearable."[19] She then relayed the news to her son, who was in the fields hoeing. He too subsequently died miraculously, while still standing up. For her own part, Madam P'ang journeyed about the countryside bidding her friends farewell, and then secluded herself, where it was never known. And with her passing ends the saga of Layman P'ang. This real-life individual was honored as China's answer to the mythical Indian businessman Vimalakirti, who combined enlightenment with the life of the market.

An even more elusive figure is the hermit Han-shan, whose name means "Cold Mountain," the site where he supposedly resided. He is an almost totally lengendary character, for we actually know nothing for sure about when he lived (the current best guess is late eighth to early ninth century). Almost everything known about him has been gleaned from his poems and from a presumably contemporaneous preface to these poems composed by a mysterious hand untraceable to any historical Chinese individual. His was some of the most confessional, yet joyous, verse penned in T'ang China, and he has been claimed by the Ch'anists as one of theirs—although he might just as easily have been a Taoist conversant in Buddhist jargon.

Han-shan embodied the archetypal hero of the Chinese imagination: a member of the rural gentry who gave up his staid family life and some sort of scholarly career to become a wandering poet. As he describes his own early life in the years before his wanderings:

> From my father and mother I inherited land enough
> And need not envy others' orchards and fields
> Creak, creak goes the sound of my wife's loom;
> Back and forth my children prattle at their play.
>
> . . .
>
> The mountain fruits child in hand I pluck;
> My paddy field along with my wife I hoe.
> And what have I got inside my house?
> Nothing at all but one stand of books.[20]

So we have a gentleman scholar, comfortably well off, with wife and children and an idyllic life undisturbed by the incursions of the world. It is all too perfect by half, and sure enough sometime before his thirtieth year his life was disrupted by an (undescribed) event so catastrophic that his wife and family turned him out:

> I took along books when I hoed the fields,
> In my youth, when I lived with my older brother.
> Then people began to talk;
> Even my wife turned against me.
> Now I've broken my ties with the world of red dust;
> I spend my time wandering and read all I want.
> Who will lend a dipper of water
> To save a fish in a carriage rut.[21]

Just when this sad event took place we do not know. However, by the time Han-shan was thirty he found himself on Cold Mountain, part of the T'ien-tai mountain range and near the town of T'ang-hsing.

> Thirty years ago I was born into the world.
> A thousand, ten thousand miles I've roamed,
> By rivers where the green grass lies thick,

> Beyond the border where the red sands fly.
> I brewed potions in a vain search for life everlasting.
> I read books, I sang songs of history,
> And today I've come home to Cold Mountain
> To pillow my head on the stream and wash my ears.[22]

He described his life in the mountains in a number of verses that often seem more Taoist than Buddhist. One of the most lyrical follows:

> Ever since the time when I hid in the Cold Mountain
> I have kept alive by eating the mountain fruits.
> From day to day what is there to trouble me?
> This my life follows a destined course.
> The days and months flow ceaseless as a stream;
> Our time is brief as the flash struck on a stone.
> If Heaven and Earth shift, then let them shift;
> I shall still be sitting happy among the rocks.[23]

He was a contradictory individual, one minute solemn in his search for Mind, and the next minute a buoyant *bon vivant*, writing verses that seem almost a T'ang version of our own *carpe diem*:

> Of course there are some people who are careful of money,
> But not I among them.
> Because I dance too much, my garment of thin cloth is
>   worn.
> My bottle is empty, for I spurt out the wine when we sing.
> Eat a full meal.
> Don't tire your feet.
> The day when weeds are sprouting through your skull,
> You will regret what you have been.[24]

The life he describes for himself is one immersed in poetry. He is the compleat poet, whose only concern is writing (not publishing) verse.

> Once at Cold Mountain, troubles cease—
> No more tangled, hung-up mind,
> I idly scribble poems on the rock cliff,
> Taking whatever comes, like a drifting boat.[25]

But if his poems were written on a rock cliff, how then were they preserved? Thereon hangs a tale, or more likely a legend. At some unknown time, Han-shan's verses (some three hundred) were collected and supplied with a "preface."[26] The person who takes credit for saving Han-shan from a country poet's oblivion identifies himself as Lu-ch'iu Yin, a high official. As it happens, the T'ang Chinese were very fussy about keeping records on such things as high officials, and a Lu-ch'iu Yin is not remembered among their ranks. Consequently, some have speculated that the author of the preface was in fact a Buddhist priest who wished to remain anonymous. At any rate, according to the story, our official first heard of Han-shan upon becoming ill just before a planned trip to a new prefecture and, after failing to be helped by a doctor, was cured by a wandering priest, who then told him that in the prefecture of his destination he would need further protection from bodily ills. Lu-ch'iu Yin asked him for the name of a master, and the priest told him to be on the lookout for two eccentric-appearing kitchen servants at the Kuo-ch'ing monastery dining hall, named Han-shan and Shih-te.

When he arrived at his new post, he immediately sought out this monastery and was amazed to learn the story was true. People around the temple said, "Yes, there is a Han-shan. He lives alone in the hills at a place called Cold Mountain, but he often comes down to the temple to visit his friend, Shih-te." The cook, Shih-te, it turned out, saved leftovers for his friend Han-shan, who would come and take them away in a bamboo tube, merrily laughing and joking along the length of the temple veranda as he carted away his booty. Once the monks caught him and exposed his system, but he only laughed all the more. His appearance was that of a starving beggar, but his wisdom was that of a man of enlightenment.

Lu-ch'iu Yin anxiously pressed on to the kitchen, where sure enough he found Han-shan and Shih-te, tending the stoves and warming themselves over the fire. When he bowed low to them, they broke into gales of laughter and shouted "HO" back at him. The other monks were scandalized and wondered aloud why a distinguished official would bow to a pair of ne'er-do-wells. But before he could explain, the pair clasped hands and bolted out of the temple. (The giggling Han-shan and Shih-te became a staple of Zen art for a millennium thereafter.) Determined to retrieve them, he arranged for the monastery to provide them permanent accommodations and left a package of clothes and incense for them. When they failed to reappear, he had a bearer carry his gifts and accompany him up into the mountains. Finally they glimpsed Han-shan, who yelled, "Thief! Thief!" at them and retreated to the opening of a cave. He then bade them farewell with, "Each of you men should strive to your utmost!" Whereupon he disappeared into the cave, which itself then closed upon him, leaving no trace. The preface says Han-shan was never seen again. In homage the disappointed Lu-ch'iu Yin had his poems collected from where they had been composed—on scraps of bamboo, wood, stones, cliffs, and on the walls of houses. Thus there came to be the collected *oeuvre* of Han-shan.

Han-shan's poems support at least part of this somewhat fanciful story. He does seem to have been Buddhist in outlook, and as one of his translators, Burton Watson, has declared, ". . . to judge from his poetry, Han-shan was a follower of the Ch'an sect, which placed great emphasis on individual effort and was less wary of emotionalism than earlier Buddhism had been. . . . Though he writes at times in a mood of serenity, at other times he appears despondent, angry, arrogant, or wildly elated. . . ."[27]

As did Layman P'ang, Han-shan seems to have believed that the Way is found in everyday-mindedness, a point of view most forcefully expounded by Ma-tsu. As Han-shan declares in one of his poems:

> As for me, I delight in the everyday Way,
> Among mist-wrapped vines and rocky caves.
> Here in the wilderness I am completely free,
> With my friends, the white clouds, idling forever.
> There are roads, but they do not reach the world;
> Since I am mindless, who can rouse my thoughts?
> On a bed of stone I sit, alone in the night,
> While the round moon climbs up Cold Mountain.[28]

Many of his verses reinforce the belief that he was indeed a follower of Southern Ch'an. For example, he seemed to believe that the mind itself is the Buddha that all seek.

> Talking about food won't make you full,
> Babbling of clothes won't keep out the cold.
> A bowl of rice is what fills the belly;
> It takes a suit of clothing to make you warm.
> And yet, without stopping to consider this,
> You complain that Buddha is hard to find.
> Turn your mind within! There he is!
> Why look for him abroad?[29]

Interestingly enough, for all his rather traditional Ch'an sentiments and admonitions, he was much more in touch with human concerns than were most followers of Ch'an. For one thing, he lived alone in the mountains, an isolated ascetic cut off from human contact, and the resulting loneliness was something those caught up in the riotous give-and-take of a Ch'an monastery never knew. He gives voice to this loneliness in a touching poem.

I look far off at T'ien-t'ai's summit,
Alone and high above the crowding peaks.
Pines and bamboos sing in the wind that sways them;
Sea tides wash beneath the shining moon.
I gaze at the mountain's green borders below
And discuss philosophy with the white clouds.
In the wilderness, mountains and seas are all right,
But I wish I had a companion in my search for the Way.[30]

The admission of loneliness and near-despair in many of his verses has always been a troublesome point for Zen commentators. The enlightened man is supposed to be immune to the misgivings of the heart, focused as he is on oneness and nondistinction. But Han-shan worried a good bit about old age, and he also missed his family, as he admits, albeit through the medium of a dream:

Last night in a dream I returned to my old home
And saw my wife weaving at her loom.
She held her shuttle poised, as though lost in thought,
As though she had no strength to lift it further.
I called. She turned her head to look,
But her eyes were blank—she didn't know me.
So many years we've been parted
The hair at my temples has lost its old color.[31]

But perhaps it is this non-Ch'an quality, this mortal touch, that elevates Han-shan to the rank of a great lyrical poet. He actually manages to be both a plausible Buddhist and a vulnerable human being. Few other poets in Chinese letters managed to combine genuine Buddhism with such memorable verse. As Burton Watson has observed, "In the works of most first-rate Chinese poets, Buddhism figures very slightly, usually as little more than a vague mood of resignation or a picturesque embellishment in the landscape—the mountain temple falling into melancholy ruin, the old monk one visits on an outing in the hills. Han-shan, however, is a striking exception to this rule. The collection of poetry attributed to him ... is permeated with deep and compelling religious feeling. For this reason he holds a place of special importance in Chinese literature. He proved that it was possible to write great poetry on Buddhist, as well as Confucian and Taoist, themes; that the cold abstractions of Mahayana philosophy could be transformed into personal and impassioned literature. . . . The language of his poems is simple, often colloquial or even slangy . . . [but] many of his images and terms are drawn from the Buddhist *sutras* or the sayings of the Southern School of Zen, whose doctrine of the Buddha as present in the minds of all men—of Buddha as the mind itself—he so often refers to. At the same time he is solidly within the Chinese poetic tradition, his language again and again echoing the works of earlier poets. . . ."[32]

With Han-shan we return repeatedly to the world of Cold Mountain, which was—as another of his translators, Arthur Waley, has pointed out—as much a state of mind as a locality. It was this, together with his advice to look within, that finally gives Han-shan his haunting voice of Ch'an. He seems not to have cared for the supercilious "masters" who dominated the competitive world of the monasteries. He invited them to join him in the rigorous but rewarding world of "Cold Mountain," where the mind was Buddha and the heart was home.

> When men see Han-shan
> They all say he's crazy
> And not much to look at—
> Dressed in rags and hides.
> They don't get what I say
> & I don't talk their language.
> All I can say to those I meet:
> "Try and make it to Cold Mountain."[33]

Priest Reading in the Moonlight.
Attributed to Ka'o (active ca. 1350 or
slightly earlier). Courtesy of Museum
of Fine Arts, Boston.

10

HUANG-PO:
MASTER OF
THE UNIVERSAL MIND

Perhaps the most thoughtful Zen philosopher of them all was Huang-po (d. 850?), who picked up where the earlier teachers had left off and brought to a close the great creative era of Ch'an. He also stood at the very edge of the tumultuous watershed in Chinese Buddhism, barely living past the 845 Great Persecution that smashed the power of all the Buddhist schools except that of the reclusive Southern Ch'anists.

Originally named Hsi-yun, the master moved at a young age from his birthplace in present-day Fukien to Mt. Huang-po in the same province, the locale that gave him his Ch'an title. His biography declares that his voice was articulate and mellifluous, his character open and simple.[1] He later decided to make a pilgrimage to see the famous Ma-tsu, but when he arrived in Kiangsi he was told that the master had died.[2] Po-chang Huai-hai was still there, however, and consequently Huang-po settled down to study with him instead.

Huang-po is known to us today primarily through the accident of having a follower obsessed by the written word. This man, Pei Hsiu, was also a high Chinese official who served as governor in two of the provinces where Huang-po at various times resided. He studied under Huang-po both times (all day and night, so he claimed) and later produced an anecdotal summary of the master's teachings now known as *On the Transmission of Mind*.[3] This document was extensive, representing one of the most detailed descriptions of an early master's thoughts. Pei Hsiu also reports in his preface (dated 858) that he sent his work back to Kuang T'ang monastery on Mt. Huang-po to have it authenticated by the old monks there who still remembered the sayings of the master.[4]

By the time of Huang-po the issue of "gradual" versus "sudden" enlightenment was decisively resolved in favor of the latter. He therefore turned instead to two major remaining questions: 1) how enlightenment fits into the mental world, and 2) how this intuitive insight can be transmitted. Before he was through he had advanced these issues significantly and had laid the philosophical basis for the next phase of Ch'an in China—to be dominated by the school of his pupil Lin-chi.

Huang-po struggled with a fundamental dilemma of Ch'an: how the wordless wisdom of intuition can be passed from generation to generation. Enlightenment necessarily has to be intuitive, and that means traditional teaching methods are useless. There are no conceptual formulations or "concepts." It is by definition wordless. It has to be realized intuitively by the novice, by himself. The masters had isolated a type of knowledge that words could not transmit. It was this transmission of wordless insight, of Mind, that obsessed Huang-po.

His teachings are well summarized by his biographer Pei Hsiu, who declared: "Holding in esteem only the intuitive method of the Highest Vehicle, which cannot be communicated in words, he taught nothing but the doctrine of the One Mind; holding that there is nothing else to teach, in that both mind and substance are void. . . . To those who have realized the nature of Reality, there is nothing old or new, and conceptions of shallowness and depth are meaningless. Those who speak of it do not attempt to explain it, establish no sects, and open no doors or windows. That which is before you is it. Begin to reason about it and you will at once fall into error."[5]

He seems to have been preoccupied with the issue of transmission even during the early days of studying under Huai-hai. His very first question to the older master reportedly was "How did the early Ch'an masters guide their followers?" Huai-hai answered this very un-Ch'an question with silence, an implied rebuke. When Huang-po pressed the point, Huai-hai called him a disappointing disciple and said he had best beware or he (Huang-po) would be the man who lost Ch'an.[6]

In a later episode, however, Huai-hai designates Huang-po as a successor in Dharma, via a famous transmission exchange in which Huang-po finally demonstrates wordless communication.

One day Huai-hai asked Huang-po, "Where have you been?" The answer was that he had been at the foot of the Ta-hsiung Mountain picking mushrooms. Huai-hai continued, "Have you seen any tigers?" Huang-po immediately roared like a tiger. Huai-hai picked up an ax as if to chop the tiger. Huang-po suddenly slapped Huai-hai's face. Huai-hai laughed heartily, and then returned to his temple and said to the assembly, "At the foot of the Ta-hsiung Mountain there is a tiger. You people should watch out. I have already been bitten today."[7]

This enigmatic utterance by Huai-hai has been taken by many to signify that Huang-po was being acknowledged as a worthy being, perhaps even a successor. The scholar Chang Chung-yuan has observed that the genius of this response was its freedom from the trap of logical assertion or negation.[8] The act signified freedom from the alternatives of words or silence. Could it be that with this incident we have finally captured a wordless transmission?

Huang-po also had a number of exchanges in later years with Nan-ch'uan (738–824), another of his seniors who had studied at the feet of old Ma-tsu. As the story is reported in *The Transmission of the Lamp:*

Some time later Huang-po was with Nan-ch'uan. All the monks in Nan-ch'uan's monastery were going out to harvest cabbage. Nan-ch'uan asked Huang-po, "Where are you going?" Huang-po answered, "I am going to pick cabbage." Nan-ch'uan went on, "What do you use to pick cabbage?" Huang-po lifted his sickle. Nan-ch'uan remarked, "You take the objective position as a guest, but you do not know how to preside as a host in the subjective position." Huang-po thereupon knocked on the ground three times with his sickle.[9]

When Blofeld translates this puzzling episode from *On the Transmission of Mind,* he comments that he has been unable to find a modern Zen master who could explain its meaning.[10] However, Nan-ch'uan's final remark questions the degree of Huang-po's enlightenment, and some assume the latter knocked on the ground to signify defeat.[11]

As did other masters, Huang-po also employed silence as a teaching device, using it to teach wordless insight by example. One particularly pointed story involves none other than his biographer, the official Pei Hsiu. In Pei Hsiu's introduction to his transcript of Huang-po's teachings he says that they first met in 843 when he invited the master to lecture at Lung-hsing Temple in Chung-ling, the district which he governed. Six years later, in 849, the governor was in charge of Wan-ling, and he again invited the master to come and teach, this time at the local K'ai-yan temple.[12]

When Huang-po arrived in Wan-ling, for what was to be the second teaching session with Pei Hsiu, the story says that the governor made the mistake of presenting the master with a written exposition of the teachings of Ch'an. Huang-po greeted this with silence, *his* "exposition" of Ch'an.

> The Prime Minister invited the Master to the city and presented his own written interpretation of Ch'an to him. The Master took it and put it on the table. He did not read it. After a short silence, he asked the Prime Minister, "Do you understand?" The minister answered, "I do not understand." The Master said, "It would be better if you could understand immediately through inner experience. If it is expressed in words, it won't be our teaching."[13]

The Transmission of the Lamp reports that after this episode at Wan-ling, the spirit of Huang-po's school became widespread south of the Yangtze River.[14]

This exchange brings out the essence of Huang-po's concerns. His most insistent conviction was that Ch'an cannot be taught, that it must be somehow gained intuitively. He was contemptuous of conceptual thought, believing it to be the greatest hindrance to achieving intuitive insight. The problem is the mistaken belief that Zen can somehow be taught and understood if only one grasps the concepts. But concepts only serve to obstruct intuition; Zen intuition can work only outside concepts. As Huang-po phrased it:

> Since Zen was first transmitted, it has never taught that men should seek for learning or form concepts. "Studying the Way" is just a figure of speech. It is a method of arousing people's interest in the early stages of their development. In fact, the Way is not something which can be studied. Study leads to the retention of concepts and so the Way is entirely misunderstood.[15]

The use of the rational mind in the study of Ch'an is only meaningful at the beginning. But once the fish of intuitive insight has been snared in the net of the rational mind's ken, the net must be discarded. Elsewhere he likens the extended use of analytical thought to the shoveling of dung.[16]

Concepts, it turns out, are only one of the mind's many

constructs. The mind also provides our perception of concrete objects, thereby "creating" them to suit its needs.

> Hills are hills. Water is water. Monks are monks. Laymen are laymen. But these mountains, these rivers, the whole world itself, together with the sun, moon, and stars—not one of them exists outside your minds! . . . Phenomena do not arise independently, but rely upon (the mental) environment (we create).[17]

Since reality is created by the mind, we will never know what is "real" and what is illusion. Examples of this are commonplace. The electron is both a wave and a particle, depending upon our point of view. Which is "reality"? Furthermore, concepts limit. By treating the world using rational constructs, we force it into a limited cage. But when we deal with it directly, it is much more complex and authentic. To continue the example, the electron may be something much more complex than either a wave or a particle, since it behaves at times like either or both. It may in fact be something for which our rationality-bound mind has no "concept."

The illusory world we think we see around us, deceptively brought to us by our untrustworthy senses, leads us to conceptual thought and to logical categories as a means to attempt its "understanding." The resulting intellectual turmoil is just the opposite of the tranquillity that is Ch'an. But avoidance of conceptual thought leads to a serene, direct, and meaningful understanding of the world around us, without unsettling mental involvement.

> Ordinary people all indulge in conceptual thought based on environmental phenomena, hence they feel desire and hatred. To eliminate environmental phenomena, just put an end to your conceptual thinking. When this ceases, environmental phenomena are void; and when these are void, thought ceases. But if you try to eliminate environment without first putting a stop to conceptual thought, you will not succeed, but merely increase its power to disturb you.[18]

What is worse, reliance on misleading perception blocks out our experience of our own pure mind.

> People in the world cannot identify their own mind. They believe that what they see, or hear, or feel, or know, is mind.

They are blocked by the visual, the auditory, the tactile, and the mental, so they cannot see the brilliant spirit of their original mind.[19]

When he was asked why Zen students should not form concepts as other people do, he replied, "Concepts are related to the senses, and when feeling takes place, wisdom is shut out."[20] Huang-po is so adamant against the deceiving world of the senses he even comes down hard on the pleasures of the gourmet.

Thus, there is sensual eating and wise eating. When the body suffers the pangs of hunger and accordingly you provide it with food, but without greed, that is called wise eating. On the other hand, if you gluttonously delight in purity and flavour, you are permitting the distinctions which arise from wrong thinking. Merely seeking to gratify the organ of taste without realizing when you have taken enough is called sensual eating.[21]

The point here seems to be that the use of the senses for pleasure is an abuse and distracts one from the illusion of the world, which itself obscures our mind from us. The ideal man he describes in terms of one who can remain passive even when confronted by a manifestation of good or of evil. He commends the person who has the character to remain aloof, even when in the Buddhist heaven or the Buddhist hell:

If he should behold the glorious sight of all the Buddhas coming to welcome him, surrounded by every kind of gorgeous manifestation, he would feel no desire to approach them. If he should behold all sorts of horrific forms surrounding him, he would experience no terror. He would just be himself, oblivious of conceptual thought and one with the Absolute. He would have attained the state of unconditioned being.[22]

Truth is elusive. It is impossible to find it by looking for it. And the world of the senses and the conceptual thought it engenders are actually impediments to discovering real truth. He provides an analogy in the story of a man who searches abroad for something that he had all along.

Suppose a warrior, forgetting that he was already wearing his pearl on his forehead, were to seek for it elsewhere, he could travel the whole world without finding it. But if someone who knew what was wrong were to point it out to him, the warrior would immediately realize that the pearl had been there all the time.[23]

He concludes that the warrior's finding his pearl had nothing to do with his searching for it, just as the final realization of intuitive wisdom has nothing to do with the graduated practice of the traditional Buddhists.

So, if you students of the Way are mistaken about your own real Mind . . . you will indulge in various achievements and practices and expect to attain realization by such graduated practices. But, even after aeons of diligent searching, you will not be able to attain to the Way. These methods cannot be compared to the sudden elimination of conceptual thought, the certain knowledge that there is nothing at all which has absolute existence, nothing on which to lay hold, nothing on which to rely, nothing in which to abide, nothing subjective or objective. It is by preventing the rise of conceptual thought that you will realize Bodhi; and, when you do, you will just be realizing the Buddha who has always existed in your own Mind![24]

The traditional practices neither help nor hinder finding the way, since they are unrelated to the final flash of sudden enlightenment—which is in your mind from the beginning, ready to be released.

What then did he teach, if there is nothing to be taught? The answer seems to be to stop seeking, for only then does wisdom come. Furthermore, to study a *doctrine* of nonattachment puts you in the compromising position of becoming attached to nonattachment itself.

If you students of the Way wish to become Buddhas, you need study no doctrines whatever, but learn only how to avoid seeking for and attaching yourselves to anything. . . . Relinquishment of everything is the Dharma, and he who understands this is a Buddha, but the relinquishment of ALL delusions leaves no Dharma on which to lay hold.[25]

But just how does Huang-po manage to practice what he preaches?

. . . [M]ost students of Zen cling to all sorts of sounds and forms. Why do they not copy me by letting each thought go as though it were nothing, or as though it were a piece of rotten wood, a stone, or the cold ashes of a dead fire? Or else, by just making whatever slight response is suited to each occasion?[26]

His final admonitions were organized by Pei Hsiu and summarized in the following list, reported as Huang-po's answer to the question of what guidance he had to offer those who found his teaching difficult.

I have NOTHING to offer. . . . All you need to remember are the following:
First, learn how to be entirely unreceptive to sensations arising from external forms, thereby purging your bodies of receptivity to externals.
Second, learn not to pay attention to any distinctions between this and that arising from your sensations, thereby purging your bodies of useless discernments between one phenomenon and another.
Third, take great care to avoid discriminating in terms of pleasant and unpleasant sensations, thereby purging your bodies of vain discriminations.
Fourth, avoid pondering things in your mind, thereby purging your bodies of discriminatory cognition.[27]

Huang-po struggled mightily with the problem of transmission. Since the doctrine was passed "mind-to-mind," he was obliged to find a transmission that somehow circumvented the need for words, something to bring a novice up against his own original nature. His contribution here was not revolutionary: He mainly advocated the techniques perfected by Ma-tsu, including roars and shouts, beatings, calling out a disciple's name unexpectedly, or just remaining silent at a critical moment to underscore the inability of words to assist. He also used the technique of continually contradicting a pupil, until the pupil finally realized that all his talking had been just so many obscuring concepts.

But just what was this mind that was being transmitted? His answer was that nothing was transmitted, since the whole point was just to jar loose the intuition of the person being "taught."

Once Huang-po was asked, "If you say that mind can be transmitted, then how can you say it is nothing?" He answered, "To achieve nothing is to have the mind transmitted to you." The questioner pressed, "If there is

nothing and no mind, then how can it be transmitted?"
Huang-po answered, "You have heard the expression
'transmission of the mind' and so you think there must be
something transmitted. You are wrong. Thus Bodhidharma
said that when the nature of the mind is realized, it is not
possible to express it verbally. Clearly, then, nothing is
obtained in the transmission of the mind, or if anything is
obtained, it is certainly not knowledge."[28]

He finally concludes that the subject cannot really even be
discussed, since there are no terms for the process that transpires.
Just as sunyata—that "emptiness" or Void whose existence means
that conceptual thought is empty and rational constructs inadequate—is not something that can be transmitted as a concept, so too
is the Dharma or teaching, as well as Mind, that essence we share
with a larger reality. Even statements that concepts are pointless
must fall back on language and consequently are actually
themselves merely make-do approximations, as are all descriptions of the process of transmission. He finally gives up on words
entirely, declaring that none of the terms he has used has any
meaning.

A transmission of Void cannot be made through words. A
transmission in concrete terms cannot be the Dharma. . . In
fact, however, Mind is not Mind and transmission is not really
transmission.[29]

He was working on the very real problem of the transmission of
understanding that operates in a part of the mind where speech and
logic cannot enter. As John Wu has pointed out, in a sense
Huang-po had come back full circle to the insights of Chuang Tzu:
good and evil are meaningless; intuitive knowledge is more
profound than speech-bound logic; there is an underlying unity
(for Chuang Tzu it was the Tao or Way; for Huang-po, the Universal
Mind) that represents the ineffable absolute.[30]
    In effect, Huang-po laid it all out, cleared the way, and defined
Ch'an once and for all. The Perennial Philosophy was never more
strongly stated. The experimental age of Ch'an thus drew to a close,
its job finished. With his death at the midpoint of the ninth century,
there was little more to be invented.[31] It was time now for Ch'an to
formalize its dialectic, as well as to meet society and make its mark
in the world. The first was taken care of by Huang-po's star pupil,
Lin-chi, and the second was precipitated by the forces of destiny.

The death of Huang-po coincided with a critical instant in Chinese history whose consequences for future generations were enormous. Once before Chinese politics had affected Ch'an, producing a situation in which Southern Ch'an would steal the march on Northern Ch'an. And now another traumatic episode in Chinese affairs would effectively destroy all Buddhist sects except Southern Ch'an, leaving the way clear for this pursuit of intuitive wisdom—once relegated to wandering teachers of *dhyana*—to become the only vital Buddhist sect left in China.

As noted previously, resentment toward Buddhism had always smoldered in Chinese society. Periodically the conservative Chinese tried to drive this foreign belief system from their soil, or failing that, at least to bring it under control. The usual complaints revolved around the monasteries' holdings of tax-free lands, their removal of able-bodied men and women from society into nonproductive monastic life, and the monastic vows of celibacy so antithetical to the Chinese ideals of the family.

The Ch'an monasteries, deliberately or not, worked hard to defuse many of these complaints. Indeed, some would say that Ch'an managed to change Buddhism into something the Chinese could partially stomach. Ch'anists were just the opposite of parasitical on society, since they practiced Po-chang Huai-hai's injunction of a day without work being a day without food. Also, the unthinking piety of traditional Buddhists was reviled by Ch'anists. Furthermore, Ch'an dispensed with much of the rigmarole and paraphernalia favored by the Buddhist sects that stuck to its Indian origins more closely.

The resentment felt toward Buddhists was summarized in a document issued in 819 by a scholar-bureaucrat named Han Yu.[32] His recital of Buddhism's failings came down particularly hard on the fact that the Buddha had not been Chinese. Han Yu advocated a complete suppression of this pernicious establishment: "Restore its people to human living! Burn its books! And convert its buildings to human dwellings!"[33] As resentment toward the worldly influence of Buddhism grew during the ninth century, there came to power an emperor who decided to act.

The Emperor Wu-tsang (r. 841–46) is now thought to have gone mad as a prelude to his persecution of the Buddhists. But his edicts were effective nonetheless. The state had begun tightening its grip on Buddhism when he came into power in 841, but in August 845 he issued the edict that ultimately had the effect of destroying traditional Buddhism and urbanized Northern Ch'an in China. Over a period of two years he destroyed 4,600 big temples and monasteries and over 40,000 smaller temples and retreats. He freed 150,000 male and female slaves or temple attendants and evicted some 265,000 monks and nuns, forcing them back into secular life. (This was out of a total Chinese population estimated to be around 27 million.) And not incidentally, the state reclaimed several million acres of property that had belonged to the monasteries. The effect of this was to obliterate virtually all the great Buddhist establishments, including the Buddhist strongholds in the capitals of Chang-an and Loyang, which were reduced to only two temples and thirty monks in each of the two cities.[34]

The irony of the Great Persecution was that it actually seemed to invigorate Southern Ch'an. For one thing, these rural Ch'an teachers had long been iconoclasts and outcasts themselves, as they disowned ostentatious temples and even the scriptures. Almost as much a philosophy as a religion, Southern Ch'an had long known how to do without imperial favor and largess. And when a further edict came down demanding that all Buddhist paraphernalia, including statues and paintings, be burned, the outcast Ch'an monasteries had the least to lose, since they had even done a bit of burning themselves—if we are to believe the story of Tan-hsia (738–824), a famous Ch'an monk who once burned a Buddhist statue for warmth. Southern Ch'an teachers just melted for a time back into secular life, from which they had never been far in any case.[35]

The result of all this was that after 846 the only sect of Buddhism with any strength at all was rural Ch'an. Chinese Buddhism literally became synonymous with Southern Ch'an—a far cry from the almost fugitive existence of the sect in earlier years. And when Buddhism became fashionable again during the Sung, Southern Ch'an became a house religion, as Northern had once been. The result was that Ch'an gradually lost its iconoclastic character. But out of this last phase of Ch'an developed one of the most powerful tools ever for enlightenment, the famous Zen koan, whose creation preserved something out of the dynamism of Ch'an's early centuries.

PART III
SECTARIANISM AND THE KOAN

. . . in which the Ch'an movement diversifies
into a variety of schools, each beholden to a master or
masters advocating an individualized path to enlightenment.
From this period of personality and experimentation
gradually emerge two main Ch'an paths, the Lin-chi and the
Ts'ao-tung (later called Rinzai and Soto in Japan). The
Lin-chi school concludes that enlightenment can be
precipitated in a prepared novice through shouts, jolts, and
mental paradoxes. The Ts'ao-tung relies more heavily
on the traditional practice of meditation to gradually release
enlightenment. The faith grows in numbers, but quality declines.
To maintain Ch'an's intellectual vigor, there emerges a new
technique, called the koan, which uses episodes from
Ch'an's Golden Age to challenge novices' mental complacency. This
invention becomes the hallmark of the later Lin-chi sect,
and through the refinement of the koan technique Ch'an enjoys
a renaissance of creativity in China.

Lin-chi. Soga Dasoku (late fifteenth century).
Courtesy of Daitoku-ji, Kyoto.

11

LIN-CHI:
FOUNDER OF RINZAI ZEN

The Great Persecution of 845 brought to a close the creative Golden Age of Ch'an, while also leaving Ch'an as the dominant form of Chinese Buddhism. In the absence of an establishment Buddhism for Ch'an to distinguish itself against, the sect proceeded to evolve its own internal sectarianism. There arose what are today known as the "five houses," regional versions of Ch'an that differed in minor but significant ways.[1] Yet there was no animosity among the schools, merely a friendly rivalry. In fact, the teachers themselves referred back to the prophecy attributed to Bodhidharma that the flower of dhyana Buddhism would one day have five petals.

The masters who founded the five schools were all individualists of idiosyncratic character. Yet the times were such that for the most part their flowers bloomed gloriously only a few decades before slowly fading. However, two of the sects did prosper and eventually went on to take over the garden. These two houses, the Lin-chi and the Ts'ao-tung, both were concerned with dialectics and became the forerunners of the two Zen sects (Rinzai and Soto) eventually to flourish in Japan. Of the two, the Lin-chi is most directly traceable back to the earlier masters, since its founder actually studied under the master Huang-po.

The master known today as Lin-chi (d. 866?) was born in the prefecture of Nan-hua, in what today is Shantung province.[2] He reportedly was brilliant, well behaved, and filled with the filial devotion expected of good Chinese boys. Drawn early to Buddhism, although not necessarily to Ch'an, he shaved his head and became a monk while still young. His early studies were of the sutras, as well as the vinaya or Buddhist rules and the sastra or commentaries. But in his early twenties he decided that he was more interested in intuitive wisdom than orthodoxy and consequently took the road in search of a master.

Thus he arrived at the monastery of Huang-po already a fully ordained monk. But his learning was traditional and his personality that of a timorous fledgling monk. For three years he dutifully attended the master's sermons and practiced all the observances of the mountain community, but his advancement was minimal. Finally the head disciple suggested that he visit Huang-po for an interview to try to gain insight. The young man obligingly went in to see the master and asked him the standard opener: "What is the real meaning of Bodhidharma's coming from the West?" Huang-po's wordless response was to lay him low with a blow of his stick.

Lin-chi scurried away in perplexity and related the story to the head disciple, who encouraged him to return, which he did twice more. But each time he received the same harsh reception. He was finally so demoralized that he announced plans to leave the monastery and seek enlightenment elsewhere. The head monk related this to Huang-po together with the opinion that this young novice showed significant promise. So when Lin-chi came to bid Huang-po farewell, the master sympathetically directed him to the monastery of a kindly nearby teacher, the master Ta-yu.

Perhaps it was all planned, but when Lin-chi arrived at the second monastery and related his unhappy treatment at the hands of Huang-po the master Ta-yu listened patiently and then declared, "Huang-po treated you with great compassion. He merely wanted to relieve your distress." Upon hearing this Lin-chi suddenly understood that Huang-po was transmitting the wordless insight to him, the understanding that Ch'an lies not in the words produced in the abbot's room but rather in the realization of his intuitive mind. It suddenly was all so obvious that the young monk could not contain his joy and declared, "So Huang-po's Buddhism is actually very simple; there's nothing to it after all!" This struck the master Ta-yu as either impertinent or a significant breakthrough, so he grabbed Lin-chi and yelled, "You scamp! A minute ago you complained that Huang-po's teaching was impossible to understand and now you say there is nothing to it. What is it you just realized? Speak quickly!" (Only in a spontaneous utterance is there real, uncalculated evidence of enlightenment.)

Lin-chi's answer was to pummel Ta-yu in the ribs three times with his fist. The older master then discharged him (or perhaps kicked him out) with the observation, "Your teacher is Huang-po, and therefore you do not concern me." Thus the enlightened young novice trudged back up the mountain to Huang-po's monastery. The master greeted him with the puzzled observation: "Haven't you come back a bit too soon? You only just left." In response Lin-chi bowed and said, "It's because you've been so kind to me that I came back so quickly," and he proceeded to relate the story of his sudden enlightenment. To which Huang-po declared, "What a big mouth that old man has. The next time I see him I'll give him a taste of my staff." To this Lin-chi yelled, "Why wait! I can give it to you now," and proceeded to slap the master's face. The startled Huang-po declared, "This crazy monk is plucking the tiger's whiskers." Whereupon Lin-chi emitted the first of what was to be a lifetime of shouts, affirming his wordless insight. The satisfied Huang-po called an attendant and said, "Take this crazy fellow to the assembly hall."

This is a perfect example of "sudden" enlightenment that took many years to achieve. Lin-chi had been a plodding, earnest young man until the moment of his "sudden" enlightenment, which occurred over a seemingly uncalculated remark by a teacher not even his own master. In fact, all Huang-po had done was to assail him with a staff. But Lin-chi was transformed suddenly from a milksop to the founder of a school, probably the greatest radicalization since the Apostle Paul was struck down on the road to Damascus.[3] Still, Lin-chi's "sudden" enlightenment had come about at the end of a highly disciplined period of preparation. As he later described it:

> In bygone days I devoted myself to the vinaya and also delved into the sutras and sastras. Later, when I realized that they were medicines for salvation and displays of doctrines in written words, I once and for all threw them away, and searching for the Way, I practiced meditation. Still later I met great teachers. Then it was, with my Dharma Eye becoming clear, that I could discern all the old teachers under Heaven and tell the false ones from the true. It is not that I understood from the moment I was born of my mother, but that, after exhaustive investigation and grinding discipline, in an instant I knew of myself.[4]

Like a reformed addict, he railed most against his own recent practices. He proceeded to denounce all the trappings of Buddhism, even the Ch'an Patriarchs themselves, as he shattered the chains of his former beliefs:

> Followers of the Way, if you want insight into Dharma as is, just don't be taken in by the deluded views of others. Whatever you encounter, either within or without, slay it at

once: on meeting a buddha slay the buddha, on meeting a patriarch slay the patriarch, on meeting an arhat slay the arhat, on meeting your parents slay your parents, on meeting your kinsman slay your kinsman, and you attain emancipation. By not cleaving to things, you freely pass through.[5]

After his enlightenment, he had many exchanges with Huang-po in which he came off ahead as often as not. It is also interesting that many of the interactions involved the manual labor of the monastery, an indication of the significance of work in Ch'an life. One famous joust between Lin-chi and Huang-po went as follows:

One day Master Lin-chi went with Huang-po to do some work in which all the monks participated. Lin-chi followed his master who, turning his head, noticed that Lin-chi was carrying nothing in his hand.
"Where is your hoe?"
"Somebody took it away."
"Come here: let us discuss something," commanded Huang-po and as Lin-chi drew nearer, he thrust his hoe into the ground and continued, "There is no one in the world who can pick up my hoe."
However, Lin-chi seized the tool, lifted it up, and exclaimed, "How then could it be in my hands?"
"Today we have another hand with us; it is not necessary for me to join in."
And Huang-po returned to the temple.[6]

This story can be interpreted many ways. John Wu says, "Obviously he was using the hoe as a pointer to the great function of teaching and transmitting the lamp of Ch'an. . . . [This was] a symbolic way of saying that in a mysterious manner the charge was now in his hands."[7] However, as Freud once remarked concerning the celebrated phallic symbolism of his stogie, "Sometimes, madam, it's just a cigar," and one suspects that in this little slapstick episode, the hoe might possibly be just a hoe.

Another exchange between Huang-po and Lin-chi may have more dialectical significance. According to the story:

One day Huang-po ordered all the monks of the temple to work in the tea garden. He himself was the last to arrive. Lin-chi greeted him, but stood there with his hands resting on the hoe.
"Are you tired?" asked Huang-po
"I just started working; how can you say that I am tired?"

Huang-po immediately lifted his stick and struck Lin-chi, who then seized the stick, and with a push, made his master fall to the ground. Huang-po called the supervisor to help him up. After doing so, the supervisor asked, "Master, how can you let such a madman insult you like that?" Huang-po picked up the stick and struck the supervisor. Lin-chi, digging the ground by himself, made this remark: "Let all other places use cremation; here I will bury you alive."[8]

Of Lin-chi's final quip, which tends to take the edge off a really first-rate absurdist anecdote, John Wu makes the following observation, "This was a tremendous utterance, the first authentic roaring, as it were, of a young lion. It was tantamount to declaring that his old conventional self was now dead and buried, with only the True Self living in him; that this death may and should take place long before one's physical decease; that it is when this death has taken place that one becomes one's True Self which, being unborn, cannot die. From that time on, there could no longer be any doubt in Huang-po's mind that his disciple was thoroughly enlightened, destined to carry on and brighten the torch of Ch'an."[9] Whether this is true or not, it does seem clear that Lin-chi's pronounced personality appealed to old Huang-po, who loved to match wits with him as he came and went around the monastery. He even allowed the young master liberties he denied others. For example, Lin-chi once showed up during the middle of a summer meditation retreat, something strictly forbidden. He then decided to leave before it was over, something equally unprecedented:

One day after half the summer session had already passed, Lin-chi went up the mountain to visit his master Huang-po whom he found reading a sutra. Lin-chi said to him:
"I thought you were the perfect man, but here you are apparently a dull old monk, swallowing black beans [Chinese characters]."
Lin-chi stayed only a few days and then bid farewell to Huang-po, who said:
"You came here after the summer session had started, and now you are leaving before the summer session is over."
"I came here simply to visit you, Master!"
Without ado, Huang-po struck him and chased him away. After having walked a few *li*, Lin-chi began to doubt his enlightenment in Ch'an, so he returned to Huang-po for the rest of the summer.[10]

Some time after Lin-chi received the seal of enlightenment from Huang-po, he decided to go his own way and departed for the province of Hopei, where he became the priest of a small temple on the banks of a river. This little temple was called "Overlooking the Ford," or *lin-chi* in Chinese, and it was from this locale that he took his name. After he was there for a time, however, some local fighting broke out, forcing him to abandon his pastoral riverbank location. (This disturbance may well have been connected with the disruptions of the 845 persecution of Buddhism.) But even when in the middle of a war he seems to have always been a man of Ch'an. There is an episode that strongly resembles the eighteenth-century essayist Dr. Samuel Johnson's kicking a stone to refute Berkeley's proposition that matter is nonexistent:

One day the Master entered an army camp to attend a feast. At the gate he saw a staff officer. Pointing to an open-air pillar, he asked: "Is this secular or sacred?"
The officer had no reply.
Striking the pillar, the Master said: "Even if you could speak, this is still only a wooden post." Then he went in.[11]

Fortunately, Ch'an was not a sect that required a lot of paraphernalia, and Lin-chi merely moved into the nearby town, where the grand marshal donated his house for a temple. He even hung up a plaque with the name "Lin-chi," just to make the master feel at home. But things may have heated up too much, for Lin-chi later traveled south to the prefecture of Ho, where the governor, Counselor Wang, honored him as a master. There is a telling conversation between the two that reveals much about the teaching of Ch'an at the time. Apparently the Ch'anists had completely abandoned even any pretense of traditional Buddhism—again a fortuitous development, considering traditional Buddhism's imminent destruction.

One day the Counselor Wang visited the Master. When he met the Master in front of the Monks' Hall, he asked: "Do the monks of this monastery read the sutras?"
"No, they don't read sutras," said the Master.
"Then do they learn meditation?" asked the Counselor.
"No, they don't learn meditation," answered the Master.
"If they neither read sutras nor learn meditation, what in the world are they doing?" asked the Counselor.
"All I do is make them become buddhas and patriarchs," said the Master.[12]

Lin-chi eventually traveled on, finally settling at the Hsing-hua temple in Taming prefecture, where he took up his final residence. It was here that a record of his sermons was transcribed by a "humble heir" named Ts'un-chiang. The result was *The Record of Lin-chi*, one of the purest exercises in the dialectics of the nondialectical understanding. But, as Heinrich Dumoulin observed, "Zen has never existed in pure experience only, without admixture of theoretical teachings or methodical practice, as it has sometimes been idealized. It could not exist in that fashion, for mysticism, like all other human experience, is dependent on the actual conditions of human life."[13] Indeed, Lin-chi was one of the first to develop what might be called a dialectic of irrationality. He loved categories and analysis in the service of nonconceptual inquiry, and what he created were guides to the uncharted seas of the intuitive mind.

Lin-chi is best known for his use of the shout. He shared the concern of Huang-po and Ma-tsu with the problem of wordless transmission and to their repertory of beatings and silences he added the yell, another way to affirm insights that cannot be reasoned. We may speculate that the shout was rather like a watered-down version of the beating, requiring less effort but still able to startle at a critical instant.[14] He seems to have been particularly fond of classifying things into groups of four, and one of his most famous classifications was of the shout itself. He once demonstrated the shout to a hapless monk as follows:

> The Master asked a monk: "Sometimes a shout is like the jeweled sword of a spirit King [i.e., extremely hard and durable]; sometimes a shout is like the golden-haired lion crouching on the ground [i.e., strong, taut, and powerful]; sometimes a shout is like a weed-tipped fishing pole [i.e., probing and attracting the unwary]; and sometimes a shout doesn't function as a shout. How do you understand this?"
> As the monk fumbled for an answer, Lin-chi gave a shout.[15]

His philosophy of the shout as a device for cutting off sequential reasoning was thus demonstrated by example. But the question those who relate this story never resolve is: Which of the four shouts was the shout he used on the student? (John Wu in *The Golden Age of Zen* speculates that this shout was of the first category, since it was meant to "cut off" the monk's sequential thought, but that seems a rather simplistic mixing of the metaphorical with the concrete.[16])

Lin-chi also was not averse to the use of the stick in the pursuit of reality, as the following example illustrates. The story also shows that the use of the stick was meaningful only if it was unexpected.

> Once the Master addressed the assembly.
> "Listen, all of you! He who wants to learn Dharma must never worry about the loss of his own life. When I was with Master Huang-po I asked three times for the real meaning of Buddhism, and three times I was struck as if tall reeds whipped me in the wind. I want those blows again, but who can give them to me now?"
> A monk came forth from the crowd, answering: "I can give them to you!"
> Master Lin-chi picked up a stick and handed it to him. When the monk tried to grab it, the Master struck him instead.[17]

There also is a story indicating that Lin-chi believed that when the shout failed to work, the stick might be required.

> The Master took the high seat in the Hall. A monk asked, "What about the cardinal principle of the Buddha-dharma?"
> The Master raised his whisk.
> The monk shouted. The Master struck him.
> Another monk asked: "What about the cardinal principle of the Buddha-dharma?"
> Again the Master raised his whisk.
> The monk shouted. The Master also shouted.
> The monk faltered; the Master struck him.[18]

Yet another series of exchanges sounds a similar theme.

> The Master asked a monk, "Where do you come from?"
> The monk shouted.
> The master saluted him and motioned him to sit down. The monk hestitated. The Master hit him.
> Seeing another monk coming, the Master raised his whisk. The monk bowed low. The Master hit him.
> Seeing still another monk coming, the Master again raised his whisk. The monk paid no attention. The Master hit him too.[19]

He was also challenged by a nun, one of the few recorded

instances of a master actually matching wits with a woman who had taken Ch'an orders.

> The Master asked a nun: "Well-come or ill-come?"
> The nun shouted.
> "Go on, go on, speak!" cried the Master, taking up his stick.
> Again the nun shouted. The Master hit her.[20]

What Lin-chi also brought to Ch'an was a dialectical inquiry into the relationship between master and pupil, together with a similar analysis of the mind states that lead to enlightenment. He seems remarkably sophisticated for the ninth century, and indeed we would be hard pressed to find this kind of psychological analysis anywhere in the West that early. The puzzling, contradictory quality about all this is that Lin-chi believed fervently in intuitive intelligence, and in the uselessness of words—even warning that questions were irrelevant:

> Does anyone have a question? If so, let him ask it now. But the instant you open your mouth you are already way off.[21]

Among his dialectical creations were various fourfold categorizations of the intangible. We have already seen his four categories of the shout. He also created the four categories of relationship between subject and object, also sometimes called the Four Processes of Liberation from Subjectivity and Objectivity. Some believe this served to structure the "four standpoints or points of view which Lin-chi used in instructing his students."[22] Lin-chi's original proposition, the basis of all the later commentary, is provided in *The Record of Lin-chi* as follows:

> At the evening gathering the Master addressed the assembly, saying: "Sometimes I take away man and do not take away the surroundings; sometimes I take away the surroundings and do not take away man; sometimes I take away both man and the surroundings; sometimes I take away neither man nor the surroundings."[23]

As Chang Chung-yuan describes these four arrangements, the first is to "take away the man but not his objective situation," i.e., to take away all interpretation and just experience the world without subjective associations.[24] (This is quite similar to the approach of the Japanese haiku poem, in which a description of something is provided completely devoid of interpretation or explicit emotional response.)

The second arrangement is to let the man remain but take away objectivity. As John Wu interprets this, "In the second stage, people of normal vision, who see mountains as mountains and rivers as rivers, must be reminded of the part that their own mind contributes to the appearance of things, and that what they naively take for objectivity is inextricably mixed with subjectivity. Once aware of subjectivity, one is initiated into the first stages of Ch'an, when one no longer sees mountains as mountains and rivers as rivers."[25] This is merely the Ch'an commonplace that "non-attachment or objectivity liberates one's self from bondage to the outside and thus leads to enlightenment."[26] As Dumoulin describes these, "In the first and second stages, illusion departs first from the subject and then from the object; clinging to subjective intellectual perception and to the objective world is overcome."[27]

Lin-chi's third stage is to "take away both the man and his objective situation. In other words, it is liberation from . . . the attachments of both subjectivity and objectivity. Lin-chi's famous 'Ho!' . . . often served this purpose."[28] In a blow of a master's staff or a shout there is nothing one can grasp, either objectively or subjectively. This is the next-to-last stage in the progression toward liberation from the mind's tyranny.

In the fourth stage we find the final condition, in which objectivity and subjectivity cease to be distinguishable. What this means is that there is no intellectuation at all, that the world simply *is*. As Dumoulin declares, "reality is comprehended in its final oneness."[29] Or as the story says: Before enlightenment, mountains are mountains and rivers are rivers; during the study of Zen, mountains are not mountains and rivers are not rivers; but when there finally is enlightenment, mountains are again mountains and rivers are rivers. In this final state the distinction and confrontation of subject and object dissolve, as we are finally at one with the nameless world.

Another of Lin-chi's famous dialectical categories is his "Fourfold Relationship possible Between Questioner and Answerer or Between Guest and Host." The point of the structure he sets up is to elucidate the interaction of master and novice, but he does so using metaphor of host and guest—where the host represents the universal Self and the guest the ego-form self.[30] Lin-chi's sermon on the subject went as follows:

A true student gives a shout, and to start with holds out a sticky lacquer tray. The teacher, not discerning that this is an objective circumstance, goes after it and performs a lot of antics with .t. The student again shouts but still the teacher is unwilling to let go. This is . . . called "the guest examines the host."

Sometimes a teacher will proffer nothing, but the instant a student asks a question, robs him of it. The student, having been robbed, resists to the death and will not let go; this is called "the host examines the guest."

Sometimes a student comes forth before a teacher in conformity with a state of purity. The teacher, discerning that this is an objective circumstance, seizes it and flings it into a pit. "What an excellent teacher!" exclaims the student, and the teacher replies, "Bah! You can't tell good from bad!" Thereupon the student makes a deep bow; this is called "the host examines the host."

Or again, a student will appear before a teacher wearing a cangue and bound with chains. The teacher fastens on still more chains and cangues for him. The student is so delighted that he can't tell what is what: this is called "the guest examines the guest."[31]

In the first category, according to Chang Chung-yuan, the ego meets the universal Self.[32] In the second category the universal Self encounters the ego-form self. In the third category, the universal Self of one meets the universal Self of another, and in the fourth category the ego of one encounters the ego of another. Or if we are to interpret this in the concrete, in the first encounter, an enlightened master meets an unenlightened novice; in the second an enlightened novice meets an unenlightened master (which did happen); in the third an enlightened master meets an enlightened novice; and in the fourth category an unenlightened master meets an unenlightened novice, to the mutual delusion of both.[33]

Lin-chi has been called the most powerful master in the entire history of Ch'an, and not without reason. His mind was capable of operating at several levels simultaneously, enabling him to overlay very practical instruction with a comprehensive dialectic. He believed in complete spontaneity, total freedom of thought and deed, and a teaching approach that has been called the "lightning" method—because it was swift and unpredictable. He was uncompromising in his approach, and he was also extremely critical of the state of Ch'an in his time—a criticism probably justified. He found both monks and masters wanting. It seems that Ch'an had become fashionable, with the result that there were many masters who were more followers of the trend than followers of the Way. So whereas Huang-po often railed against other sects of Buddhism, Lin-chi reserved his ire for other followers of Ch'an (there being few other Buddhist sects left to criticize).

He even denounced his own students, who often mimicked his shouting without perceiving his discernment in its use. He finally had to set standards for this, announcing to the assembly one day that henceforth only those who could tell the enlightened from the unenlightened would have the right to shout.

> "You all imitate my shouting," he said, "but let me give you a test now. One person comes out from the eastern hall. Another person comes out from the western hall. At their meeting, they simultaneously shout. Do you possess enough discernment to distinguish the guest from the host [i.e., the unenlightened from the enlightened]? If you have no such discernment, you are forbidden hereafter to imitate my shouting.[34]

His major concern seems to have been that his students resist intellection. Lin-chi himself was able to speculate philosophically while still a natural man, using conceptual thought only when it served his purpose. But perhaps his students could not, for he constantly had to remind them that striving and learning were counterproductive.

> "Followers of Tao!" Lin-chi said, "the way of Buddhism admits of no artificial effort; it only consists in doing the ordinary things without any fuss—going to the stool, making water, putting on clothes, taking a meal, sleeping when tired. Let the fools laugh at me. Only the wise know what I mean."[35]

Or as he said at another time:

> The moment a student blinks his eyes, he's already way off. The moment he tries to think, he's already differed. The moment he arouses a thought, he's already deviated. But for the man who understands, it's always right here before his eyes.[36]

The problem, he believed, was that too many teachers had started "teaching" and explaining rather than forcing students to experience truth for themselves. Thus these teachers had no right to criticize their monks, since they themselves had failed in their responsibility.

> There are teachers all around who can't distinguish the false from the true. When students come asking about . . . the [objective] surroundings and the [subjective] mind, the blind old teachers immediately start explaining to them. When they're railed at by the students they grab their sticks and hit them, [shouting], "What insolent talk!" Obviously you teachers yourselves are without an eye so you've no right to get angry with them.[37]

And finally, in his old age, Lin-chi became something of a monument himself, a testing point for enlightenment in a world where true teachers were rare. He even complained about it.

> Hearing everywhere of old man Lin-chi, you come here intending to bait me with difficult questions and make it impossible for me to answer. Faced with a demonstration of the activity of my whole body, you students just stare blankly and can't move your mouths at all; you're at such a loss you don't know how to answer me. You go around everywhere thumping your own chests and whacking your own ribs, saying, "I understand Ch'an! I understand the Way!" But let two or three of you come here and you can't do a thing. Bah! Carrying that body and mind of yours, you go around everywhere flapping your lips like winnowing fans and deceiving villagers.[38]

His school prospered, becoming the leading expression of Ch'an in China as well as a vital force in the Zen that later arose among Japan's samurai. And his dialectical teachings became the philosophical basis for later Zen, something he himself probably would have deplored. (Later teachers seem to have given Lin-chi's categories more importance than he actually intended, for he professed to loathe systems and was in fact much more concerned with enlightenment as pure experience.) In any case, when he decided that his days were through he put on his finest robes, seated himself in the meditation posture, made a brief statement, and passed on. The year is said to have been 866 or 867.

Tung-shan, Wading the Stream (detail).
Attributed to Ma Yuan (ca. 1150–1230). Courtesy
of the Tokyo National Museum.

12

TUNG-SHAN AND TS'AO-SHAN:
FOUNDERS OF SOTO ZEN

Virtually all the masters encountered up to this point have been traceable to Ma-tsu, descendant in Dharma of the legendary Huai-jang and his master, the Sixth Patriarch, Hui-neng. This was the line that became Japanese Rinzai Zen, many centuries later. However, Hui-neng had another follower, a shadowy figure remembered as Ch'ing-yuan Hsing-ssu (d. 740) whose line also was perpetuated to present-day Japan.[1] His foremost pupil was Shih-t'ou (700–90), and a common description of the eighth-century Ch'an establishment was: "In Kiangsi the master was Ma-tsu; in Hunan the master was Shih-t'ou. People went back and forth between them all the time, and those who never met these two great masters were completely ignorant."[2] Shih-t'ou jousted with Ma-tsu, and they often swapped students. Ma-tsu sent his pupils on their way with a wink and the advice that Shih-t'ou was "slippery."[3] This legendary master was forebear of three of the five "houses" of Ch'an arising after the Great Persecution of 845, although the only one of the three surviving is the Ts'ao-tung, which arose during the later T'ang (618–907) and early Five Dynasties (907–960) period and remains today as Japanese Soto.

One of the cofounders of the Ts'ao-tung house was known as Tung-shan Liang-chieh (807–869), who was born in present day Chekiang but eventually found his way to what is now northern Kiangsi province.[4] As did most great masters, he took Buddhist orders early, and one of the most enduring stories of his life has him confounding his elders—an event common to many spiritual biographies. He began as a novice in the Vinaya sect, an organization often more concerned with the letter of the law than its spirit. One day he was asked to recite the Heart Sutra, but when he came to the phrase "There is no eye, ear, nose, tongue, body, or mind," he wonderingly touched his own face and then inquired of his master, "I have eyes, ears, nose, tongue, and so forth; how, then, can the sutra say there are no such things?"[5] The Vinaya master was dumbfounded by his iconoclasm and suggested that his bent of mind would be more readily cultivated in the Ch'an sect. So off he went to Mt. Sung, where he subsequently was ordained at the precocious age of twenty-one.

Afterward he traveled across China, typical for young monks of the age. Ironically enough, considering that his line eventually rivaled Ma-tsu's, his first stop was the monastery of Nan-ch'uan, one of the foremost disciples of Ma-tsu. As he arrived, Nan-ch'uan was announcing a memorial service to be conducted the next day on the anniversary of his master's death, a standard Chinese custom.

> Nan-ch'uan remarked, "When we serve food for Master Ma-tsu tomorrow, I do wonder whether he will come for it." None of the monks made a reply but [Tung-shan] came forth out of the crowd and said, "As soon as he has companions he will come." Hearing this, Nan-ch'uan praised him: "Although this man is young, he is worthy of being trained." [Tung-shan] said to him, "Master, you should not make a slave out of an honorable person."[6]

Tung-shan studied briefly with Nan-ch'uan making a name for himself in the process and then traveled on. He later landed at the monastery of a teacher named Yun-yen, but after a successful period of study he announced his intention to again continue down the road. Yun-yen, however, protested losing his star pupil.

> "After you leave here, it will be very hard for us to see each other again," said Master Yun-yen.
> "It will be very hard for us not to see each other again," answered [Tung-shan]. . . . Then Yun-yen said to him, "You must be very careful, as you are carrying this great thing."
> [Tung-shan] was puzzled. Later when he was crossing the water and saw his image reflected, he suddenly understood the teaching of Yun-yen.[7]

By the year 860 Tung-shan had a monastery of his own and was besieged by disciples. He subsequently moved to Tung-shan (Mt.

Tung) in what is today Kiangsi province, the locale that provided his historic name. His respect for Yun-yen's enigmatic wisdom was explained years later.

> One day, when the Master was conducting the annual memorial service for Master Yun-yen, a monk asked him:
> "What instruction did you receive from the late Master Yun-yen?"
> "Although I was there with him, he gave me no instruction," answered the Master.
> "Then why should you conduct the memorial service for him, if he did not instruct you?" persisted the monk. . . .
> "It is neither for his moral character nor his teaching of Dharma that I respect him. What I consider important is that he never told me anything openly."[8]

Yet Tung-shan does not seem completely against the cultivation of enlightenment, as were some of the other, more radical Ch'anists. Take, for example, the following reported encounter:

> A government officer wanted to know whether there was anyone approaching Ch'an through cultivation. The Master answered: "When you become a laborer, then there will be someone to do cultivation."[9]

The officer's question would have elicited a shout from Lin-chi, a blow from Huang-po, and advice from Chao-chou to go wash his rice bowl.

Although Tung-shan may have avoided the deliberate absurdities of the Lin-chi masters, his utterances are often puzzling nonetheless. Part of the reason is that he preferred the metaphor to the concrete example. Unlike the repartee of the absurdist Lin-chi masters, his exchanges are not deliberately illogical. Instead we find a simple reluctance to say anything straight. But if you follow the symbolic language, you realize it is merely another clever way of never teaching with words, while still using language. His frequent speaking in metaphors can be appreciated by the following exchange, which uses language emeshed in symbols.

> Monk: "With what man of Tao should one associate, so that one will hear constantly what one has never heard?"
> The Master: "That which is under the same coverlet with you."

Monk: "This is still what you, Master, can hear yourself. What is it that one will hear constantly which one has never heard?"
The Master: "It is not the same as wood and stone." . . .
Monk: "Who is he in our country that holds a sword in his hand?"
The Master: "It is Ts'ao-shan."
Monk: "Whom do you want to kill?"
The Master: "All those who are alive will die."
Monk: "When you happen to meet your parents, what should you do?"
The Master: "Why should you have any choice?"
Monk: "How about yourself?"
The Master: "Who can do anything to me?"
Monk: "Why should you not kill yourself, too?"
The Master: "There is no place on which I can lay my hands."[10]

The Ch'an teachers deliberately avoided specifics, since these might cause students to start worrying about the precise definition of words and end up bogged down in conceptual quandries, neglecting their real nature—which cannot be reached using words.[11] But further than this, the monk thinks he will trap the master by asking him if his injunction to kill includes his own parents. (Remember Lin-chi's "On meeting your parents, slay your parents.") But Tung-shan answered by accusing the monk—indirectly—of making discriminations. As for self-murder, Tung-shan maintains his immaterial self-nature is indestructible.[12]

The dialectic of Tung-shan, subsequently elaborated by his star pupil, Ts'ao-shan, represents one of the last great expressions of Chinese metaphysical thought. He defined a system of five positions or relations between the Particular or Relative and the Universal or Absolute, defined as follows.[13]

In the first state, called the Universal within the Particular, the Absolute is hidden and obscured by our preoccupation with the world of appearances. However, the world of appearances is in fact a part of the larger world of Absolute reality. When we have achieved a true understanding of the objective world we realize that it is no more real than our senses make it, and consequently it represents not absolute reality but merely our perception. This realization leads to the second phase.

In the second state, called the Particular within the Universal, we recognize that objective reality must always be perceived through our subjective apparatus, just as the Absolute must be approached through the relative, since all particularities merely exemplify the Absolute. Even good and bad are part of this same Universality. It is all *real*, but simply that—no values are attached, since it is all part of existence. This, says the scholar John Wu, is the state of enlightenment.[14]

In dialectical terms, this rounds out the comparison of the Particular and the Universal, with each shown to be part of the other. But they must ultimately be resolved back into *sunyata*, the Void that encompasses everything. Neither the Universal or Absolute, nor the particulars that give it physical form, are the ultimate reality. They both are merely systems in the all-encompassing Void.

The third and fourth stages he defines exemplify achieving enlightenment by Universality alone and achieving enlightenment by Particularity alone. The third stage, enlightenment through Universality, leads one to meditate on the Absolute, upon the single wordless truth that defines the particular around us as part of itself. (It sounds remarkably similar to the Tao.) This meditation is done without props, language, or any of the physical world (the particular) surrounding us.

Enlightenment through the Particular, through experience with the phenomenal world, was the fourth stage. This received the most attention from the Lin-chi sect—whose masters would answer the question "What is the meaning of Ch'an?" with "The cypress tree in the courtyard" or "Three pounds of flax."[15]

At the fifth stage, enlightenment reaches the Void, the state that cannot be contained in a concept, since all concepts are *inside* it. When you finally reach this state of wordless insight, you realize that both words *and* wordlessness are merely part of this larger reality. Action and nonaction are equally legitimate responses to the world. Tung-shan demonstrated this when he was asked, "When a snake is swallowing a frog, should you save the frog's life?" To this he answered, "To save the frog is to be blind [i.e., to ultimate oneness and therefore to discriminate between frog and snake]; not to save the frog is not to let form and shadow appear [i.e., to ignore the phenomena].[16] Perhaps Tung-shan was demonstrating that he was free of discrimination between either option.[17]

The question of the subjective and the objective, the Universal and the Particular, permeated Tung-shan's teachings.

> Once the Master asked a monk what his name was. The monk answered that his name was so-and-so. The Master then asked: "What one is your real self?"

"The one who is just facing you."

"What a pity! What a pity! The men of the present day are all like this. They take what is in the front of an ass or at the back of a horse and call it themselves. This illustrates the downfall of Buddhism. If you cannot recognize your real self objectively, how can you see your real self subjectively?"

"How do you see your real self subjectively?" the monk immediately asked.

"You have to tell me that yourself."

"If I were to tell you myself, it would be seeing myself objectively. What is the self that is known subjectively?"

"To talk about it in such a way is easy to do, but to continue our talking makes it impossible to reach the truth."[18]

There also is a poem, known as the *Pao-ching San-mei*, traditionally attributed to Tung-shan.[19] One quatrain will give the flavor of the verse:

> The man of wood sings,
> The woman of stone gets up and dances,
> This cannot be done by passion or learning,
> It cannot be done by reasoning.[20]

This has been interpreted as the idea of Universality penetrating into Particularity. The wooden man singing and the stone maiden dancing are explained as evidence of the power of Universality.[21]

Tung-shan had a number of distinguishing qualities. He often used Taoist language in his teachings, quoting Chuang Tzu to make a point. Reportedly he never used the shout or the stick to shock a novice into self-awareness. And whereas his dialogues often used metaphors that at first appear obscure, there are never the deliberate absurdities of the Lin-chi masters, who frequently answered a perfectly reasonable question with a deliberate inanity merely to demonstrate the absurdity of words. Unlike the Lin-chi masters, he seems less concerned with the process of transmission than with what exactly is transmitted. Tung-shan viewed words as did Chuang Tzu, namely as the net in which to catch the fish. Whereas the Lin-chi masters viewed enlightenment as a totality, Tung-shan teachers believed that enlightenment arrived in stages, and they were concerned with identifying what these stages were. This was, in fact, the purpose of his five categories of Particularity and Universality, which became a part of the historic dialectic of Zen enlightenment. Ironically, with the emergence of the idea of stages, we seem back to a concept of "gradual" enlightenment—arrived at because the Chinese mind could not resist theoretical speculations.

Tung-shan's deathbed scene was almost worthy of comic opera. One day in the third month of 869 he made known his resolve to die and, shaving his head and donning his formal robes, ordered the gong to be struck as he seated himself in meditation. But his disciples began sobbing so disturbingly that he finally despaired of dying in peace and, opening his eyes, chided them.

> Those who are Buddhists should not attach themselves to externalities. This is the real self-cultivation. In living they work hard; in death they are at rest. Why should there be any grief?[22]

He then instructed the head monk to prepare "offerings of food to ignorance" for everyone at the monastery, intending to shame all those who still clung to the emotions of the flesh. The monks took a full week to prepare the meal, knowing it was to be his last supper. And sure enough, upon dining he bade them farewell and, after a ceremonial bath, passed on.

The most famous disciple of Tung-shan, Master Ts'ao-shan (840–901), was born as Pen-chi on the Fukien coast. Passing through an early interest in Confucianism, he left home at nineteen and became a Buddhist. He was ordained at age twenty-five and seems to have found frequent occasion to visit Tung-shan. Then one day they had an encounter that catapulted Ts'ao-shan into the position of favored pupil. The exchange began with a question by Tung-shan:

> "What is your name?"
> "My name is [Ts'ao-shan]."
> "Say something toward Ultimate Reality."
> "I will not say anything."
> "Why don't you speak of it?"
> "It is not called [Ts'ao-shan]."[23]

It is said that Tung-shan gave Ts'ao-shan private instruction after this and regarded his capability highly. The anecdote, if we may venture a guess, seems to assert that the Universal cannot be reached through language, and hence he could only converse about his objective, physical form.

After several years of study, Ts'ao-shan decided to strike out on his own, and he announced this intention to Tung-shan. The older master then inquired:

> "Where are you going?"
> "I go where it is changeless."
> "How can you go where it is changeless?"
> "My going is no change."[24]

Ts'ao-shan subsequently left his master and went wandering and teaching. Finally, in late summer of 901, the story says that Ts'ao-shan one evening inquired about the date, and early the next morning he died.

Although the recorded exchanges between Tung-shan and Ts'ao-shan are limited to the two rather brief encounters given, the younger master actually seems to have been the moving force behind the dialectical constructions of the Ts'ao-tung school. The ancient records, such as *The Transmission of the Lamp*, all declare that Ts'ao-shan was inspired by the Five States of Universality and Particularity to become a great Buddhist. As Dumoulin judges, "It was [Ts'ao-shan] who first, in the spirit of and in accordance with the master's teachings, arranged the five ranks in their transmuted form and explained them in many ways. . . . The fundamental principles, however, stem from [Tung-shan], who for that reason must be considered to be their originator."[25]

The ultimate concern of both the Ts'ao-tung and Lin-chi doctrines was enlightenment. The difference was that Ts'ao-tung masters believed quiet meditation was the way, rather than the mind-shattering techniques of Lin-chi. Ts'ao-tung (Soto Zen) strives to soothe the spirit rather than deliberately instigate psychic turmoil, as sometimes does the Lin-chi (Rinzai). The aim is to be in the world but not of it; to occupy the physical world but transcend it mentally, aloof and serene.

A further difference has been identified by the British scholar Sir Charles Eliot, who concludes that whereas Lin-chi "regards the knowledge of the Buddha nature . . . as an end in itself, all-satisfying and all-engrossing, the [Ts'ao-tung] . . . held that it is necessary to have enlightenment after Enlightenment, that is to say that the inner illumination must display itself in a good life."[26] Thus Eliot suggests the Ts'ao-tung took something of an interest in what you do, in distinction to the Lin-chi school, which preferred to focus on inner wisdom.

The Ts'ao-tung sect, at least in its early forms, was fully as dialectical in outlook as was the Lin-chi. In this it was merely carrying on, to some extent, the example of its forebear Shih-t'ou, who was himself remembered as deeply interested in theoretical and intellectual speculations. Today the Ts'ao-tung sect is differentiated from the Lin-chi primarily by its methods for teaching novices. There is no disagreement about the goal, merely about the path.

It is interesting that the whole business of the Five Ranks seems not to have survived the Sung Dynasty. Ts'ao-tung's real contribution was essentially to revive the approach of Northern Ch'an, with its stress on meditation, intellectual inquiry, stages of enlightenment, and the idea that Ch'an is not entirely inner-directed but may also have some place in the world at large. This is the real achievement of Ts'ao-tung, and the quality that enabled it to survive and become Soto.

Yun-men Wen-yen (left) and his Teacher
Hsueh-feng I-ts'un (detail). Attributed to Ma Yuan
(ca. 1150–1230). Courtesy of Tenryu-ji, Kyoto.

13

KUEI-SHAN, YUN-MEN, AND FA-YEN:
THREE MINOR HOUSES

The "five houses" or sects of Ch'an that arose after the Great
Persecution of 845 did not all appear simultaneously, nor did they
enjoy equal influence. Whereas the Lin-chi and the Ts'ao-tung
were destined to survive and find their way to Japan, the three other
houses were treated less kindly by history. Nonetheless, in the
search for enlightenment, each of the three other houses
contributed techniques, insights, and original ideas that enriched
the Zen tradition. It is with the stories of the masters who founded
the three extinct houses that we close out the era preceding the
Sung Dynasty and the rise of the koan.

KUEI-SHAN, FOUNDER OF THE KUEI-YANG SECT

This earliest of the five houses was founded by a contemporary of
Huang-po and follower of the Ma-tsu tradition known by the name
Kuei-shan (771-853). Under his original name, Ling-yu, he left
home at fifteen to become a monk, studying under a local Vinaya
master in present-day Fukien province. He later was ordained at
Hangchow, where he assiduously absorbed the *vinaya* and sutras
of both Theravada and Mahayana.[1] Then at age twenty-three he
traveled to Kiangsi and became a pupil of the famous Ch'an
lawgiver Po-chang Huai-hai.

The moment of Kuei-shan's enlightenment at the hands of
Huai-hai is a Zen classic. As the story goes:

One day as he was waiting upon [Huai-hai], the latter asked
him to poke the stove, to see whether there was any fire left in

it. Kuei-shan poked but found no fire. [Huai-hai] rose to poke it himself, and succeeded in discovering a little spark. Showing it to his disciple, he asked, "Is this not fire?" Thereupon Kuei-shan became enlightened.[2]

Just why this seemingly trivial incident should trigger enlightenment is clearly a matter that must be approached intuitively.[3]

Kuei-shan received his name from Mt. Kuei, where he was sent to found a monastery by Po-chang Huai-hai. The circumstances of his selection reveal almost more than we would wish to know about the Ch'an monastic world at the beginning of the ninth century. It happened that Huai-hai was considering the idea of founding a new monastery on Mt. Kuei in Hunan province. However, he was uncertain whether the venture would flourish, and consequently he turned for advice to a wandering fortuneteller named Ssu-ma.[4] This seer responded that Mt. Kuei was an ideal location and would support fifteen hundred monks. However, Huai-hai himself would not prosper there, since "You are a bony, ascetic man and it is a fleshy, sensuous mountain." The advice was to find somebody else.

Huai-hai consented and began calling in his candidates for Ssu-ma to examine. The first to be summoned was the head monk—whom Ssu-ma asked to produce a deep cough and then walk several steps. The wizened old mystic watched carefully and then whispered to Huai-hai that this was not the man. Next to be called in was Kuei-shan, currently administrator of the monastery. Ssu-ma took one look and nodded his approval to Huai-hai. That night Huai-hai summoned Kuei-shan and assigned his new mission: "Go to Mt. Kuei and found the monastery that will perpetuate my teachings."

When the head monk discovered he had been passed over he was outraged and at the next morning's convocation demanded that Huai-hai justify this slight. The master replied:

"If you can make an outstanding response in front of the assembly, you shall receive the appointment." [Huai-hai] then pointed to a pitcher and said to him, "Do not call this a pitcher. What, instead, should you call it?" [The head monk] answered, "It cannot be called a wooden wedge." Master [Huai-hai] did not accept this, and turned to [Kuei-shan], demanding his answer. [Kuei-shan] kicked the pitcher and knocked it over. Master [Huai-hai] laughed and said, "Our head monk has lost his bid for Mount Kuei."[5]

The head monk's reply had been intellectualizing wordplay, caught up in the world of names and categories. Kuei-shan's reply was spontaneous, wordless, and devoid of distinctions. His was a mind that could transcend rationality.

Kuei-shan did establish the monastery and from it a short-lived school. However, Kuei-shan's memory was perpetuated largely through a brilliant pupil later known as Yang-shan (807–883) owing to his founding a monastery on Mt. Yang in Kiangsi province. Together their teachings became known as the Kuei-yang school, the first of the "five houses."

The exchanges between Kuei-shan and Yang-shan reported in *The Transmission of the Lamp* are among the most electric in all Ch'an. In the following they joust over the distinction between function of wisdom (which is revealed through action) and substance or self-nature (which is revealed through nonaction).

> Once when all the monks were out picking tea leaves the Master said to Yang-shan, "All day as we were picking tea leaves I have heard your voice, but I have not seen you yourself. Show me your original self." Yang-shan thereupon shook the tea tree.
>
> The Master said, "You have attained only the function, not the substance." Yang-shan remarked, "I do not know how you yourself would answer the question." The Master was silent for a time. Yang-shan commented, "You, Master, have attained only the substance, not the function." Master Kuei-shan responded, "I absolve you from twenty blows!"[6]

Commentators differ on who won this exchange and whether Kuei-shan was really satisfied. Another story relates similar fast-witted but serious repartee.

> Two Ch'an monks came from [a rival] community and said, "There is not a man here who can understand Ch'an." Later, when all the monks went out to gather firewood, Yang-shan saw the two, who were resting; he took a piece of firewood and asked them, "Can you talk (about it)?" As both remained silent, Yang-shan said to them, "Do not say that there is no one here who can understand Ch'an."
>
> When he returned to the monastery, Yang-shan reported to the master, "Today, two Ch'an monks were exposed by me." The master asked, "How did you expose them?" Yang-shan related the incident and the master said, "I have now exposed you as well."[7]

The translator Charles Luk suggests that Kuei-shan had "exposed" Yang-shan by showing that he still distinguished between himself and the other monks.

Yet another story, reminiscent of Nan-ch'uan, further dramatizes the school's teaching of nondiscrimination. The report recounts a present that Kuei-shan sent to Yang-shan, now also a master and co-founder of their school:

> Kuei-shan sent [Yang-shan] a parcel containing a mirror. When he went to the hall, [Yang-shan] held up the mirror and said to the assembly, "Please say whether this is Kuei-shan's or Yang-shan's mirror. If someone can give a correct reply, I will not smash it." As no one answered, the master smashed the mirror.[8]

Kuei-shan's answer to one pupil who requested that he "explain" Ch'an to him was to declare:

> If I should expound it explicitly for you, in the future you will reproach me for it. Anyway, whatever I speak still belongs to me and has nothing to do with you.[9]

This monk, who later became the famous master Hsiang-yen, subsequently burned his sutras and wandered the countryside in despair. Then one day while cutting grass he nicked a piece of broken tile against some bamboo, producing a sharp snap that suddenly triggered his enlightenment. In elation he hurried back to his cell in the abandoned monastery where he was living and burned incense to Kuei-shan, declaring, "If you had broken the secret to me then, how could I have experienced the wonderful event of today."[10]

The real contribution of the Kuei-yang sect is agreed to be the final distinction Yang-shan made between the Ch'an of meditation (based on the Lankavatara Sutra) and instantaneous Ch'an (that completely divorced from the sutras). In this final revision of Ch'an history, "traditional" or "Patriarchal" Ch'an was redefined as the anti-sutra establishment of the Southern school, while the teaching of the Lankavatara, which actually had been the basis of the faith until the middle of the eighth century, was scorned as an aberration. He emphasized, in a sense, Ch'an's ultimate disowning of Buddhism—through a new, manufactured "history."

Kuei-shan died in the prescribed manner: After a ritual ablution he seated himself in the meditation posture and passed on with a smile. He was buried on Mt. Kuei, home of his monastery. His followers and those of his pupil Yang-shan composed the Kuei-yang school, an early attempt to formalize the anti-sutra position of Ma-tsu.[11] However, they were supplanted by other much more successful followers of Huai-hai, such as Huang-po and Lin-chi, whose school became the real perpetuator of Ma-tsu's iconoclasm.

THE YUN-MEN SECT

The Master Yun-men (862/4–949) was born in Kiangsu province (some say Chekiang) to a family whose circumstances forced them to place him in a Vinaya temple as a novice. But his inquiring mind eventually turned to Ch'an, and off he went to a master, with his first target being the famous Mu-chou, disciple of Huang-po. (Mu-chou is remembered as the monk who sent Lin-chi in for his first three withering interviews with Huang-po.) For two days running, Yun-men tried to gain entry to see the master, but each time he was ejected. The third day he succeeded in reaching Mu-chou, who grabbed him and demanded, "Speak! Speak!" But before Yun-men could open his mouth, the master shoved him out of the room and slammed the door, catching his leg and breaking it in the process. The unexpected bolt of pain shooting through Yun-men's body suddenly brought his first enlightenment.[12]

He journeyed on, studying with several famous masters, until finally he inherited a monastery from a retiring master who sensed his genius. Yun-men was one of the best-known figures from Ch'an's waning Golden Age, and stories of his exchanges with monks became a major source of koans.[13] He loathed words and forbade his followers to take notes or write down his sermons. (However, his talks were secretly recorded by a follower who attended in a paper robe and kept notes on the garment.) As did the earlier masters, he struggled mightily with the problem of how to prevent novices from becoming attached to his words and phrases.

[Yun-men] came to the assembly again and said: "My work here is something that I cannot help. When I tell you to penetrate directly into all things and to be non-attached to them, I have already concealed what is within you. Yet you all continue looking for Ch'an among my words, so that you may achieve enlightenment. With myriad deviations and artificialities, you raise endless questions and arguments. Thus, you merely gain temporary satisfactions from verbal contests, repeatedly quarrel with words, and deviate even further from Ch'an. When will you obtain it, and rest?"[14]

He firmly believed that all teaching was useless; that all explanations do more harm than good; and that, in fact, nothing worthwhile can ever be taught.

The Master said, "If I should give you a statement that would teach you how to achieve Ch'an immediately, dirt would already be spread on top of your head. . . . To grasp Ch'an, you must experience it. If you have not experienced it, do not pretend to know. You should withdraw inwardly and search for the ground upon which you stand; thereby you will find out what Truth is."[15]

One of Yun-men's sermons reveals much about the growing pains of Ch'an. The seriousness of the novices seems to have been steadily deteriorating, and his characterization of the run-of-the-mill novices of his time presents a picture of waning dynamism. Success was clearly bringing a more frivolous student to the monasteries, and we sense here the warning of a man who rightly feared for the future quality of Ch'an.

Furthermore, some monks, idle and not serious in their studies, gather together trying to learn the sayings of the ancients, and attempt to reveal their own nature through memorizing, imagining, prophesying. These people often claim that they understand what Dharma is. What they actually do is simply talk themselves into endless entanglements and use meditation to pass the time.[16]

He also felt the traditional pilgrimages from master to master had become hardly more than a glorified version of sightseeing.

Do not waste your time wandering thousands of [miles], through this town and that, with your staff on your shoulder, wintering in one place and spending the summer in another. Do not seek out beautiful mountains and rivers to contemplate. . . . [T]he fundamental thing for you to do is to obtain the essence of Ch'an. Then your travels will not have been in vain. If you find a way to guide your understanding under a severe master . . . wake up, hang up your bowl-bag, and break your staff. Spend ten or twenty years of study under him until you are thoroughly enlightened.[17]

He also advised that they try to simplify their search, that they try to realize how uncomplicated Ch'an really is.

> Let me tell you that anything you can directly point at will not lead you to the right trail. . . . Besides dressing, eating, moving bowels, releasing water, what else is there to do?[18]

Yun-men was one of the most dynamic masters of the late ninth and early tenth century, providing new twists to the historic problem of nonlanguage transmission. *His* celebrated solution was the so-called one-word answer. Several of these are preserved in the two major koan collections of later years. Two of the better-known follow:

> A monk asked Yun-men, "What is the teaching that transcends the Buddha and patriarchs?" Yun-men said, "A sesame bun."[19]

> A monk asked Yun-men, "What is Buddha?" Yun-men replied, "A dried piece of shit."[20]

The "one-word" was his version of the blow and the shout. R. H. Blyth is particularly fond of Yun-men and suggests he may have had the keenest intellect of any Ch'an master—and even goes so far as to declare him the greatest man China has produced.[21]

At the very least Yun-men was in the great tradition of the iconoclastic T'ang masters, with a touch that bears comparison to Huang-po. And he probably was wise in attempting to stop copyists, for his teachings eventually were reduced to yet another abominable system, as seemed irresistible to the Chinese followers of the five houses. A later disciple produced what is known as the "Three propositions of the house of Yun-men." It is not difficult to imagine the barnyard response Yun-men would have had to this "systematization" of his thought.[22] The school of this "most eloquent of Ch'an masters" lasted through the Sung dynasty, but its failure to find a transplant in Japan eventually meant that history would pass it by. Nonetheless, the cutting intellect of Yun-men was one of the bright stars in the constellation of Ch'an, providing what is possibly its purest antirational statement.

THE FA-YEN SECT

The master known as Fa-yen (885–958), founder of the third short-lived house of Ch'an, need not detain us long. Fa-yen's novel method for triggering enlightenment was to repeat back the questioner's own query, thereby isolating the words and draining them of their meaning. It was his version of the shout, the silence, the single word. And whereas the Lin-chi school was concerned with the Four Processes of Liberation from Subjectivity and Objectivity and the Ts'ao-tung school constructed the five relations between Particularity and Universality, the Fa-yen school invented the Six Attributes of Being.[23] The Six Attributes of Being (totality and differentiation, sameness and difference, becoming and disappearing) were adapted from the doctrine of another Buddhist sect, and in fact later attempts by one of Fa-yen's disciples to combine Ch'an and Pure Land Buddhism have been credited with accelerating the disappearance of his school.

According to The Transmission of the Lamp, the master remembered as Fa-yen was born as Wen-i, near Hangchow. He became a Ch'an novice at age seven and was ordained at twenty. Learned in both Buddhist and Confucianist literature (though not, significantly enough, in the Taoist classics), he then got the wanderlust, as was common, and headed south to seek out more Ch'an teachers. He ended up in Kiangsi province in the city of Fu-chou, where to escape the floodings of a rainstorm he found himself one evening in a local monastery. He struck up a conversation with the master there, who suddenly asked him:

> "Where are you going, sir?"
> "I shall continue my foot travels along the road."
> "What is that which is called foot travel?"
> "I do not know."
> "Not-knowing most closely approaches the Truth."[24]

The Transmission of the Lamp states that he was enlightened on the spot and decided to settle down for a period of study. He eventually became a famous teacher himself, shepherding as many as a thousand students at one time.

One of his most often repeated exchanges concerned the question of the difference between the "moon" (i.e., enlightenment) and the "finger pointing at the moon," (i.e., the teaching leading to enlightenment). It was a common observation that students confused the finger pointing at the moon with the moon itself, which is to say they confused talk about enlightenment with the state. One day a monk came along who thought he was smart enough to get around the dilemma.

A monk asked, "As for the finger, I will not ask you about it. But what is the moon?"

The Master said, "Where is the finger that you do not ask about?"

So the monk asked, "As for the moon, I will not ask you about it. But what is the finger?"

The Master said, "The moon!"

The monk challenged him, "I asked about the finger; why should you answer me, 'the moon'?"

The Master replied, "Because you asked about the finger."[25]

At age seventy-four Fa-yen died in the manner of other great masters, calmly and seated in the meditation posture. Part of the lineage of Shih-t'ou and an offshoot of the branch of Ch'an that would become Soto, he was a kindly individual with none of the violence and histrionics of the livelier masters. However, his school lasted only briefly before passing into history. Nonetheless, a number of disciples initially perpetuated his memory, and his wisdom is preserved in various Sung-period compilations of Ch'an sermons.

*Boy on a Water Buffalo, Recalling the
Zen Parable of Looking for the Ox While Riding
the Ox.* Attributed to Sekkyakushi (fourteenth century).
Courtesy of the Smithsonian Institution, Freer
Gallery of Art, Washington, D.C.

14

TA-HUI:
MASTER OF THE KOAN

To confront the koan—the most discussed, least understood teaching concept of the East—is to address the very essence of Zen itself. In simple terms the koan is merely a brief story—all the encounters between two monks related here could be koans. During the Sung Dynasty (960–1279) these stories were organized into collections, commented upon, and structured into a system of study—which involved meditating on a koan and arriving at an intuitive "answer" acceptable to a Zen master. Faced with the threatening intellectualism of the Sung scholars, Ch'anists created the koan out of the experience of the older masters, much the way a liferaft might be constructed from the timbers of a storm-torn ship. But before we examine this raft, it would be well to look again at the ship.

It will be recalled that Ch'an grew out of both Buddhism and Taoism, extracting from them the belief that a fundamental unifying quality transcends all the diversity of the world, including things that appear to be opposite. However, Ch'an taught that this cannot be understood using intellectualism, which rationally makes distinctions and relates to the world by reducing it to concepts and systems. One reason is that all rationality and concepts are merely part of a larger, encompassing Reality; and trying to reach this Reality intellectually is like trying to describe the outside of a building while trapped inside.

There is, however, a kind of thought—not beholden to concepts, systems, discriminations, or rationality—that *can* reach this new understanding. It is intuition, which operates in a mode entirely different from rationality. It is holistic, not linear; it is unself-conscious and noncritical; and it doesn't bother with any of the rational systems of analysis we have invented for ourselves. But since we can't call on it at our pleasure, the next best thing we can do is clear the way for it to operate—by shutting off the rational part of the mind. Then intuition starts hesitantly coming out of the shadows. Now, if we carefully wait for the right moment and then suddenly create a disturbance that momentarily short-circuits the rational mind—the way shock suppresses our sense of pain in the first moments of a serious accident—we may get a glimpse of the intuitive mind in full flower. In that instant we *intuitively* understand the oneness of the world, the Void, the greater Reality that words and rationality have never allowed us to experience.

The Zen teachers have a very efficient technique for making all this happen. They first discredit rationality for a novice by making him feel foolish for using it. Each time the novice submits a rational solution to a koan, he receives a humiliating rebuff. After a while the strain begins to tell. In the same way that a military boot camp destroys the ego and self-identity of a recruit, the Zen master slowly erodes the novice's confidence in his own logical powers.

At this point his intuitive mind begins overcoming its previous repression. Distinctions slowly start to seem absurd, because every time he makes one he is ridiculed. Little by little he dissolves his sense of object and subject, knower and known. The fruit now is almost ready to fall from the tree. (Although enlightenment cannot be *made to happen*, it can be *made possible*.) Enter at this point the unexpected blow, the shout, the click of bamboo, the broken leg. If the student is caught unawares, rationality may be momentarily short-circuited and suddenly he glimpses—Reality.

The irony is that what he glimpses is no different from what he saw before, only now he understands it intuitively and realizes how simplistic and confining are rational categories and distinctions. Mountains are once again mountains; rivers are once again rivers. But with one vital difference: Now he is *not attached to them*. He travels through the world just as always, but now he is at one with it: no distinctions, no critical judgments, no tension. After all that preparatory mental anguish there is no apparent external change. But internally he is enlightened: He thinks differently, he understands differently, and ultimately he lives differently.

Ch'an began by working out the question of what this enlightenment really is. Prior to Ma-tsu the search was more for the nature of enlightenment than for its transmission. This was the doctrinal phase of Ch'an. As time went by, however, the concern shifted more and more from defining enlightenment—which the Ch'an masters believed had been done sufficiently—to struggling with the process. After Ma-tsu, Ch'an turned its attention to "auxiliary means" for helping along transmission: paradoxical words and actions, shouts, beatings, and eventually the koan.[1]

The koan, then, is the final step in the "auxiliary means." A succinct analysis of the koan technique is provided by Ruth F. Sasaki in *Zen Dust*: "Briefly, [koans] consisted of questions the early masters had asked individual students, together with the answers given by the students; questions put to the masters by students in personal talks or in the course of the masters' lectures, together with the masters' answers; statements of formulas in which the masters had pointed to the profound Principle; anecdotes from the daily life of the masters in which their attitudes or actions illustrated the functioning of the Principle; and occasionally a phrase from a sutra in which the Principle or some aspect of it was crystallized in words. By presenting a student with one or another of these koans and observing his reaction to it, the degree or depth of his realization could be judged. The koans were the criteria of attainment."[2]

Called *kung-an* in Chinese (meaning a "case" or a problem), the koan was a response to two major challenges that beset Ch'an in the Sung era: First, the large number of students that appeared at Ch'an monasteries as a result of the demise of other sects meant that some new means was needed to preserve personalized attention (some masters reportedly had one thousand or even two thousand followers at a monastery); and second, there was a noticeable decline in the spontaneity of both novices *and* masters. The masters had lost much of the creative fire of Ch'an's Golden Age, and the novices were caught up in the intellectual, literary world of the Sung, to the point that intellectualism actually threatened the vitality of the sect.

The koan, then, was the answer to this dilemma. It systematized instruction such that large numbers of students could be treated to the finest antirational tradition of the Ch'an sect, and it rescued the dynamism of the earlier centuries. Although mention of *kung-an* occurs in the Ch'an literature before the end of the T'ang era (618–907), the reference was to a master's use of a particularly effectual question on more than one student. This was still an instance of a master using his *own* questions or paradoxes. The koan in its true form—that is, the use of a classic incident from the literature, posed as a conundrum—is said to have been created when a descendant of Lin-chi, in the third generation, interviewed a novice about some of Lin-chi's sayings.[3] This systematic use of the existing literature was found effective, and soon a new teaching technique was in the making.

Examples of classic koans already have been seen throughout this book, since many of the exchanges of the early masters were later isolated for use as kung-an. But there are many, many others. Perhaps the best-known koan of all time is the exchange between Chao-chou (778–897) and a monk:

A monk asked Chao-chou. "Does a dog have Buddha nature [i.e., is a dog capable of being enlightened]?" Chao-chou answered, "Mu [a word whose strict meaning is "nothing-ness"]."[4]

Quick, what does it mean? Speak! Speak! If you were a Ch'an novice, a master would be glaring at you demanding an immediate, intuitive answer. (A favored resolution of this, incidentally, is simply "Mu," but bellowed with all the force of the universe's inherent Oneness behind it. And if you try to fake it, the master will know.) Or take another koan, drawn completely at random.

When the monks assembled before the noon meal to hear his lecture, the Master Fa-yen [885–958] pointed at the bamboo blinds. Two monks simultaneously went and rolled them up. Fa-yen said, "One gain, one loss."[5]

Don't think! Respond instantly! Don't say a word unless it's right. Don't make a move that isn't intuitive. And above all, don't analyze.

Yun-men [862/4–949] asked a monk, "Where have you come here from?" The monk said, "From Hsi-ch'an." Yun-men said, "What words are being offered at Hsi-ch'an these days?" The monk stretched out his hands. Yun-men struck him. The monk said, "I haven't finished talking." Yun-men then extended his own hands. The monk was silent, so Yun-men struck him.[6]

You weren't there. You're not the monk. But now you've got to do something to show the master you grasp what went on in that exchange. What was spontaneous to the older masters you must grasp in a secondhand, systematized situation. And if you can't answer the koan right (it should be stressed, incidentally, there is not necessarily a fixed answer), you had best go and meditate, try to grasp it nonintellectually, and return tomorrow to try again.

Off you go to meditate on "Mu" or "One gain, one loss," and the mental tension starts building. Even though you know you aren't supposed to, you analyze it intellectually from every angle. But that just heightens your exasperation. Then suddenly one day something dawns on you. Elated, you go to the master. You yell at him, or bark like a dog, or kick his staff, or stand on your hands, or recite a poem, or declare, "The cypress tree in the courtyard," or perhaps you just remain silent. He will know (intuitively) if you have broken through the bonds of reason, if you have transcended the intellect.

There's nothing quite like the koan in the literature of the world: historical episodes that have to be relived intuitively and responded to. As Ruth F. Sasaki notes, "Collections of 'old cases,' as the koans were sometimes called, as well as attempts to put the koans into a fixed form and to systematize them to some extent, were already being made by the middle of the tenth century. We also find a few masters giving their own alternate answers to some of the old koans and occasionally appending verses to them. In many cases these alternate answers and verses ultimately became attached to the original koans and were handled as koans supplementary to them."[7] Ironically, koans became so useful, indeed essential, in the perpetuation of Ch'an that they soon were revered as texts. Collections of the better koans appeared, and next came accretions of supporting commentaries—when the whole point was supposed to be circumventing reliance on words! But commentaries always seemed to develop spontaneously out of Ch'an.

Today two major collections of koans are generally used by students of Zen. These are the Mumonkan (to use the more familiar Japanese name) and the Hekiganroku (again the Japanese name) or Blue Cliff Record.[8] Masters may work a student through both these collections as he travels the road to enlightenment, with a new koan being assigned after each previous one has been successfully resolved.

The Blue Cliff Record was the first of the two collections. It began as a grouping of one hundred kung-an by a master named Hsueh-tou Ch'ung-hsien (980–1052) of the school of Yun-men. This master also attached a small poem to each koan, intended to direct the student toward its meaning. The book enjoyed sizable circulation throughout the latter part of the eleventh century, and sometime thereafter a Lin-chi master named Yuan-wu K'o-ch'in (1063–1135) decided to embellish it by adding an introduction to each koan and a long-winded commentary on both the koan and the poem supplied by the previous collector. (In the case of the poem we now have commentary on commentary—the ultimate achievement of the theologian's art! However, masters today often omit Yuan-wu's commentaries, giving their own interpretation instead.[9]) The commentator, Yuan-wu, was the teacher of Ta-hui, the dynamic master of the Lin-chi lineage whom we will meet here.

The Mumonkan, a shorter work, was assembled in 1228 by the Ch'an monk Wu-men Hui-k'ai (1183–1260) and consists of forty-eight koans, together with an explanatory comment and a verse. Some of the koans in the Mumonkan also appear in the Blue Cliff Record. The Mumonkan is usually preferred in the Japanese summer, since its koans are briefer and less fatiguing.[10]

The koan was an invention of the Sung Dynasty (960–1279), an era of consolidation in the Chinese empire after the demise of the T'ang and passage of a war-torn interlude known as the Five Dynasties (907–60). Although Sung Ch'an seemed to be booming, Buddhism in general continued the decline that began with the Great Persecution of 845. For example, the number of registered monks dropped from around 400,000 in 1021 to approximately half that number a scant half-century later.[11] But the monks who did come probably had higher education than previously, for the Sung educational system was the world's best at the time. Colleges were established nationwide, not just in the sophisticated metropolitan areas, and scholarship flourished. Whether this was good for Ch'an is not a simple question. The hardy rural monks who had passed beyond the Buddhist scriptures made Ch'an what it was. Could the powers of the antirational be preserved in an atmosphere where the greatest respect was reserved for those who spent years memorizing the Chinese classics? The answer to this was to rest with the koan.

The Ch'an master Ta-hui (1089–1163), who perfected the koan technique, was rumored to be a reincarnation of Lin-chi. Born in Anhwei province, located about halfway between the older capitals of the north and the Ch'an centers in the south, he was said to be both pious and precocious, becoming a devoted monk at age seventeen while assiduously reading and absorbing the teachings of the five houses.[12] At age nineteen, he began his obligatory travels, roaming from master to master. One of his first teachers reportedly interviewed him on the koans in the collection now known as the Blue Cliff Record, but he did so by not speaking a word and thereby forcing Ta-hui to work them out for himself. Ta-hui also experimented with the Ts'ao-tung teachings, but early on began to question the straitlaced, quietistic approach of that house. He finally was directed to the Szechuan teacher Yuan-wu K'o-ch'in of the Lin-chi school, beginning the association that would move him to the forefront of the struggle to save Ch'an via the koan.

Ta-hui experienced his first enlightenment under Yuan-wu, in the master's temple in the Northern Sung capital of Pien-liang. As the story is reported:

> One day when Yuan-wu had taken the high seat in the lecture hall, he said: "A monk asked Yun-men: 'From whence come all the buddhas?' Yun-men answered: 'The East Mountain walks over the water.' But if I were asked, I would not answer that way. 'From whence come all the buddhas?' A fragrant breeze comes of itself from the south, and in the palace pavilion a refreshing coolness stirs." At these words [Ta-hui] suddenly attained enlightenment.[13]

After this he grew in experience and wisdom, eventually taking over many temple duties from Yuan-wu. He soon became a part of the Ch'an establishment in the north and in 1126 was even presented with an official robe and title from a minister.

Then suddenly, in the midst of this tranquillity, outside forces intervened to change dramatically the course of Chinese history. For many years previous, China had been threatened by nomadic peoples from the north and west, peoples whom the Chinese haughtily identified as "barbarians." The Sung emperors, cloistered gentlemen in the worst sense of the term, had maintained peace in their slowly shrinking domain by buying off belligerent neighbors and occasionally even ceding border territories. They thought their troubles finally might be easing somewhat when their hostile neighbors were overwhelmed by a new warring tribe from Manchuria. But after a series of humiliating incidents, the Chinese found themselves with merely a new enemy, this time more powerful than any before. China was at last on the verge of being overwhelmed, something it had forestalled for many centuries. Even the invention of gunpowder, which the Chinese now used to fire rocket-propelled arrows, could not save them. Before long the barbarians marched on the capital, and after some years of Chinese attempts at appeasement, the invaders carried off the emperor and his entire court to Manchuria. The year was 1127, which marked the end of the Chinese dynasty now known as the Northern Sung (960–1127).

After this disheartening setback a son of the former emperor moved south and set up a new capital in the coastal city of Hangchow, whose charms the Chinese were fond of comparing favorably with heaven (in the refrain, "Heaven above; Hangchow below"). This new regime, known as the Southern Sung (1127–1279), witnessed yet another transformation of Ch'an. Among other things, Southern Ch'an came to resemble eighth-century Northern Ch'an, in its close association with the court and the intelligentsia.

When political discord forced the Northern Sung government to flee south, the master Yuan-wu was assigned a monastery in the southern province of Kiangsi by the emperor, and Ta-hui accompanied him there, again as head monk. After four years, Ta-hui again decided to migrate—this time alone—to Szechuan and there to build a secluded hermitage. After another move he was summoned in 1137 by the prime minister, himself also a former pupil of Yuan-wu, to come and establish a temple near the new southern capital of Hangchow. Before long he had collected almost two thousand disciples and was becoming known as the reincarnation of Lin-chi, possibly because he was giving new life to the Lin-chi sect. But then his politics got him in trouble and he was banished for almost fifteen years to various remote outposts, during which time he began to write extensively.[14] Finally, in 1158, he was ordered back to Hangchow to take over his old temple. Since by then old age was encroaching, he was permitted to retire at this temple and live off imperial patronage. It is said that his pupils swelled to seventeen hundred when he returned and that when he died in 1163 he left ninety-four enlightened heirs.[15]

Ta-hui is regarded today as the great champion of the koan method, and he was celebrated during his life for a running disagreement he had with the Ts'ao-tung (later Soto) school. In a sense, this dispute drew the distinctions that still divide Zen into two camps. The issue seems to have boiled down to the matter of what one does with one's mind while meditating. The Ts'ao-tung masters advocated what they called Silent Illumination (mo-chao) Ch'an, which Ta-hui preferred to call Silent Illumination Hetero-dox (mo-chao-hsieh) Ch'an. The Ts'ao-tung master Cheng-chueh, with whom he argued, believed that enlightenment could be achieved through sitting motionless and slowly bringing tranquil-lity and empty nonattachment to the mind. The koans were recognized to be useful in preserving the original spirit of Ch'an, but their brain-fatiguing convolutions were not permitted to disturb the mental repose of meditation. Ta-hui, in contrast, believed that this silent meditation lacked the dynamism so essential to the sudden experience of enlightenment. His own approach to enlightenment came to be called Introspecting-the-

Koan (k'an-hua) Ch'an, in which meditation focused on a koan.[16]

Another of Ta-hui's objections to the Silent Illumination school seems to have been its natural drift toward quietism, toward the divorcing of men from the world of affairs. This he believed led nowhere and was merely renouncing humanity rather than illuminating it.

> These days there's a breed of shaven-headed outsiders [i.e., rival masters] whose own eyes are not clear, who just teach people to stop and rest and play dead. . . . They teach people to "keep the mind still," to "forget feelings" according to circumstances, to practice "silent illumination." . . . To say that when one has put things to rest to the point that he is unawares and unknowing, like earth, wood, tile, or stone, this is not unknowing silence—this is a view of wrongly taking too literally words that were (only) expedient means to free bonds.[17]

He seemed to be counseling never to forget that meditation is only a means, not an end. Instead Ta-hui advocated meditating deeper and ever deeper into a koan, focusing on the words until they "lose their flavor." Then finally the bottom falls out of the bucket and enlightenment hits you. This "Introspecting the Koan" form of Ch'an (called Kanna Zen by the Japanese) became the standard for the Rinzai sect, whose students were encouraged to meditate on a koan until it gradually infiltrated the mind. As one commentator has explained, "The essential is to immerse oneself patiently and wholeheartedly in the koan, with unwavering attention. One must not be looking for an answer but looking at the koan. The 'answer,' if it comes, will come of its own accord."[18] As described by Ta-hui:

> Just steadily go on with your koan every moment of your life. . . . Whether walking or sitting, let your attention be fixed upon it without interruption. When you begin to find it entirely devoid of flavor, the final moment is approaching: do not let it slip out of your grasp. When all of a sudden something flashes out in your mind, its light will illumine the entire universe, and you will see the spiritual land of the Enlightened Ones. . . .[19]

The important thing is to concentrate totally on a koan. This concentration need not necessarily be confined to meditation, as Ta-hui illustrates using one of the more celebrated one-word statements of Yun-men.

A monk asked Yun-Men, "What is Buddha?" Yun-Men said, "A dry piece of shit." Just bring up this saying. . . . Don't ask to draw realization from the words or try in your confusion to assess and explain. . . . Just take your confused unhappy mind and shift it onto "A dry piece of shit." Once you hold it there, then the mind . . . will naturally no longer operate. When you become aware that it's not operating, don't be afraid of falling into emptiness. . . . In the conduct of your daily activities, just always let go and make yourself vast and expansive. Whether you're in quiet or noisy places, constantly arouse yourself with the saying "A dry piece of shit." As the days and months come and go, of itself your potential will be purified and ripen. Above all you must not arouse any external doubts besides: when your doubts about "A dry piece of shit" are smashed, then at once doubts numerous as the sands of the Ganges are all smashed.[20]

Although Ta-hui was a strong advocate of the koan, he was staunchly against its being used in a literary sense. Whenever a student starts analyzing koans intellectually, comparing one against another, trying to understand rationally how they affect his nonrational intelligence, he misses the whole point. The only way it can work is if it is fresh. Only then does it elicit a response from our spontaneous intelligence, our intuitive mind.

But the Sung trend toward intellectualism was almost irresistible. The prestige of the Chinese "gentleman"—who could quote the ancient poets, compose verse himself, and analyze enlightenment—was the great nemesis of Ch'an.

Gentlemen of affairs who study the path often understand rationally without getting to the reality. Without discussion and thought they are at a loss, with no place to put their hands and feet—they won't believe that where there is no place to put one's hands and feet is really a good situation. They just want to get there in their minds by thinking and in their mouths to understand by talking—they scarcely realize they've already gone wrong.[21]

Equally bad was the Ch'an student who memorized koans rather than trying to understand them intuitively.

A gentleman reads widely in many books basically in order to augment his innate knowledge. Instead, you have taken to memorizing the words of the ancients, accumulating them in your breast, making this your task, depending on them for something to take hold of in conversation. You are far from knowing the intent of the sages in expounding the teachings. This is what is called counting the treasure of others all day long without having half a cent of your own.[22]

Ta-hui rightly recognized in such scholarship an impending destruction of Ch'an's innate vigor. At one point, in desperation, he even destroyed the original printing blocks for the best-known koan collection of the time, the Blue Cliff Record compiled by his master, Yuan-wu.[23] But the trend continued nonetheless.

Ch'an was not over yet, however. It turns out that the sect did not continue to fly apart and diversify as might be suspected, but rather it actually consolidated. Although the Kuei-yang and Fa-yen houses fizzled comparatively quickly, the Yun-men lasted considerably longer, with an identifiable line of transmission lasting virtually throughout the Sung Dynasty. The Ts'ao-tung house languished for a while, but with Silent Illumination Ch'an it came back strongly during the Sung Dynasty. Lin-chi split into two factions in the early eleventh century, when two pupils of the master Ch'u-yuan (986–1036) decided to go their own way. One of these masters, known as Huang-lung Hui-nan (1002–1069), started a school which subsequently was transmitted to Japan by the Japanese master Eisai, where it became known as Oryo Zen. However, this school did not last long in China or Japan, becoming moribund after a few generations. The other disciple of Ch'u-yuan was a master named Yang-ch'i Fang-hui (992–1049), whose school (known in Japanese as Yogi Zen) eventually became the *only* school of Chinese Ch'an, absorbing all other sects when the faith went into its final decline after the Sung. Ta-hui was part of this school, and it was the branch of the Lin-chi sect that eventually took hold in Japan.

In closing our journey through Chinese Ch'an we must note that the faith continued on strongly through the Sung largely because the government began selling ordinations for its own profit. Ch'an also continued to flourish during the Mongol-dominated Yuan Dynasty (1279–1309), with many priests from Japan coming to China for study. During the Ming Dynasty (1368–1644), it merged with another school of Buddhism, the Pure Land salvationist sect, and changed drastically. Although Ming-style Chinese Ch'an still persists today, mainly outside China, its practice bears scant resemblance to the original teachings. For the practice of the classical Ch'an described here we must now turn to Japan.

PART IV
ZEN
IN JAPAN

. . . in which Ch'an is imported to Japan by
traditional Buddhists disillusioned with the spiritual
decadence of existing Japanese sects. Through a fortuitous
association with the rising military class, Ch'an is eventually
elevated to the most influential religion of Japan. Before
long, however, it evolves into a political and cultural rather
than a spiritual force. Although some Japanese attempt
to restore Ch'an's original vigor by deliberately attacking
its "High Church" institutions, few Japanese Zen teachers respect
its original teachings and practice. Japanese teachers
contribute little to the Ch'an (Zen) experience until finally,
in the eighteenth century, a spiritual leader appears who
not only restores the original vitality of the faith, but goes on
to refine the koan practice and revolutionize the
relationship of Zen to the common people. This inspired
teacher, Hakuin, creates modern Zen.

Japanese Priest Traveling. Kano Tsunenobu
(1636–1713). Private collection.

15
EISAI:
THE FIRST JAPANESE MASTER

There is a twelfth-century story that the first Japanese monk who journeyed to China to study Ch'an returned home to find a summons from the Japanese court. There, in a meeting reminiscent of the Chinese sovereign Wu and the Indian Bodhidharma some seven hundred years before, Japan's emperor commanded him to describe the teachings of this strange new cult. The bemused monk (remembered by the name Kakua) replied with nothing more than a melody on his flute, leaving the court flabbergasted.[1] But what more ideal expression of China's wordless doctrine?

As in the China entered by Bodhidharma, medieval Japan already knew the teachings of Buddhism. In fact, the Japanese ruling classes had been Buddhist for half a millennium before Ch'an officially came to their attention. However, contacts with China were suspended midway during this time, leaving Japanese Buddhists out of touch with the many changes in China—the most significant being Ch'an's rise to the dominant Buddhist sect.[2] Consequently the Japanese had heard almost nothing about this sect when contacts resumed in the twelfth century. To their amazement they discovered that Chinese Buddhism had become Ch'an. The story of Ch'an's transplant in Japan is also the story of its preservation, since it was destined to wither away in China.

Perhaps we should review briefly how traditional Buddhism got to Japan in the first place. During the sixth century, about the time of Bodhidharma, a statue of the Buddha and some sutras were transmitted to Japan as a gift/bribe from a Korean monarch seeking military aid. He claimed Buddhism was very powerful although difficult to understand. Not all Japanese, however, were overjoyed with the appearance of a new faith. The least pleased were those employed by the existing religion, the Japanese cult of Shinto, and they successfully discredited Buddhism for several decades. But a number of court intrigues were underway at the time, and one faction got the idea that Buddhism would be helpful in undermining the Shinto-based ruling clique. Eventually this new faction triumphed, and by the middle of the seventh century, the Japanese were constructing Buddhist temples and pagodas.[3]

Other imports connected with these early mainland contacts were Chinese writing and the Chinese style of government. The Japanese even recreated the T'ang capital of Ch'ang-an, consecrated at the beginning of the eighth century as Nara, their first real city. The growing Buddhist establishment soon overwhelmed Nara with a host of sects and temples, culminating in 752 with the unveiling of a bronze meditating Buddha larger than any statue in the world.

Japan was now awash in thirdhand Buddhism, as Chinese missionaries patronizingly expounded Sanskrit scriptures they themselves only vaguely understood. Buddhism's reputation for powerful magic soon demoralized the simple religion of Shinto, with its unpretentious shrines and rites, and this benign nature reverence was increasingly pushed into the background. The impact of Buddhism became so overwhelming that the alarmed emperor finally abandoned Nara entirely to the Buddhists, and at the close of the eighth century set up a new capital in central Japan, known today as Kyoto.

The emperor also decided to discredit the Nara Buddhists on their own terms, sending to China for new, competing sects. Back came emissaries with two new schools, which soon assumed dominance of Japanese Buddhism. The first of these was Tendai, named after the Chinese T'ien-t'ai school. Its teachings centered on the Lotus Sutra, which taught that the human Buddha personified a universal spirit, evidence of the oneness permeating all things. The Tendai school was installed on Mt. Hiei, in the outskirts of Kyoto, giving birth to an establishment eventually to number several thousand buildings. The monks on Mt. Hiei became the authority on Buddhist matters in Japan for several centuries thereafter, and later they also began meddling in affairs of state, sometimes even resorting to arms. Tendai was, and perhaps to some degree still is, a faith for the fortunate few. It did not stress an idealized hereafter, since it served a class—the idle aristocracy—perfectly comfortable in the present world. In any case, it became the major Japanese Buddhist sect during the Heian era (794–1185), a time of aristocratic rule.

The other important, and also aristocratic, version of Buddhism preceding Zen was called Shingon, from the Chinese school

Chen-yen, a magical-mystery sect thriving on secrecy and esoteric symbolism. It appealed less to the intellect than did Tendai and more to the taste for entertainment among the bored aristocrats. Although Shingon monasteries often were situated in remote mountainous areas, the intrigue of their engaging ceremonies (featuring efflorescent iconography, chants, and complex liturgies) and their evocative mandalas (geometrical paintings full of symbolism) made this sect a theatrical success. This so-called Esoteric Buddhism of Shingon grew so popular that the sober Tendai sect was obliged to start adding ritualistic complexity into its own practices.[4]

The Japanese government broke off relations with China less than a hundred years after the founding of Kyoto, around the middle of the ninth century. From then until the mid-twelfth century mainland contacts virtually ceased, and consequently both Japanese culture and Japanese Buddhism gradually evolved away from their Chinese models. The Japanese aristocracy became obsessed with aesthetics, finery, and refined lovemaking accompanied by poetry, perfumes, and flowers.[5] They distilled the vigorous T'ang culture to a refined essence, rather like extracting a delicate liqueur from a stout potion.

The Buddhist church also grew decadent, even as it grew ever more powerful and ominous. The priesthood became the appointment of last resort for otherwise unemployable courtiers, and indeed Buddhism finally degenerated largely into an entertainment for the ruling class, whose members were amused and diverted by its rites. This carefree aristocracy also allowed increasing amounts of wealth and land to slip into the hands of corrupt religious establishments. For their own part, the Buddhists began forming armies of monks to protect their new wealth, and they eventually went on to engage in inter-temple wars and threaten the civil government.

During this time, the Japanese aristocracy preserved its privileged position through the unwise policy of using an emerging military class to maintain order. These professional soldiers seem to have arisen from the aristocracy itself. Japanese emperors had a large number of women at their disposal, through whom they scattered a host of progeny, not all of which could be maintained idle in Kyoto. A number of these were sent to the provinces, where they were to govern untamed outlying areas. This continued until one day the court in Kyoto awoke to find that Japan was in fact controlled by these rural clans and their mounted warriors, the samurai.[6]

In the middle of the twelfth century, the samurai effectively seized Japan, and their strongman invented for himself the title of shogun, proceeding to institute what became almost eight centuries of unbroken warrior rule. The age of the common man had arrived, and one of the shogun's first acts was to transfer the government away from aristocratic Kyoto, whose sophisticated society made him uncomfortable, to a warrior camp called Kamakura, near the site of modern Tokyo. The rule of Japan passed from perfumed, poetry-writing aesthetes to fierce, often illiterate swordsmen.

Coincident with this coup, the decadence and irrelevance of traditional Buddhism had begun to weigh heavily upon a new group of spiritual reformers. Before long Tendai and Shingon were challenged by new faiths recognizing the existence and spiritual needs of the common people. One form this reformation took was the appearance of new sects providing spiritual comfort to the masses and the possibility of eternal salvation through some simple act, usually the repetition of a sacred chant. One, and later two, such sects (Jodo and Jodo Shin) focused on the Buddhist figure Amida, whose Paradise or "Pure Land" in the hereafter was open to all those calling upon his name (by chanting a sort of Buddhist "Hail Mary" called the nembutsu, "Praise to Amida Buddha"). Another simplified sect preached a fundamentalist return to the Lotus Sutra and was led by a firebrand named Nichiren, who also created a chant for his largely illiterate followers. A formula guaranteeing Paradise had particular appeal to the samurai, whose day-to-day existence was dangerous and uncertain. The scandalized Tendai monks vigorously opposed this home-grown populist movement, occasionally even burning down temples to discourage its growth. But the Pure Land and Nichiren sects continued to flourish, since the common people finally had a Buddhism all their own.

There were others, however, who believed that the aristocratic sects could be reformed from within—by importing them afresh from China, from the source. These reformers hoped that Buddhism in China had maintained its integrity and discipline during the several centuries of separation. And by fortunate coincidence, Japanese contacts with the mainland were being reopened, making it again allowable to undertake the perilous sea voyage to China. But when the first twelfth-century Japanese pilgrims reached the mainland, they were stunned to find that traditional Buddhism had been almost completely supplanted by Ch'an. Consequently, the Japanese pilgrims returning from China perforce returned with Zen, since little else remained. However, Zen was not originally brought back to replace traditional Buddhism, but rather as a stimulant to restore the rigor that had drained out of monastic life, including formal meditation and respect or discipline.[7]

Credit for the introduction of Lin-chi Zen (called Rinzai) in Japan is traditionally given to the aristocratic priest and traveler Myoan

Eisai (1141–1215).[8] He began his career as a young monk in the Tendai complex near Kyoto, but in the summer of 1168 he accompanied a Shingon priest on a trip to China, largely to sightsee and to visit the home of the T'ien-t'ai sect as a pilgrim. However, the T'ien-t'ai school must have been a mere shadow of its former self by this time, and naturally enough Eisai became familiar with Ch'an. But he was hardly a firebrand for Zen, for when he returned to Japan he continued practice of traditional Buddhism.

Some twenty years later, in 1187, Eisai again journeyed to China, this time planning a pilgrimage on to India and the Buddhist holy places. But the Chinese refused him permission to travel beyond their borders, leaving Eisai no choice but to study there. He finally attached himself to an aging Ch'an monk on Mt. T'ien-t'ai and managed to receive the seal of enlightenment before returning to Japan in 1191, quite probably the first Japanese ever certified by a Chinese Ch'an master. He was not, however, totally committed to Zen. His Ch'an teacher was also occupied with other Buddhist schools, and what Eisai brought back was a Buddhist cocktail blended from several different traditions.[9] But he did proceed to build a temple to the Huang-lung (Japanese Oryo) branch of the Lin-chi sect on the southernmost Japanese island, Kyushu (the location nearest China), in the provincial town of Hakata. Almost as important, he also brought back the tea plant (whose brew was used in China to keep drowsy monks awake during meditation), thereby instituting the long marriage of Zen and tea.

Although his provincial temple went unchallenged, later attempts to introduce this new sect into Kyoto, the stronghold of traditional Buddhism, met fierce resistance from the establishment, particularly Tendai. But Eisai contended that Zen was a useful sect and that the government would reap practical benefits from its protection. His spirited defense of Zen, entitled "Propagation of Zen for the Protection of the Country," argued that its encouragement would be good for Japanese Buddhism and therefore good for Japan.[10]

As in India, so in China its teaching has attracted followers and disciples in great numbers. It propagates the Truth as the ancient Buddha did, with the robe of authentic transmission passing from one man to the next. In the matter of religious discipline, it practices the genuine method of the sages of old. Thus the Truth it teaches, both in substance and appearance, perfects the relationships of master and disciple. In its rules of action and discipline, there is no confusion of right and wrong. . . . Studying it, one discovers the key to all forms of

Buddhism; practicing it, one's life is brought to fulfillment in the attainment of enlightenment. Outwardly it favors discipline over doctrine, inwardly it brings the Highest Inner Wisdom. This is what the Zen sect stands for.[11]

He also pointed out how un-Japanese it would be to deny Zen a hearing: Japan has been open-minded in the past, why should she reject a new faith now?

In our country the [emperor] shines in splendor and the influence of his virtuous wisdom spreads far and wide. Emissaries from the distant lands of South and Central Asia pay their respects to his court. Lay ministers conduct the affairs of government; priests and monks spread abroad religious truth. Even the truths of the Four Hindu Vedas are not neglected. Why then reject the five schools of Zen Buddhism?[12]

Eisai was the classic tactician, knowing well when to fight and when to retire, and he decided in 1199 on a diversionary retreat to Kamakura, leaving behind the hostile, competitive atmosphere of aristocratic Kyoto. Through his political connections, he managed to get installed as head of a new temple in Kamakura, beginning Zen's long association with the Japanese warrior class.

Eisai seems to have done well in Kamakura, for not long after he arrived, the current strongman gave him financing for a Zen temple in Kyoto, named Kennin-ji and completed in 1205. Eisai returned the favor by assisting in the repair of temples ravaged by the recent wars. It was reportedly for a later, hard-drinking ruler that Eisai composed his second classic work, "Drink Tea and Prolong Life," which championed the medicinal properties of this exotic Chinese beverage, declaring it a restorative that tuned up the body and strengthened the heart.

In the great country of China they drink tea, as a result of which there is no heart trouble and people live long lives. Our country is full of sickly-looking, skinny persons, and this is simply because we do not drink tea. Whenever one is in poor spirits, one should drink tea. This will put the heart in order and dispel all illness. When the heart is vigorous, then even if the other organs are ailing, no great pain will be felt. . . . The heart is the sovereign of the five organs, tea is the chief of the bitter foods, and bitter is the chief of the tastes. For this reason the heart loves bitter things, and when it is doing well all the other organs are properly regulated. . . . When, however, the whole body feels weak, devitalized, and depressed, it is a sign that the heart is ailing. Drink lots of tea, and one's energy and spirits will be restored to full strength.[13]

This first Zen teacher was certainly no Lin-chi. He was merely a Tendai priest who imported Lin-chi's sect from China hoping to bring discipline to his school; he established an ecumenical monastery at which both Zen and esoteric Tendai practices were taught; he consorted with leaders whose place was owed to a military *coup d'état*; and he appeared to advocate Zen on transparently practical, sometimes almost political, grounds. He compromised with the existing cults to the end, even refusing to lend aid to other, more pure-minded advocates of Ch'an who had risen in Kyoto in the meantime.[14] But Eisai was a colorful figure whom history has chosen to remember as the founder of Zen in Japan, as well as (perhaps equally important) the father of the cult of tea.

Eisai ended his days as abbot of the Kyoto temple of Kennin-ji and leader of a small Zen community that was careful not to quarrel with the powers of Tendai and Shingon, which also had altars in the temple. Eisai's "Zen" began in Japan as a minor infusion of Buddhism's original discipline, but through an accommodation with the warrior establishment, he accidentally planted the seeds of Ch'an in fertile soil. Gradually the number of Zen practitioners grew, as more and more of the samurai recognized in Zen a practical philosophy that accorded well with their needs. As Paul Varley has explained: "Zen . . . stresses cultivation of the intuitive faculties and places a high premium on discipline and self-control. It rejects rational decision-making as artificial and delusory, and insists that action must come from emotion. As such, Zen proved particularly congenial to the medieval *samurai*, who lived with violence and imminent death and who sought to develop such things as 'spontaneity of conduct' and a 'tranquility of heart' to meet the rigours of his profession. Under the influence of Zen, later *samurai* theorists especially asserted that the true warrior must be constantly prepared to make the ultimate sacrifice of his life in the service of his lord—without a moment's reflection or conscious consideration."[15]

It can only be ironic that what began in China as a school of meditation, then became an iconoclastic movement using koans to beat down the analytical faculties finally emerged (in an amalgam with other teachings) in Japan as a psychological mainstay for the soldiers of a military dictatorship. There was, however, another Japanese school of Zen that introduced its practice in a form more closely resembling original Ch'an. This was the movement started by Dogen, whose life we may now examine.

Dogen, Self-Portrait. Courtesy
of Eihei-ji, Fukui, Japan.

16

DOGEN:
FATHER OF JAPANESE
SOTO ZEN

The Soto master Dogen (1200–53) is probably the most revered figure in all Japanese Zen. Yet until recently he has been comparatively unknown abroad, perhaps because that great popularizer of Zen in the West, D. T. Suzuki, followed the Rinzai school and managed to essentially ignore Dogen throughout his voluminous writings. But it was Dogen who first insisted on intensive meditation, who produced the first Japanese writings explaining Zen practice, and who constructed the first real Zen monastery in Japan, establishing a set of monastic rules still observed. Moreover, the strength of his character has inspired many Zen masters to follow. Indeed, it is hard to contradict the scholar Dumoulin, who declared him "the strongest and most original thinker that Japan has so far produced."[1]

Born January 2 of the year 1200 an illegitimate son of a noble Fujiwara mother and a princely father, Dogen's circumstances from the start were aristocratic.[2] Around him swirled the literary life of the court, the powerful centuries-old position of the Fujiwara, and the refined decadence of ancient Kyoto. Although his father died when he was two, his privileged education continued at the hands of his mother and half-brother. He most certainly learned to read and write classical Chinese, as well as to versify and debate—all skills that he would one day put to extensive use. His poetic sensitivity (something traditionally prized by the Japanese above logic and precision of thought) was encouraged by all he met in the hothouse atmosphere of ancient Kyoto.

This idyllic, protected life was shattered at age seven with the sudden death of his mother. But she set the course of his life when, at the last, she bade him become a monk and reach out to suffering mankind. A popular tradition has it that at his mother's funeral Dogen sensed in the rising incense the impermanence of all things. After the shock of his mother's death he was adopted by an uncle as family heir and set on the way to a reluctant career in statecraft. But as he approached age twelve, the time when a formal ceremony would signify his entry into the male circle of aristocracy, his reservations overwhelmed him and he slipped away to visit another uncle, a priest living in the foothills of Mt. Hiei. When Dogen begged to be allowed to turn his back on the aristocratic world of Kyoto and fulfill his mother's dying wish by becoming a monk the family was dismayed. But finally they relented, and he was ordained the following year as a Tendai brother on Mt. Hiei.

Already a scholar of the Chinese classics, he now turned to the literature of Tendai Buddhism. But soon he was snagged on a problem that has haunted theologians East and West for many centuries. In Christian terms it is the Calvinist question of whether man is already saved by predestination or whether he must earn his salvation. Dogen formulated this in a Buddhist context as follows:

As I study both the exoteric and the esoteric schools of Buddhism, they maintain that man is endowed with the Dharma-nature by birth. If this is the case, why had the Buddhas of all ages—undoubtedly in possession of enlightenment—to seek enlightenment and engage in spiritual practice?[3]

In other words, if man already has the Buddha nature, why must he struggle to realize it by arduous disciplines? Conversely, if the Buddha nature must be acquired, how can it be inherent in all things, as was taught?

This perplexing paradox, which no one in Japan's Tendai "Vatican" on Mt. Hiei could resolve, finally drove Dogen wandering in search of other teachers. He initially stopped at Eisai's temple, Kennin-ji, long enough to be taught the basics of Rinzai Zen practice, but then he traveled on. Eventually, though, he returned to Kennin-ji, and in 1217, began Zen study under Eisai's disciple, Myozen (1184–1225). Of his relationship with this Rinzai master he later declared:

Ever since I awakened to the Bodhi-mind and sought the supreme Truth I made many visits to Buddhist masters throughout the country. It was thus that I happened to meet the Venerable Myozen at Kennin-ji. Nine years quickly passed as I studied the Way under him. During that period I had the opportunity to learn from him, to some extent, the training methods of the Rinzai Zen sect. To the Venerable Myozen, leading disciple of my late master Eisai, was rightly transmitted the highest supreme Law and he was unparalleled among his fellow disciples in learning and virtue.[4]

Dogen may have been impressed as much by the legend of Eisai as by the shouting and beating of the Rinzai sect, for he often sprinkled stories about Eisai through his writings and sermons thereafter.

But Dogen still could not find contentment, even with the Rinzai he received at Kennin-ji, and at age twenty-three he resolved to go to China and experience Ch'an teachings firsthand. So in the spring of 1223 he and Myozen shipped out for China, intending to visit Buddhist establishments there. (Another reason for his hasty decision to go to China for study may have been a series of political upheavals involving armed monks, which resulted in some of his high-placed relations being banished—while a series of executions took place.)[5]

After a rough but speedy voyage across the East China Sea, they arrived at Ming-chou, down the coast from the Sung capital of Hangchow. Myozen could not wait and headed straight for the Ch'an complex on Mt. T'ien-t'ung. However, the more cautious Dogen chose to stay aboard ship until midsummer, easing himself into Chinese life slowly. But even there he experienced an example of Ch'an fervor and devotion that impressed him deeply, if only because it was so different from what he had seen in Japan. This lesson was at the hands of a sixty-year-old Chinese cook from a Ch'an monastery who visited the ship to purchase some Japanese mushrooms. Dogen became involved in an animated conversation with the old monk and, since his monastery was over ten miles away, out of courtesy invited him to stay the night on board ship. However, the old *tenzo* monk (one in charge of monastery meals) insisted on returning, saying duty called. But, Dogen pressed, surely there must be others who could cook in such a large monastery, and besides cooking was hardly the point of Zen. As Dogen later recalled his own words:

"Venerable sir! Why don't you do *zazen* [Zen meditation] or study the *koan* of ancient masters? What is the use of working so hard as a *tenzo* monk?"

On hearing my remarks, he broke into laughter and said, "Good foreigner! You seem to be ignorant of the true training and meaning of Buddhism." In a moment, ashamed and surprised at his remark, I said to him, "What are they?"

"If you understand the true meaning of your question, you will have already realized the true meaning of Buddhism," he answered. At that time, however, I was unable to understand what he meant.[6]

Such were the exchanges between Japanese Buddhist scholars and Ch'an monastery cooks in the early thirteenth century.

In midsummer of 1223, Dogen finally moved ashore and entered the temple on Mt. T'ien-t'ung called Ching-te-ssu. His intense study brought no seal of enlightenment, but it did engender severe disappointment with the standards of Ch'an monasteries in China. Although the school that Dogen found was a branch of Lin-chi traceable back to the koan master Ta-hui, different from the fading school Eisai had encountered, Dogen later would denounce impartially the general run of all Ch'an masters he met in China.

Although there are in China a great number of those who profess themselves to be the descendants of the Buddhas and patriarchs, there are few who study truth and accordingly there are few who teach truth. . . . Thus those people who have not the slightest idea of what the great Way of the Buddhas and patriarchs is now become the masters of monks. . . . Reciting a few words of Lin-chi and Yun-men they take them for the whole truth of Buddhism. If Buddhism had been exhausted by a few words of Lin-chi and Yun-men, it could not have survived till today.[7]

After studying for two years while simultaneously nosing about other nearby monasteries, Dogen finally decided to travel, hoping others of the "five houses" had maintained discipline. (He also seems to have experienced some discrimination as a foreigner in China.) But the farther he went, the more despondent he became; nowhere in China could he find a teacher worthy to succeed the ancient masters. He finally resolved to abandon China and return to Japan.

But at this moment fate took a turn that—in retrospect—had enormous importance for the future of Japanese Buddhism. A monk he met on the road told him that T'ien-t'ung now had a new abbot, a truly enlightened master namd Ju-ching (1163–1228). Dogen returned to see and was received warmly, being invited by Ju-ching to ignore ceremony and approach him as an equal. The twenty-five-year-old Japanese monk was elated, and settled down at last to undertake the study he had come to China for. The master Ju-ching became Dogen's ideal of what a Zen teacher should be, and the habits—perhaps even the eccentricities—of this aging teacher were translated by Dogen into the model for monks in Japan.

Ju-ching was, above all things, uncompromising in his advocacy of meditation or zazen. He might even have challenged Bodhidharma for the title of its all-time practitioner, and it was from Ju-ching's Ch'an (which may also have included koan study) that Dogen took his cue. Although Ch'an was still widespread, Ju-ching seems to have been the only remaining advocate of intensive meditation in China, and a chance intersection of history brought this teaching to Japan. Significantly, he was one of the few Ts'ao-tung masters ever to lead the important T'ien-t'ung monastery, traditionally headed by a member of the Lin-chi school. Ju-ching was a model master: strict but kindly; simple in habits, diet, dress; immune to the attractions of court recognition; and an uncompromising advocate of virtually round-the-clock meditation.

But he never asked anything of his monks he did not also demand of himself, even when advanced in years. He would strike nodding monks to refresh their attention, while lamenting that age had so diminished the strength in his arm it was eroding his ability to create good monks. Ju-ching would meditate until eleven in the evening and then be up again by two-thirty or three the next morning, back at zazen. He frequently developed sores on his backside from such perpetual sitting, but nothing deterred him. He even declared the pain made him love zazen all the more.

The story of Dogen's final enlightenment at the hands of Ju-ching is a classic of Japanese Zen. In the meditation hall one early morning all the monks were sitting in meditation when the man next to Dogen dozed off—a common enough occurrence in early-morning sessions. But when Ju-ching came by on a routine inspection and saw the sleeping monk, he was for some reason particularly rankled and roared out, "Zazen means the dropping away of mind and body! What will you get by sleeping?" Dogen, sitting nearby, was at first startled, but then an indescribable calm, an ecstatic joy washed over him. Could it be that this was the moment he had been hoping for? Could it be that the fruit had been ready to fall from the tree, with this just the shake needed?

Dogen rushed to Ju-ching's room afterward and burned incense, to signify his enlightenment experience. Throwing himself at the master's feet, he declared, "I have experienced the dropping away of mind and body."

Ju-ching immediately recognized his enlightenment to be genuine (modern masters reportedly can discern a novice's state merely by the way he rings a gong) and he replied, "You have indeed dropped body and mind."

"But wait a minute," Dogen cautioned. "Don't sanction me so easily. How do you really know I've achieved enlightenment?"

To which Ju-ching replied simply, "Body and mind have dropped away."

Dogen bowed in acknowledgment of his acknowledgment. And thus, in May 1225, was the greatest Zen teacher in Japan enlightened. In the fall Ju-ching conferred upon Dogen the seal of patriarchal succession of his line of the Ts'ao-tung sect.[8]

Dogen stayed on for two more years studying under Ju-ching, but finally he decided to return again to Japan. When they parted, Ju-ching gave his Japanese protégé the patriarchal robe, his own portrait (called *chinso*, a symbol of transmission), and bade him farewell. So did Dogen return to Japan in the fall of 1227, taking with him the koan collection Blue Cliff Record, which he copied his last night in China. But he also brought the fire of a powerful idea, pure meditation, that formed the basis for the Japanese Soto school of Zen.

Dogen returned to Eisai's old temple of Kennin-ji, where he proceeded to write the minor classic *A Universal Recommendation for Zazen*, introducing the idea of intense meditation to his countrymen.

You should pay attention to the fact that even the Buddha Sakyamuni had to practice zazen for six years. It is also said that Bodhidharma had to do zazen at Shao-lin temple for nine years in order to transmit the Buddha-mind. Since these ancient sages were so diligent, how can present-day trainees do without the practice of zazen? You should stop pursuing words and letters and learn to withdraw and reflect on yourself. When you do so, your body and mind will naturally fall away, and your original Buddha-nature will appear.[9]

It was the opening shot in a campaign to make pure Zen the meaningful alternative to the decadent traditional Buddhism of the aristocracy and the new salvationist sect of Pure Land. But first the

Japanese had to be taught how to meditate, so he wrote a meditation "handbook" that explained exactly how and where to undertake this traditional Buddhist practice. His directions are worth quoting at length.

> Now, in doing zazen it is desirable to have a quiet room. You should be temperate in eating and drinking, forsaking all delusive relationships. Setting everything aside, think neither of good nor evil, right nor wrong. Thus, having stopped the various functions of your mind, give up the idea of becoming a Buddha. This holds true not only for zazen but for all your daily actions.
>
> Usually a thick square mat is put on the floor where you sit and a round cushion on top of that. You may sit in either the full or half lotus position. In the former, first put your right foot on your left thigh and then your left foot on your right thigh. In the latter, only put your left foot on the right thigh. Your clothing should be worn loosely but neatly. Next, put your right hand on your left foot and your left palm on the right palm, the tips of the thumbs lightly touching. Sit upright, leaning to neither left nor right, front nor back. Your ears should be on the same plane as your shoulders and your nose in line with your navel. Your tongue should be placed against the roof of your mouth and your lips and teeth closed firmly. With your eyes kept continuously open, breathe quietly through your nostrils. Finally, having regulated your body and mind in this way, take a deep breath, sway your body to left and right, then sit firmly as a rock. Think of nonthinking. How is this done? By thinking beyond thinking and nonthinking. This is the very basis of zazen.[10]

This first little essay was meant to provide Japan a taste of the real Zen he had experienced in China, and it was the beginning of an astounding literary output. Dogen asserted that since the Buddha had meditated and Bodhidharma had meditated, the most valuable thing to do is meditate. Not surprisingly, he received a cold response from the other schools in Kyoto, both the Tendai sects and the other "Zen" teachers who, like Eisai, taught a "syncretic" Zen of compromise with establishment Buddhism. His rigid doctrine was socially awkward for the syncretic Zen monks at Kennin-ji—who seasoned their practice with chants and esoteric ceremonies—and Dogen finally decided to spare them further embarrassment by retiring to a mountain retreat.

Off he went to another temple, An'yoin, where he began to elaborate on the role of meditation in Zen practice, writing another essay, entitled *"Bendowa"* or "Lecture on Training," designed to provide a more dialectical defense for *zazen*. Written in the form of eighteen questions and answers, the "Lecture on Training" was intended to further justify the intense meditation he had described earlier. This essay later became the initial section of a massive book today known as the *Shobogenzo (Treasure of Knowledge Regarding the True Dharma)*, which was guarded as a secret treasure of the Soto school for many centuries.

> Question: . . . For most people the natural way to enlightenment is to read the scriptures and recite the *nembutsu* [Praise to Amida Buddha]. Since you do nothing more than sit cross-legged, how can this mere sitting be a means of gaining enlightenment?

> Answer: . . . Of what use is it to read the scriptures and recite the *nembutsu*? It is useless to imagine that the merits of Buddhism come merely from using one's tongue or voice; if you think such things embrace all of Buddhism, the Truth is a long way from you. You should only read the scriptures so as to learn that the Buddha was teaching the necessity of gradual and sudden training and that from this you can realise enlightenment; do not read them so as to make a show of wisdom with useless intellection. . . . Just to continually repeat the *nembutsu* is equally useless, for it is a frog who croaks both day and night in some field. . . . They who do nothing . . . more than study the scriptures . . . never understand this, so just stop it and thereby cure your delusions and doubts. Just follow the teachings of a true master and, through the power of Zazen, find the utterly joyful enlightenment of Buddha.[11]

It is not surprising to find Dogen firm in the belief that meditation is superior to the practices of two competing movements: the traditional sutra veneration of the Tendai sect and the Pure Land schools' chanting of the *nembutsu* to Amida Buddha. But what about the Rinzai Zen teaching that enlightenment is sudden and cannot be induced by gradual practice? He next attacks this position:

Question: Both in India and China, from the beginning of time to the present day, some Zen teachers have been enlightened by such things as the sound of stones striking bamboos, whilst the color of plum blossoms cleared the minds of others. The [Buddha] was enlightened at the sight of the morning star, whilst [his follower] Ananda understood the Truth through seeing a stick fall. As well as these, many Zen teachers of the five schools after the Sixth Patriarch were enlightened by only so much as a word. Did all of them practise Zazen?

Answer: From olden times down to the present day, all who were ever enlightened, either by colors or sounds, practised Zazen without Zazen and became instantaneously enlightened.[12]

What exactly is he saying here? It would seem that he is convoluting the early teaching of the Southern sect, which proposed that "meditation" is a mind process that might also be duplicated by other means. Dogen seems to be arguing that zazen is efficacious since all who became enlightened were really "meditating" in daily life, whether they realized it or not. The Southern school claimed that dhyana could be anything and therefore it seemed ancillary; Dogen claims it could be anything and therefore it is essential.

Dogen also came back to his original doctrinal dilemma, the question that had sent him wandering from teacher to teacher in Japan while still a youth: Why strive for enlightenment if all creatures are Buddhas to begin with? He finally felt qualified to address his own quandary.

Question: There are those who say that one has only to understand that this mind itself is the Buddha in order to understand Buddhism, and that there is no need to recite the scriptures or undergo bodily training. If you understand that Buddhism is inherent in yourself, you are already fully enlightened and there is no need to seek for anything further from anywhere. If this is so, is there any sense in taking the trouble to practice Zazen?

Answer: This is a very grievous mistake, and even if it should be true and the sages should teach it, it is impossible for you to understand it. If you would truly study Buddhism, you must transcend all opinions of subject and object. If it is possible to be enlightened simply by knowing that the self is, in its self-nature, the Buddha, then there was no need for Shakyamuni to try so diligently to teach the Way.[13]

Whether this answer resolves the paradox will be left to the judgment of others. But for all his intensities and eccentricities, Dogen was certainly a powerful new thinker, clearly the strongest dialectician in the history of Japanese Zen. He was also a magnetic personality who attracted many followers, and by 1233 he had so outgrown the space at An'yoin that a larger temple was imperative (which became available thanks to his aristocratic connections). His next move was to Kosho-ji, a temple near Kyoto, where he spent the succeeding ten years in intense literary creativity, where he constructed the first truly independent Zen monastery in Japan, and where he found a worthy disciple, Koun Ejo (1198–1280), who served as head monk and ultimately as his successor. It was here, beginning in 1233, that Dogen finally recreated Chinese Ch'an totally in Japan, right down to an architectural replica of a Sung-style monastery and an uncompromising discipline reminiscent of his old Chinese master Ju-ching.

After settling in at Kosho-ji he began, in late 1235, a fundraising drive for the purpose of building the first Zen-style monks' hall (sodo) in Japan. He believed that this building, viewed by the lawgiver Po-chang Huai-hai as the heart of a Ch'an monstery, was essential if he were to effectively teach meditation. The doors would be open to all, since the onetime aristocrat Dogen was now very much a man of the people, welcoming rich and poor, monks and laymen, men and women.[14]

When the meditation hall opened in 1236, Dogen signaled the occasion by posting a set of rules for behavior reminiscent of Huai-hai's laws set down in eighth-century China. A quick skim of these rules tells much about the character of the master Dogen.

No monk shall be admitted to this meditation hall unless he has an earnest desire for the Way and a strong determination not to seek fame and profit. . . . All monks in this hall should try to live in harmony with one another, just as milk blends well with water. . . . You should not walk about in the outside world; but if unavoidable, it is permissible to do so once a month. . . . Keep the supervisor of this hall informed of your whereabouts at all times. . . . Never speak ill of others nor find fault with them. . . . Never loiter in the hall. . . . Wear only robes of plain material. . . . Never enter the hall drunk with wine. . . . Never disturb the training of other monks by inviting outsiders, lay or clerical, into the hall. . . .[15]

Dogen maintained this first pure Zen monastery for a decade, during which time he composed forty more sections of his classic *Shobogenzo*. And during this time the tree of Zen took root in Japanese soil firmly and surely.

But things could not go smoothly forever. Dogen's powerful friends at court protected him as long as they could, but eventually his popularity became too much for the jealous Tendai monks on Mt. Hiei to bear. To fight their censure he appealed to the emperor, claiming (as had Eisai before him) that Zen was good for Japan. But the other schools immediately filed opposing briefs with the emperor and the court, culminating in a judiciary proceeding with distinguished clerics being convened to hear both sides. As might have been expected they ruled against Dogen, criticizing him for being obsessed with *zazen* and ignoring the sutras, etc. It probably was this political setback that persuaded him to quit the Kyoto vicinity in 1243 and move to the provinces, where he could teach in peace.[16]

He camped out in various small Tendai monasteries (where he wrote another twenty-nine chapters of the *Shobogenzo*) until his final temple, called Eihei-ji, or Eternal Peace, was completed in the mountains of present-day Fukui prefecture. This site became the center of Soto Zen in Japan, the principal monastery of the sect. Dogen himself was approaching elder statesmanhood, and in 1247 he was summoned to the warrior headquarters of Kamakura by none other than the most powerful man in Japan, the warrior Hojo Tokiyori. The ruler wanted to learn about Zen, and Dogen correctly perceived it would be unhealthy to refuse the invitation.

The warriors in Kamakura would most likely have been familiar with the syncretic Rinzai Zen of Eisai, which focused on the use of the koan. For his own part, Dogen did not reject the koan out of hand (he left a collection of three hundred); rather he judged it a device intended to create a momentary glimpse of *satori*, or enlightenment, whose real value was mainly as a metaphor for the enlightenment experience—an experience he believed could be realized in full only through gradual practice.

In the pursuit of the Way [Buddhism] the prime essential is sitting (*zazen*). . . . By reflecting upon various "public-cases" (koan) and dialogues of the patriarchs, one may perhaps get the sense of them but it will only result in one's being led astray from the way of the Buddha, our founder. Just to pass the time in sitting straight, without any thought of acquisition, without any sense of achieving enlightenment—this is the way of the Founder. It is true that our predecessors recommended both the koan and sitting, but it was the sitting that they particularly insisted upon. There have been some who attained enlightenment through the test of the koan, but the true cause of their enlightenment was the merit and effectiveness of sitting. Truly the merit lies in the sitting.[17]

Dogen spent the winter of 1247–48 in Kamakura teaching meditation, and was in turn offered the post of abbot in a new Zen monastery being built for the warrior capital. But Dogen politely declined, perhaps believing the salvationist sects and the syncretic Zen of Eisai were still too strong among the samurai for his pure meditation to catch hold.[18] Or possibly he sensed his health was beginning to fail and he wanted to retire to his beloved mountain monastery, where the politics of Kyoto and Kamakura could not reach.

Maybe Dogen's many nights of intense meditation in heat and cold had taken their toll, or the long hours of writing and rewriting his manual of Zen had sapped his strength. In any case, his health deteriorated rapidly after Kamakura until finally, in 1253, all realized that the end was near. He appointed the faithful head monk Ejo his successor at Eihei-ji, and on the insistence of his disciples was then taken to Kyoto for medical care. However, nothing could be done, and on August 28 he said farewell, dying in the grand tradition—sitting in zazen.

In the long run, Dogen seems the one we should acknowledge as the true founder of Zen in Japan; pure Zen first had to be introduced before it could grow. But at the time of Dogen's death it was not at all obvious that Soto Zen, or any Zen for that matter, would ever survive to become an independent sect in Japan.[19] Perhaps Dogen felt this too, for his later writings became increasingly strident in their denunciation of the salvationist sects and the syncretic Rinzai schools. He thought of himself as above sectarianism, claiming that zazen was not a sect but rather an expression of pure Buddhism. And perhaps it was after all only an accident that the teacher who taught him to meditate happened to be a member of the Ts'ao-tung school.

After Dogen's death, his small community persevered in the mountains, isolated and at first preserving his teaching. But eventually internal disputes pulled the community apart, and the temple fell inactive for a time. Furthermore, his teaching of intensive meditation was soon diluted by the introduction of rituals from the esoteric schools of traditional Buddhism. In this new form it began to proselytize and spread outward, particularly in provincial areas, where its simplicity appealed to common folk.[20] It also welcomed women, something not necessarily stressed in all the Buddhist sects. Although Soto was by this time pretty much a thing of the past in China, with the last recognized Chinese Soto master dying about a century after Dogen, the school prospered in Japan, where today it has three followers for every one of Rinzai.

Ch'an still had Rinzai masters in China, however, and in the next phase of Zen they would start emigrating to teach the Japanese in Kamakura. The result was that Soto became the low-key home-grown Zen, while Rinzai became a vehicle for importing Chinese culture to the warrior class. It is to this dynamic period of warrior Rinzai Zen that we must now look for the next great masters.

Ikkyu. Bokusai Shoto (d. 1492). Courtesy
of the Tokyo National Museum.

17

IKKYU:
ZEN ECCENTRIC

The earliest Japanese masters brought Ch'an from China in the hope that its discipline would revitalize traditional Buddhism. Since Eisai's temple was the first to include Ch'an practice, he has received credit for founding Japanese Rinzai Zen. History, however, has glorified matters somewhat, for in fact Eisai was little more than a Tendai priest who dabbled a bit in Ch'an practice and enjoyed a gift for advancing himself with the Kamakura warlords. Nor was Dogen inspired to establish the Soto sect in Japan. He too was merely a reformer who chanced across a Chinese Soto master devoted to meditation. It was the powerful discipline of meditation that Dogen sought to introduce into Japan, not a sectarian branch of Zen. Only later did Dogen's movement become a proselytizing Zen sect. These and other thirteenth-century Japanese reformers imported Ch'an for the simple reason that it was the purest expression of Buddhism left in China. During the early era Zen focused on Kyoto and Kamakura and was mainly a reformation within the Tendai school. The Japanese understanding of Ch'an was hesitant and inconclusive—to the point that few Japanese of the mid-thirteenth century actually realized a new form of Buddhism was in the making.[1]

Over the next century and a half, however, a revolution began, as Zen at first gradually and then precipitously became the preoccupation of Japan's ruling class. The Zen explosion came about via a combination of circumstances. We have seen that the warrior ruler Hojo Tokiyori (1227–63) was interested in the school and offered Dogen a temple in Kamakura, an invitation Dogen refused. However, in 1246 an émigré Ch'an master from the Chinese mainland named Lan-ch'i (1212–78) appeared in Japan uninvited, having heard of Japanese interest in Ch'an. He went first to Kyoto, where he found Zen still subject to hostile sectarianism, and then to Kamakura, where he managed in 1249 to meet Tokiyori. The Japanese strongman was delighted and proceeded to have the temple of another sect converted to a Zen establishment, making Lan-ch'i abbot. Shortly after, Tokiyori completed construction of a Sung-style Zen monastery in Kamakura, again putting Lan-ch'i in charge. This Chinese monk, merely one of many in his native China, had become head of the leading Zen temple in Japan. When word got back, a host of enterprising Chinese clerics began pouring into the island nation seeking their fortune.[2]

Thus began the next phase of early Japanese Zen, fueled by the invasion of Chinese Ch'an monks. This movement occupied the remainder of the thirteenth century and was spurred along by unsettled conditions in China—namely the imminent fall of the Southern Sung Dynasty to the Mongols and a concurrent power struggle within Ch'an itself, which induced monks from the less powerful establishments to seek greener pastures.[3] In 1263 a senior Ch'an cleric named Wu-an (1197–1276) arrived in Kamakura and was also made an abbot by Tokiyori.[4] The first monk, Lan-ch'i, thereupon moved to Kyoto and began proselytizing in the old capital. Wu-an subsequently certified Tokiyori with a seal of enlightenment, making the military strongman of Japan an acknowledged Ch'an master. Tokiyori's interest in Zen did not go unnoticed by the warriors around him, and his advocacy, combined with the influx of Chinese monks appearing to teach, initiated the Zen bandwagon in Kamakura.

Tokiyori died in 1263, and his young son Tokimune (1251–84), who came to power five years later, initially showed no interest in Zen practice. But he was still in his teens in 1268 when there appeared in Japan envoys from Kublai Khan demanding tribute. The Mongols were at that moment completing their sack of China, and Japan seemed the next step. Undeterred, the Japanese answered all Mongol demands with haughty insults, with the not-unexpected result that in 1274 Kublai launched an invasion fleet. Although his ships foundered in a fortuitous streak of bad weather, the Japanese knew that there would be more. It was then that Tokimune began strengthening his discipline through Zen meditation and toughening his instincts with koans. He studied under a newly arrived Chinese master whose limited Japanese necessitated their communicating through a translator. (When the enlightened Chinese found cause to strike his all-powerful student, he prudently pummeled the interpreter instead.)[5] The samurai also began to take an interest in Zen, which naturally appealed to the warrior mentality because of its emphasis on discipline, on experience over education, and on a rough-and-tumble practice including debates with a master and blows for the loser—all congenial to men of simple, unschooled tastes. For their own part, the perceptive Chinese missionaries, hampered by the language barrier, rendered Zen as simplistic as possible to help the faith compete with the salvationist sects among the often illiterate warriors.

In 1281 the Mongols launched another invasion force, this time 100,000 men strong, but they were held off several weeks by the steel-nerved samurai until a typhoon (later named the Kamikaze or "Divine Wind") providentially sank the fleet. The extent to which Zen training aided this victory can be debated, but the courage of Tokimune and his soldiers undoubtedly benefited from its rigorous discipline. The Japanese ruler himself gave Zen heavy credit and immediately began building a commemorative Zen monastery in Kamakura.

By the time of Tokimuni's premature death in 1284, Rinzai Zen had been effectively established as the faith of the Kamakura rulers. His successor continued the development of Zen establishments, supported by new Chinese masters who also began teaching Chinese culture (calligraphy, literature, ink painting, philosophy) to the Kamakura warriors along with their Zen. Since the faith was definitely beginning to boom, the government prudently published a list of restrictions for Zen monasteries, including an abolition of arms (a traditional problem with the other sects) and a limit on the number of pretty boys (novices) that could be quartered in a compound to tempt the monks. The maximum number of monks in each monastery also was prescribed, and severe rules were established governing discipline. Out of this era in the late thirteenth century evolved an organization of Zen temples in Kyoto and Kamakura based on the Sung Chinese model of five main monasteries (called the "five mountains" or gozan) and a network of ten officially recognized subsidiary temples. Furthermore, Chinese culture became so fashionable in Kamakura that collections of Sung art began appearing among the illiterate provincial warriors—an early harbinger of the Japanese evolution of Zen from asceticism to aesthetics.[6]

The creation of the gozan system at the end of the thirteenth century gave Zen a formal role in the religious structure of Japan. Zen was now fashionable and had powerful friends, a perfect combination to foster growth and influence. On the sometimes pointed urging of the government, temples from other sects were converted to Zen establishments by local authorities throughout Japan.[7] The court and aristocracy in Kyoto also began taking an interest in pure, Sung-style Rinzai. Temples were built in Kyoto (or converted from other sects), and even the cloistered emperors began to meditate (perhaps searching less for enlightenment than for the rumored occult powers). When the Kamakura regime collapsed in the mid-fourteenth century and warriors of the newly ascendent Ashikaga clan returned the seat of government to Kyoto, the old capital was already well acquainted with Zen's political importance. However, although Rinzai Zen had made much visible headway in Japan—the ruling classes increasingly meditated on koans, and Chinese monks operated new Sung-style monasteries—the depth of understanding seems disappointingly superficial overall. The gozan system soon turned so political, as monasteries competed for official favor, that before long establishment Zen was almost devoid of spiritual content. In many ways, Japanese Zen became decadent almost from the start. The immense prestige of imported Chinese art and ideas, together with the powerful role of the Zen clerics as virtually the only group sufficiently educated to oversee relations with the continent, meant that early on, Zen's cultural role became as telling as its spiritual place.

Perhaps the condition of Zen is best illustrated by noting that the most famous priest of the era, Muso Soseki (1275–1351), was actually a powerful political figure. This Zen prelate, who never visited China, came to prominence when he served first an ill-fated emperor—subsequently deposed—and later the Ashikaga warrior who deposed him. Muso was instrumental in the Japanese government's establishment of regular trade with the mainland. He was also responsible for a revision of the gozan administrative system, establishing (in 1338) official Zen temples in all sixty-six provinces of Japan and spreading the power base of the faith. Although Muso is today honored as an important Japanese master, he actually preferred a "syncretic" Zen intermingled with esoteric rites and apparently understood very little of real Zen. A prototype for many Zen leaders to come, he was a scholar, aesthetician, and architect of some of the great cultural monuments in Kyoto, personally designing several of the capital's finest temples and landscape gardens.

Thus by the mid-fourteenth century Zen had become hardly more than an umbrella for the import of Chinese technology, art, and philosophy.[8] The monks were, by Muso's own admission, more often than not "shaven-headed laymen" who came to Zen to learn painting and to write a stilted form of Chinese verse as part of a *gozan* literary movement. The overall situation has been well summarized by Philip Yampolsky: "The monks in temples were all poets and literary figures. . . . [T]he use of *koans*, particularly those derived from the [Blue Cliff Record], became a literary and educational device rather than a method for the practice of Zen."[9] He further notes that ". . . with the *gozan* system frozen in a bureaucratic mold, priests with administrative talents gained in ascendency. In the headquarters temples men interested in literary pursuits withdrew completely from temple affairs and devoted themselves exclusively to literature. To be sure, priests gave lectures and continued to write commentaries. But the *gozan* priests seemed to concern themselves more and more with trivialities. By the mid-fifteenth century Zen teaching had virtually disappeared in the temples, and the priests devoted themselves mainly to ceremonial and administrative duties."[10] Authentic Zen practice had become almost completely emasculated, overshadowed by the rise of a Zen-inspired cultural movement far outstripping Chinese prototypes.

The political convolutions of fourteenth-century Japan, as well as the organizational shenanigans of the official Rinzai Zen sect, need not detain us further.[11] We need only note that the *gozan* system, which so effectively gave Zen an official presence throughout Japan, also meant that the institution present was Zen in name only. Significantly, however, a few major monasteries elected not to participate in the official system. One of the most important was the Daitoku-ji in Kyoto, which managed, by not becoming part of the establishment, to maintain some authenticity in its practice. And out of the Daitoku-ji tradition there came from time to time a few Zen monks who still understood what Zen was supposed to be about, who understood it was more than painting, gardens, poetry, and power. Perhaps the most celebrated of these iconoclastic throwbacks to authentic Zen was the legendary Ikkyu Sojun (1394–1481).

The master Ikkyu, a breath of fresh air in the stifling, hypocritical world of institutionalized Zen, seems almost a reincarnation of the early Ch'an masters of the T'ang.[12] However, his penchant for drinking and womanizing is more reminiscent of the Taoists than the Buddhists. Historical information on Ikkyu and his writings is spread among various documents of uneven reliability. The major source is a pious chronicle allegedly compiled by his disciple

Bokusai from firsthand information. Whereas this document has the virtue of being contemporaneous with his life, it has the drawback of being abbreviated and selectively edited to omit unflattering facts. Then there is a collection of tales from the Tokugawa era (1615–1868) which are heavily embellished when not totally apocryphal. The picaresque character created in the Tokugawa Tales led one commentator to liken Ikkyu to the fabulous Sufi philosopher-vagabond Nasrudin, who also became a vehicle to transmit folk wisdom.[13] These tales seem to have developed around Ikkyu simply because his devil-may-care attitude, combined with his antischolarly pose, made him a perfect peg on which to hang all sorts of didactic (not to mention Rabelaisian) anecdotes. Finally, there is a vast body of his own poetry and prose, as well as a collection of calligraphy now widely admired for its spontaneity and power.

Bokusai's chronicle identifies Ikkyu's mother as a lady-in-waiting at the imperial palace of Emperor Gokomatsu, who chose from time to time to "show her favor." When she was discovered to be with child, the empress had her sent away, charging that she was sympathetic to a competing political faction. Consequently, the master Ikkyu was born in the house of a commoner on New Year's Day of the year 1394, the natural son of an emperor and a daughter of the warrior class.

At age five his mother made him acolyte in a Zen monastery, a move some suggest was for his physical safety, lest the shogun decide to do away with this emperor's son as a potential threat. His schooling in this gozan era was aristocratic and classical, founded on Chinese literature and the Buddhist sutras. By age eleven he was studying the Vimalakirti Sutra and by thirteen he was intensively reading and writing Chinese poetry. One of his works, written at age fifteen and entitled "Spring Finery," demonstrates a delicate sensibility reminiscent of John Keats:

> How many passions cling to this wanderer's sleeves?
> Multitudes of falling blossoms mark the passion of Heaven
>   and Earth.
> A perfumed breeze across my pillow; Am I asleep or awake?
> Here and now melt into an indistinct Spring dream.[14]

The poet here has returned from a walk only to find the perfume of flowers clinging to his clothes, confusing his sense of reality and place. It recalls Keats' nightingale—"Fled is that music:—Do I wake or sleep?" In this early poem we catch a glimpse of the sensualist Ikkyu would one day become.

At age eighteen he became a novice to a reclusive monk of the Myoshin-ji branch of Zen in Kyoto; but when his mentor died two years later he wandered for a time disconsolate and suicide-prone. Then at twenty-two he decided to try for an interview with Kaso Soton (1352–1428), the Daitoku-ji-trained master known to be the sternest teacher in Japan. As was traditional, the master at first shut him out and refused an audience. Ikkyu resolved to wait outside until death, "taking the dew for his roof and the grasses for his bed." He slept at night under an empty boat and stood all day in front of Kaso's retreat. After Kaso repeatedly failed to discourage him, even once dousing him with water, the master relented and invited Ikkyu in for an interview. They were made for each other and for many years thereafter Ikkyu and Kaso "pursued deep matters tirelessly."

Ikkyu came to revere Kaso, probably one of the few authentic masters of the age, and he stayed to serve this teacher for almost a decade, even though life with Kaso was arduous. Since they lived near a major lake, Ikkyu would each night meditate in a borrowed fisherman's boat until dawn. When his purse "went flat," he would journey to the capital and sell incense or cheap clothing to poor housewives—afterwards returning to the monastery in the same straw sandals, hat, and cloak.[15] After three years Kaso gave him the Zen name Ikkyu, a recognition of his progress.

Ikkyu's enlightenment occurred in his twenty-sixth year when, while meditating in the boat, he was startled by the cry of a crow. He rushed back at dawn and reported this to his master.

> Kaso responded, "You have reached the stage of an *arhat* [one who has overcome ego], but not that of a Master, novice."
>
> Ikkyu replied, "Then I'm perfectly happy as an *arhat* and don't need to be a Master."
>
> Kaso responded, "Well, then, you really are a Master after all."[16]

Although it was customary for monks to receive a certificate from their master attesting to their enlightenment, the matter of Ikkyu's certificate is problematical. He himself refused to give out certificates, and he is depicted in Bokusai's chronicle as periodically taking out his own and requesting it be destroyed by his disciples—after which it seemed to miraculously appear again several years later. The quantity of invention and accretion attached to

Ikkyu's disappearing certificate has fostered speculation that he never, in fact, actually received a seal.

In any case, he probably *would* have destroyed his own seal of enlightenment in later years. His life grew progressively more unconventional with time, just the opposite of most. Beginning as a classicist in the finest Kyoto tradition, he had gone on to become a spiritual recluse in the mountains under a harsh meditation master. After all this training he then took the road, becoming a wandering monk in the traditional T'ang mode.

Well, almost in the traditional mode. He seemed to wander into brothels and wine shops almost as often as into Zen temples. He consorted with high and low, merchant and commoner, male and female. Our record of these explorations, both geographic and social, is in his writings, particularly his poetry. He also harbored a vendetta against the complacency and corruption of Japanese Zen and its masters, particularly the new abbot of Daitoku-ji, an older man named Yoso who had once been a fellow disciple of his beloved Kaso.

When Ikkyu was forty-six he was invited by Yoso to head a subtemple in the Daitoku-ji compound. He accepted, much to the delight of his admirers, who began bringing the temple donations in gratitude. However, after only ten days Ikkyu concluded that Daitoku-ji too had become more concerned with ceremony than with the preservation of Zen, and he wrote a famous protest poem as a parting gesture—claiming he could find more of Zen in the meat, drink, and sex traditionally forbidden Buddhists.

> For ten days in this temple my mind's been in turmoil,
> My feet are entangled in endless red tape.
> If some day you get around to looking for me,
> Try the fish-shop, the wine parlor, or the brothel.[17]

Ikkyu's attack on the commercialization of Zen was not without cause. The scholar Jan Covell observes that in Ikkyu's time, "Rinzai Zen had sunk to a low point and enlightenment was 'sold,' particularly by those temples associated with the Shogunate. Zen temples also made money in *sake*-brewing and through usury. In the mid-fifteenth century one Zen temple, Shokoku-ji, furnished all the advisers to the Shogunate's government and received most of the bribes. The imperial-sanctioned temple of Daitoku-ji was only on the fringe of this corruption, but Ikkyu felt he could not criticize it enough."[18]

Ironically, Ikkyu also attacked the writing of "Zen" poetry—in his poems. He was really attacking the literary *gozan* movement, the preoccupation of monks who forsook Zen to concentrate on producing forgettable verse in formal Chinese. They put their poetry before, indeed in place of, Zen practice. Ikkyu used his poetry (later collected as the "Crazy Cloud Poems" or *Kyoun-shu*) as a means of expressing his enlightenment, as well as his criticism of the establishment. It also, as often as not, celebrated sensual over spiritual pleasures.

Whereas the T'ang masters created illogic and struggled with intuitive transmission, Ikkyu cheerfully gave in to the existential life of the senses. In the introduction to one poem he told a parable explaining his priorities.

Once upon a time there was an old woman who supported a retired hermit for some twenty years. For a long time, she sent a young girl to serve his food. One day she told the girl to throw her arms around the monk and ask him how he felt. When the girl did so, the monk told her, "I am like a withered tree propped up against a cold boulder after three winters without warmth." The girl went back to the old woman and made her report. "Twenty years wasted feeding a phony layman!" exclaimed the woman. Then she ran him off and burnt his hut to the ground.

The grandmotherly old woman tried to give that rascal a ladder.
To provide the pure monk with a nice bride.
If tonight I were to be made such a proposition,
The withered willow would put forth new spring growth.[19]

A particularly lyrical exploration of sensuality is found in a poem entitled "A Woman's [Body] has the Fragrance of Narcissus," which celebrates the essence of sexuality.

One should gaze long at [the fairy] hill then ascend it.
Midnight on the Jade bed amid [Autumn] dreams
A flower opening beneath the thrust of the plum branch.
Rocking gently between the fairy's thighs.[20]

Ikkyu's amours seem to have produced a number of natural progeny. In fact, there is the legend that one of Ikkyu's most devoted followers, a monk named Jotei, was in fact his illegitimate son. According to the Tokugawa Tales, there was a once-rich fan maker in Sakai whose business had declined to the point that he had to sell his shop and stand on the streetcorner hawking fans. Then one day Ikkyu came by carrying some fans decorated with his own famous calligraphy and asked the man to take them on commission. Naturally they all sold immediately and, by subsequent merchandising of Ikkyu's works, the man's business eventually was restored. In gratitude he granted Ikkyu his daughter, from which union sprang Ikkyu's natural son, Jotei.

This story is questionable but it does illustrate the reputation Ikkyu enjoyed, both as artist and lover. Furthermore, he wrote touching and suspiciously fatherly poems to a little girl named Shoko.

> Watching this four-year-old girl sing and dance,
> I feel the pull of ties that are hard to dismiss,
> Forgetting my duties I slip into freedom.
> Master Abbot, whose Zen is this?[21]

When Ikkyu was in his seventies, during the disastrous civil conflict known as the Onin war, he had a love affair with a forty-year-old temple attendant named Mori. On languid afternoons she would play the Japanese *koto* or harp and he the wistful-sounding *shakuhachi*, a long bamboo flute sometimes carried by monks as a weapon. This late-life love affair occasioned a number of erotic poems, including one that claims her restoration of his virility (called by the Chinese euphemism "jade stalk") cheered his disciples.

> How is my hand like Mori's hand?
> Self confidence is the vassal, Freedom the master.
> When I am ill she cures the jade stalk
> And brings joy back to my followers.[22]

Ikkyu also left a number of prose fables and sermons that portray a more sober personality than does his often iconoclastic verse. One classic work, written in 1457 and called "Skeletons," has become a Zen classic. In the section given below he explores the Buddhist idea of the Void and nothingness:

Let me tell you something. Human birth is analogous to striking up a fire—the father is flint, the mother is stone and the child is the spark. Once the spark touches a lamp wick it continues to exist through the "secondary support" of the fuel until that is exhausted. Then it flickers out. The lovemaking of the parents is the equivalent of striking the spark. Since the parents too have "no beginning," in the end they, too, will flicker out. Everything grows out of empty space from which all forms derive. If one lets go the forms then he reaches what is called the "original ground." But since all sentient beings come from nothingness we can use even the term "original ground" only as a temporary tag.[23]

It seems unfortunate that Ikkyu's prose is not better known today.[24] In fact the best-known accounts of Ikkyu are the apocryphal tales that attached to him during the Tokugawa era. A typical episode is the following, entitled "Ikkyu Does Magic," in which the picaresque Zen-man uses his natural resources to thwart the bluster of a haughty priest from one of the scholarly aristocratic sects—just the thing guaranteed to please the common man.

Once Ikkyu was taking the Yodo no Kawase ferry on his way to Sakai. There was a yamabushi [mountain ascetic of Esoteric Buddhism] on board who began to question him.

"Hey, Your Reverence, what sect are you?"

"I belong to the Zen sect," replied Ikkyu.

"I don't suppose your sect has miracles the way our sect does?"

"No, actually we have lots of miracles. But if it's miracles, why don't you show the sort of miracles that your people have?"

"Well," said the yamabushi, "By virtue of my magic powers I can pray up Fudo [a fierce guardian deity of Buddhism] before your very eyes and make him stand right there on the prow of the boat."

And, with the beads of his rosary the man began to invoke first Kongo and then Seitaka [Esoteric Buddhist deities]. At this, all the passengers began to look back and forth wondering what was going to happen. Then, just as he had said, there on the prow of the boat, the form of Fudo appeared surrounded by a halo of dancing flames.

Then the yamabushi made a ferocious face and told him, "You'd all better offer him a prayer." This made the other passengers very uneasy—all that is but Ikkyu, who was completely unruffled.

"Well," spat out the yamabushi, "How about you, Zen monk? How are you going to deal with my miracle?"

"By producing a miracle of my own. From my very body I will cause water to issue forth and extinguish the flames of your Fudo. You'd better start your prayers up again." And Ikkyu began to pee mightily all over the flames until at last the yamabushi's magic was counteracted and the entire image melted away. Thereupon the passengers on the boat all bowed to Ikkyu for his wonderful display.[25]

Ironically, the real-life Ikkyu spent his twilight years restoring Daitoku-ji after its destruction (along with the rest of Kyoto) from the ten-year Onin war (1467–77), by taking over the temple and using his contacts in the merchant community to raise funds. He had over a hundred disciples at this time, a popularity that saddened him since earlier (and, he thought, more deserving) masters had had many fewer followers. Thus in the last decade of his life he finally exchanged his straw sandals and reed hat for the robes of a prestigious abbot over a major monastery. His own ambivalence on this he confessed in a poem:

> Fifty years a rustic wanderer,
> Now mortified in purple robes.[26]

Ikkyu's contributions to Zen culture are also significant. He helped inspire the secular Zen ritual known today as the tea ceremony, by encouraging the man today remembered as its founder. He also supported one of the best-known dramatists of the Nō theater and was himself a master calligrapher, an art closely akin to painting in the Far East and regarded by many as even more demanding.[27] He even created a soybean dish (natto) now a staple of Zen monastic cuisine.

But as his biographer James Sanford has pointed out, the real life of this truly great Japanese master has all but eluded us. His poetry is in classical Chinese and virtually unknown; his prose lies largely unread; and the Tokugawa legend of Ikkyu is almost entirely apocryphal. This last travesty has extended even to fictionalizing his role as a child at the monastery; there is now a popular television cartoon series in Japan about the irrepressible acolyte Ikkyu. Sanford speculates that his attraction for contemporary Japanese is that, in the legend of Ikkyu, "it is possible for the modern Japanese mind to re-discover 'native' examples of, and justification for, individualism—a term and concept whose full assimilation into modern Japanese culture has for over fifty years been blocked by a legacy of residual Neo-Confucian norms left over from [Japan's repressive past]."[28]

It does seem true that the Zen-man Ikkyu represents a safety valve in Japanese society, both then and now. He brought the impulsive candor of Zen to the world of affairs, demonstrating by example that after enlightenment it is necessary to return to a world where mountains are again mountains, rivers again rivers. And by rejecting official "Zen," Ikkyu may well have been the most Zenlike of all Japanese masters.

Hakuin. Portrait by a disciple. Courtesy of
Matsugaoka Bunko, Kamakura. Reprinted by permission from
Zen and Japanese Culture, D. T. Suzuki.

18

HAKUIN:
JAPANESE MASTER
OF THE KOAN

The closing era of the Japanese middle ages, in the decades following Ikkyu's death, is now known as the Century of the Country at War. Japan became a land of quarreling fiefdoms, and Zen, too, drifted for want of leadership and inspiration. The eventual reunification of the country late in the sixteenth century was led by a brutal military strategist named Oda Nobunaga (1534–82). As part of his takeover he obliterated the militaristic Buddhist complex on Mt. Hiei by one day simply slaughtering all its monks and burning the establishment to the ground, thereby ending permanently the real influence of Buddhism in Japanese politics. Nobunaga was succeeded by an even more accomplished militarist, Toyotomi Hideyoshi (1536–98), who brought to the shogunate a flair for diplomacy and cunning compromise. Hideyoshi solidified Japan only to have yet another warlord, Tokugawa Ieyasu (1542–1616), maneuver its rule into the hands of his own family—inaugurating the two and a half centuries of totalitarian isolationism known today as the Tokugawa era (1615–1868). He also moved the capital to the city whose modern name is Tokyo, at last leaving historic Kyoto in repose.

Under the Tokugawa a new middle class of urban merchants and craftsmen arose, and with it came a version of Zen for common people, with masters who could touch the concerns of the working class. Among these beloved masters must certainly be remembered the monk Takuan (1573–1645) from Ikkyu's rebuilt Daitoku-ji temple, who introduced Zen teachings to this new audience, and the wandering teacher Bankei (1622–93), whose kindly, mystical interpretation of oneness through *zazen* earned him wide fame.

Overall, however, Rinzai Zen remained spiritually dormant until the middle of the Tokugawa era, when there appeared one of the most truly inspired Zen teachers of all time.

The master Hakuin (1686–1769) was born as Sugiyama Iwajiro in Hara, a small village at the base of Mt. Fuji. He was the youngest of five children in a family of modest means, an origin that may have helped him understand the concerns of the poor. As he tells his story, he was seven or eight when his mother took him to hear a priest from the salvationist Nichiren sect preach on the tormenting Buddhist hells. He was terrified and secretly began day and night reciting the Lotus Sutra (which claims to protect from the perils of fire or water those who chant the proper incantation). The fear of hell, with its boiling caldrons, so permeated his young mind that he even became leary of the traditional Japanese bath, then often taken in a round tub fired from the bottom with wood. He claimed this fear of the bath finally convinced him to become a monk.

> One day when I was taking a bath with my mother, she asked that the water be made hotter and had the maid add wood to the fire. Gradually my skin began to prickle with the heat and the iron bath-cauldron began to rumble. Suddenly I recalled the descriptions of the hells that I had heard and I let out a cry of terror that resounded through the neighborhood.
>
> From this time on I determined to myself that I would leave home to become a monk. To this my parents would not consent, yet I went constantly to the temple to recite the sutras. . . .[1]

But after several years of study and chanting, he was dismayed to find he still felt pain (when he tested himself one day with a hot poker). He resolved to intensify his devotion and at age fifteen he entered a local Zen temple (against his parents' wishes) and was ordained as a monk. Hakuin pursued his study of the Lotus Sutra, the primary scripture venerated at this temple (an illustration of how far Japanese Zen had traveled from its tradition of meditation and koans), but after a year he concluded it was just another book, no different from the Confucian classics. He therefore began to drift from temple to temple until, at nineteen, he experienced another spiritual crisis. In a book of religious biographies he came across the story of the Chinese monk Yen-t'ou (828–87), who had been attacked and murdered by bandits, causing him to emit screams heard a full three miles away. Hakuin was plunged into depression.

> I wondered why such an enlightened monk was unable to escape the swords of thieves. If such a thing could happen to a

man who was like a unicorn or phoenix among monks, a dragon in the sea of Buddhism, how was I to escape the staves of the demons of hell after I died? What use was there in studying Zen?[2]

He thereupon took up his staff and set out as an itinerant seeker, only to meet disappointment after disappointment—until finally he decided to put his future in the hands of chance. One day as the abbot of a temple was airing its library outside, Hakuin decided to select a book at random and let it decide his fate. He picked a volume of biographies of Chinese Ch'an worthies and opening it read of an eleventh-century Lin-chi master who kept awake in meditation by boring into his own thigh with a wood drill. The story galvanized Hakuin, and he vowed to pursue Zen training until enlightenment was his.

Hakuin claims that at age twenty-four he had his first really moving *satori* experience. He was in a temple in Niigata prefecture, meditating on the "Mu" koan (Q: "Does a dog have Buddha-nature? A: "Mu!"), and so intense was his concentration that he even forgot sleeping and eating. Then one day . . .

Suddenly a great doubt manifested itself before me. It was as though I were frozen solid in the midst of an ice sheet extending tens of thousands of miles. A purity filled my breast and I could neither go forward nor retreat. To all intents and purposes I was out of my mind and the Mu alone remained. Although I sat in the Lecture Hall and listened to the Master's lecture, it was as though I were hearing a discussion from a distance outside the hall. At times it felt as though I were floating through the air.

This state lasted for several days. Then I chanced to hear the sound of the temple bell and I was suddenly transformed. It was as if a sheet of ice had been smashed or a jade tower had fallen with a crash.[3]

Elated with his transformation, he immediately trekked back to an earlier master and presented a verse for approval. The master, however, was not impressed.

The Master, holding my verse up in his left hand, said to me: "This verse is what you have learned from study. Now show me what your intuition has to say," and he held out his right hand.

I replied: "If there were something intuitive that I could show you, I'd vomit it out," and I made a gagging sound.

The Master said: "How do you understand Chao-chou's Mu?"

I replied: "What sort of place does Mu have that one can attach arms and legs to it?"

The Master twisted my nose with his fingers and said: "Here's some place to attach arms and legs." I was nonplussed and the Master gave a hearty laugh.[4]

Again and again he tried to extract a seal from this master, but always in vain. One of these fruitless exchanges even left him lying in a mud puddle.

One evening the Master sat cooling himself on the veranda. Again I brought him a verse I had written. "Delusions and fancies," the Master said. I shouted his words back at him in a loud voice, whereupon the Master seized me and rained twenty or thirty blows with his fists on me, and then pushed me off the veranda.

This was on the fourth day of the fifth month after a long spell of rain. I lay stretched out in the mud as though dead, scarcely breathing and almost unconscious. I could not move; meanwhile the Master sat on the veranda roaring with laughter.[5]

He finally despaired of receiving the seal of enlightenment from this teacher, although he did have further spiritual experiences under the man's rigorous guidance—experiences Hakuin interpreted, perhaps rightly, as *satori*. Feeling wanderlust he again took to the road, everywhere experiencing increasingly deep *satori*. In southern Ise he was enlightened when suddenly swamped in a downpour. Near Osaka he was further enlightened one evening in a temple monks' hall by the sound of falling snow. In Gifu prefecture he had an even deeper experience during walking meditation in a monks' hall. He also had a mental and physical collapse about this time, no doubt resulting from the strain of his intensive asceticism. After his father's death in 1716, he studied in Kyoto for a time, but the next year he returned to the Shoin-ji temple near his original home at Hara. Weary of life at thirty-two, he still was undecided about his future. Back at the temple where he had started, he no longer had any idea of what to do. Then a revelation appeared:

One night in a dream my mother came and presented me with a purple robe made of silk. When I lifted it, both sleeves seemed very heavy, and on examining them I found an old mirror, five or six inches in diameter, in each sleeve. The reflection from the mirror in the right sleeve penetrated to my heart and vital organs. My own mind, mountains and rivers, the great earth seemed serene and bottomless. . . . After this, when I looked at all things, it was as though I were seeing my own face. For the first time I understood the meaning of the saying, "The [enlightened spirit] sees the Buddha-nature within his eye."[6]

With this dream he finally achieved full *satori*. He resolved that the old ramshackle temple would be his final home. He had found enlightenment there and there he would stay, his own master at last.

And sure enough, Hakuin never moved again. Instead, the people of Japan—high and low—came to see *him*. His simple country temple became a magnet for monks and laymen seeking real Zen. By force of his own character, and most certainly without his conscious intention, he gradually became the leading religious figure in Japan. By the end of his life he had brought the koan practice back to a central place in Zen and had effectively created modern Rinzai.

Hakuin was the legitimate heir of the Chinese koan master Ta-hui, and the first teacher since to actually expand the philosophical dimensions of Zen. It will be recalled that Ta-hui advocated "Introspecting-the-Koan" meditation, called *k'an-hua* Ch'an in Chinese and Kanna Zen in Japanese, which he put forth in opposition to the "Silent Illumination" meditation of the Soto school. Hakuin himself claimed that he first tried the quietistic approach of tranquil meditation (albeit on a koan), but he was unable to clear his mind of all distractions.

When I was young the content of my *koan* meditation was poor. I was convinced that absolute tranquility of the source of the mind was the Buddha Way. Thus I despised activity and was fond of quietude. I would always seek out some dark and gloomy place and engage in dead sitting. Trivial and mundane matters pressed against my chest and a fire mounted in my heart. I was unable to enter wholeheartedly into the active practice of Zen.[7]

Thus Hakuin concluded that merely following Ta-hui's injunction to meditate on a koan was not the entire answer. He then decided the only way that Zen could be linked meaningfully to daily life was if a practitioner could actually meditate while going about daily affairs.

This idea was rather radical, although it probably would not have unduly disturbed the T'ang masters. Hakuin was again extending both the definition of enlightenment, as it intersects with the real world, and the *means* of its realization. He was saying to meditate on a koan in such a manner that you can continue your daily life but be oblivious to its distractions. He invoked the Chinese masters to support the idea.

> The Zen Master Ta-hui has said that meditation in the midst of activity is immeasurably superior to the quietistic approach. . . . What is most worthy of respect is a pure *koan* meditation that neither knows nor is conscious of the two aspects, the quiet and the active. This is why it has been said that the true practicing monk walks but does not know he is walking, sits but does not know he is sitting.[8]

Hakuin redefined meditation to include a physically active aspect as well as merely a quiet, sitting aspect. And under this new definition anyone, even laymen, could meditate at any time, in any place. Hakuin did not exclude sitting in meditation; he tried to broaden the definition to include the kind of thing he believed would *really* produce meaningful enlightenment. In addition, meditation in action takes away the excuse of most laymen for not practicing introspection—and what is more, it brings respect from others.

> Do not say that worldly affairs and pressures of business leave you no time to study Zen under a Master, and that the confusions of daily life make it difficult for you to continue your meditation. Everyone must realize that for the true practicing monk there are no worldly cares or worries. Supposing a man accidentally drops two or three gold coins in a crowded street swarming with people. Does he forget about the money because all eyes are upon him? . . . A person who concentrates solely on meditation amid the press and worries of everyday life will be like the man who has dropped the gold coins and devotes himself to seeking them. Who will not rejoice in such a person?[9]

Hakuin realized that meditating in the middle of distractions was initially more difficult—with fewer short-term rewards—than sitting quietly alone. However, if you want to make the heightened awareness of Zen a part of your life, then you must meditate in daily life from the very first. Just as you cannot learn to swim in the ocean by sitting in a tub, you cannot relate your Zen to the world's pressures, stress, and tensions if it is forever sheltered in silent, lonely isolation. If this is difficult at first, persevere and look toward the ultimate rewards.

> Frequently you may feel that you are getting nowhere with practice in the midst of activity, whereas the quietistic

approach brings unexpected results. Yet rest assured that those who use the quietistic approach can never hope to enter into meditation in the midst of activity. Should by chance a person who uses this approach enter into the dusts and confusions of the world of activity, even the power of ordinary understanding which he had seemingly attained will be entirely lost. Drained of all vitality, he will be inferior to any mediocre, talentless person. The most trivial matters will upset him, an inordinate cowardice will afflict his mind, and he will frequently behave in a mean and base manner. What can you call accomplished about a man like this?[10]

Quietistic meditation is easier, naturally, but a person who practices it will turn out to be just as insecure and petty as someone not enlightened at all. What is equally important, "leisure-time" meditation that separates our spiritual life from our activities is merely hiding from reality. You cannot come home from the job and suddenly turn on a meditation experience. He cites the case of someone who excuses himself to meditate, but who is then so harried and tense it does no good.

Even should there be such a thing as . . . reaching a state where the great illumination is released by means of dead sitting and silent illumination . . . people are so involved in the numerous duties of their household affairs that they have scarcely a moment in which to practice concentrated meditation. What they do then is to plead illness and, neglecting their duties and casting aside responsibilities for their family affairs, they shut themselves up in a room for several days, lock the door, arrange several cushions in a pile, set up a stick of incense, and proceed to sit. Yet, because they are exhausted by ordinary worldly cares, they sit in meditation for one minute and fall asleep for a hundred, and during the little bit of meditation that they manage to accomplish, their minds are beset by countless delusions.[11]

But what is worse, these people then blame their careers, assuming they need more isolation. But this is like the aspiring ocean swimmer in the tub mistakenly desiring less water.

[They] furrow their brows, draw together their eyebrows, and before one knows it they are crying out: "Our official duties interfere with our practice of the Way; our careers prevent our Zen meditation. It would be better to resign from office, discard our seals, go to some place beside the water or under the trees where all is peaceful and quiet and no one is about, there in our own way to practice *dhyana* contemplation, and escape from the endless cycle of suffering." How mistaken these people are![12]

Having determined meditation in the midst of activity is the only meaningful practice, he next addressed the question of how to go about it. He explained that we can do it by *making* our activities into meditation.

What is this true meditation? It is to make everything: coughing, swallowing, waving the arms, motion, stillness, words, action, the evil and the good, prosperity and shame, gain and loss, right and wrong, into one single *koan*.[13]

He gave an example of how to change the implements of daily living into a Buddhist metaphor, in this case by a warrior's making his clothes, sword, and saddle into a meditation hall of the mind.

Make your skirt and upper garments into the seven- or nine-striped monks' robe; make your two-edged sword into your resting board or desk. Make your saddle your sitting cushion; make the mountains, rivers, and great earth the sitting platform; make the whole universe your own personal meditation cave. . . . Thrusting forth the courageous mind derived from faith, combine it with the true practice of introspection.[14]

If meditation bears no relationship to life, what good is it? It is merely self-centered gratification. This he condemned, pointing out that if everyone did nothing but meditate on his own inner concerns, society at large would fall apart. And ultimately Zen would be blamed. Furthermore, this inner-directed preoccupation with self-awareness is bad Zen.

Hakuin similarly taught that a Zen which ignored society was hollow and meaningless, and its monks of no use to anybody. He was particularly stern with conventional Zen students, who were content in their own enlightenment and ignored the needs of others. "Meditation in action" for the monk meant the same as for a layman, with one significant difference. Whereas the layman could bring meditation to his obligatory life of affairs, the monk must bring the life of the world to his meditation. Just to hide and meditate on your own original nature produces inadequate enlightenment, while also shutting you off from any chance to help other people, other sentient beings. The ancient masters knew, said Hakuin, that a person truly enlightened could travel through the world and not be distracted by the so-called five desires (wealth, fame, food, sleep, and sex). The enlightened being is aware of, but not enticed by, sensual gratification.

The Third Patriarch [Seng-ts'an, d. 606] has said: "If one wishes to gain true intimacy with enlightenment, one must not shun the objects of the senses." He does not mean here that one is to delight in the objects of the senses but, just as the wings of a waterfowl do not get wet even when it enters the water, one must establish a mind that will continue a true koan meditation without interruption, neither clinging to nor rejecting the objects of the senses.[15]

But Hakuin asked something of a Zen novice even more difficult than that asked by the Chinese masters of old—who merely demanded that a monk reject the world, turn his back, and shut out its distractions. In contrast, Hakuin insists that he meditate while out in the world, actively immersing himself in its attractions. The older Ch'an masters advised a monk to ignore the world, to treat it merely as a backdrop to his preoccupation with inner awareness; Hakuin says to test your meditation outside, since otherwise it serves for nothing. And today Rinzai monks are expected to silently meditate during all activities, including working in the yard of the monastery, harvesting vegetables, or even walking through the town for their formal begging.

Hakuin not only redefined meditation, he also revitalized koan practice among full-time Zen monks and ultimately brought on a renaissance of Rinzai Zen itself. He formalized the idea of several stages of enlightenment (based on his own experience of increasingly deep satori) as well as a practice that supported this growth. But most of all Hakuin was dismayed by what he considered to be the complete misunderstanding of koan practice in Japan. Monks had memorized so many anecdotes about the ancient Chinese masters that they thought they could signify the resolution of a koan by some insincere theatrics.

[O]f the monks who move about like clouds and water, eight or nine out of ten will boast loudly that they have not the slightest doubt about the essential meaning of any of the seventeen hundred koans that have been handed down. . . . If you test them with one of these koans, some will raise their fists, others will shout "katsu," but most of them will strike the floor with their hands. If you press them just a little bit, you will find that they have in no way seen into their own natures, have no learning whatsoever, and are only illiterate, boorish, sightless men.[16]

Hakuin breathed new life back into koan theory. For instance, he seems the first Japanese master to take a psychological interest in the koan and its workings. He believed a koan should engender a "great doubt" in the mind of a novice, and through this great doubt lead him to the first enlightenment or kensho.[17] Initially he had advocated the "Mu" koan for beginners, but late in life he came up with the famous "What is the sound of one hand clapping?"[18] As he described this koan in a letter to a laywoman:

What is the Sound of the Single Hand? When you clap together both hands a sharp sound is heard; when you raise the one hand there is neither sound nor smell. . . .

This is something that can by no means be heard with the ear. If conceptions and discriminations are not mixed within it and it is quite apart from seeing, hearing, perceiving, and knowing, and if, while walking, standing, sitting, and reclining, you proceed straightforwardly without interruption in the study of this koan, then in the place where reason is exhausted and words are ended, you will suddenly . . . break down the cave of ignorance. . . . At this time the basis of mind, consciousness, and emotion is suddenly shattered.[19]

But this is not the end; rather it is the beginning. After a disciple has penetrated this koan, he receives koans of increasing difficulty. From Hakuin's own experience he knew that satori experiences could be repeated and could become ever deeper and more meaningful. Although he himself never chose to overtly systematize and categorize koans, his heirs did not hesitate to do so, creating the structure that is modern Rinzai Zen.

How did Zen finally emerge, after all the centuries and the convolutions? As Hakuin's descendants taught Zen, a monk entering the monastery was assigned a koan chosen by the master. He was expected to meditate on this koan until his kensho, his first glimmer of satori, which might require two to three years. After this a new phase of study began. The monk was then expected to work his way through a program of koans, requiring as much as a decade more, after which he might meditate on his own, in seclusion, for a time longer.[20]

The master worked with monks individually (a practice reputedly left over from the time when Chinese-speaking masters had to communicate in writing) via a face-to-face interview (senzen) reminiscent of a Marine Corps drill instructor harassing a recruit. The monk would bow to the master, seat himself, and submit his attempt at resolution of the koan. The master might either acknowledge his insight, give him some oblique guidance, or simply greet him with stony silence and ring for the next recruit—signifying an unsatisfactory answer.

Hakuin made his disciples meditate; he made them struggle through koan after koan; he made monastic discipline as rigorous as possible; and he taught that it is not enough merely to be interested in yourself and your own enlightenment. But he insisted that if you follow all his teachings, if you meditate the right way and work through increasingly difficult koans, you too can find the enlightenment he found, an enlightenment that expressed itself in an enormous physical vitality.

> Even though I am past seventy now my vitality is ten times as great as it was when I was thirty or forty. My mind and body are strong and I never have the feeling that I absolutely must lie down to rest. Should I want to I find no difficulty in refraining from sleep for two, three, or even seven days, without suffering any decline in my mental powers. I am surrounded by three- to five-hundred demanding students, and even though I lecture on the scriptures or on the collections of the Masters' sayings for thirty to fifty days in a row, it does not exhaust me.[21]

Hakuin was a prolific writer and always aware of his audience. For his lay followers, he wrote in simple Japanese and related his teachings to the needs and limitations of secular life. For his monk disciples he wrote in a more scholarly style. And finally, we have many long elegant letters composed for various dignitaries of government and the aristocracy.

He also was an artist of note, producing some of the most powerful Zen-style paintings of any Japanese. Like his writings, these works are vigorous, impulsive, and dynamic. He seems to have been an inspiration for many later Zen artists, including Sengai (1750–1837) and the Zen poet Ryokan (1758–1831).[22]

Hakuin died in his sleep at age eighty-three. During his life he had reestablished Rinzai Zen in Japan in a form fully as rigorous as ever practiced in the monasteries of T'ang and Sung China, and he had simultaneously discovered a way this Zen could be made accessible to laymen, through meditation in activity. Whereas previous Japanese teachers had let koan practice atrophy in order to attract a greater number of followers, Hakuin simultaneously made Zen both more authentic and more popular. His genius thereby saved traditional Zen in its classical form, while at last making it accessible and meaningful in modern life.

Tea Bowl. Attributed to Donyu (1599–1656).
Courtesy of the Smithsonian Institution, Freer
Gallery of Art, Washington D.C.

19

REFLECTIONS

What is the resilience of Zen that has allowed it to survive and flourish over all the centuries, even though frequently at odds philosophically with its milieu? And why have the insights of obscure rural teachers from the Chinese and Japanese Middle Ages remained pertinent to much of modern life in the West? On the other hand, why has there been a consistent criticism of Zen (from early China to the present day) condemning it as a retreat from reality—or worse, a preoccupation with self amidst a world that calls for social conscience?

These questions are complex, but they should be acknowledged in any inquiry into Zen thought. They are also matters of opinion: those wishing to see Zen as unwholesome are fixed in their critical views, just as those committed to Zen practice are unshakably steadfast. What follows is also opinion, even though an attempt has been made to maintain balance.

SOCIAL CONSCIENCE IN ZEN

A distinguished modern Zen master was once asked if Zen followers looked only inward, with no concern for others. He replied that in Zen the distinction between oneself and the world was the first thing to be dissolved. Consequently, mere self-love is impossible; it resolves naturally into a love of all things. Stated in this way, Zen teachings become, in a twinkling, a profound moral philosophy. Where there is no distinction between the universe and ourselves, the very concept of the ego is inappropriate. We cannot think of ourselves without simultaneously thinking of others. Zen is not, therefore, an obsession with the self, but rather an obsession with the universe, with all things—from nature to the social betterment of all. Although Zen initially forces a novice to focus on his own mind, this is only to enable him or her to attain the insight to merge with all things, great and small. True Zen introspection eventually must lead to the dissolution of the self. When this occurs, we no longer need the chiding of a Golden Rule.

It is fair to question whether this particular view of social conscience, which might be described as more "passive" than "active," adequately refutes the charge of "me-ism" in Zen. But perhaps less is sometimes more in the long run. There is no great history of Zen charity, but then there have been few if any bloody Zen Crusades and little of the religious persecution so common to Western moral systems. Perhaps the humanism in Zen takes a gentler, less flamboyant form. In the scales of harm and help it seems as noble as any of the world's other spiritual practices.

ZEN AND CREATIVITY

Zen gained from Taoism the insight that total reliance on logical thought stifles the human mind. Logic, they found, is best suited to analyzing and categorizing—functions today increasingly delegated to the computer. Whereas the logical mode of thought can only manipulate the world view of given paradigm, intuition can inspire genuine creativity, since it is not shackled by the nagging analytical mind, which often serves only to intimidate imaginative thought. Zen struggled relentlessly to deflate the pomposity of man's rationality, thereby releasing the potential of intuition. Although much research has arisen in recent times to pursue the same effect—from "brainstorming" to drugs—Zen challenged the problem many centuries ago, and its powerful tools of meditation and the koans still taunt our modern shortcuts.

ZEN AND MIND RESEARCH

That Zen ideas should find a place in psychoanalysis is not surprising. Meditation has long been used to still the distraught mind. Japanese researchers have studied the effects of meditation on brain activity for many years, and now similar studies are also underway in the West. The connection between Zen "enlightenment" and a heightened state of "consciousness" has been examined by psychologists as diverse as Erich Fromm and Robert Ornstein. But perhaps most significantly, our recent research in the hemispheric specialization of the brain—which suggests our left hemisphere is the seat of language and rationality while the right dominates intuition and creativity— appears to validate centuries-old Zen insights into the dichotomy of thought. Zen "research" on the mind's complementary modes may well light the path to a fuller understanding of the diverse powers of the human mind.

ZEN AND THE ARTS

At times the ancient Chinese and Japanese art forms influenced by Zen seem actually to anticipate many of the aesthetic principles we now call "modern." Sixteenth-century Zen ceramics could easily pass as creations of a contemporary potter, and ancient Chinese and Japanese inks and calligraphies recall the modern monochrome avant-garde. Zen stone gardens at times seem pure abstract expressionism, and the Zen-in-fluenced landscape gardens of Japan can manipulate our perception using tricks only recently understood in the West. Japanese haiku poetry and Nō drama, created under Zen influence, anticipate our modern distrust of language; and contemporary architecture often echoes traditional Japanese design—with its preference for clean lines, open spaces, emphasis on natural materials, simplicity, and the integration of house and garden.

Aesthetic ideals emerging from Zen art focus heavily on naturalness, on the emphasis of man's relation to nature. The Zen artists, as do many moderns, liked a sense of the materials and process of creation to come through in a work. But there is a subtle difference. The Zen artists frequently included in their works devices to ensure that the message reached the viewer. For example, Zen ceramics are always intended to force us to experience them directly and without analysis. The trick was to make the surface seem curiously imperfect, almost as though the artist were careless in the application of a finish, leaving it uneven and rough. At times the glaze seems still in the process of flowing over a piece, uneven and marred by ashes and lumps. There is no sense of "prettiness": instead they feel old and marred by long use. But the artist consciously is forcing us to experience the piece for itself, not as just another item in the category of bowl. We are led into the process of creation, and our awareness of the piece is heightened—just as an unfinished painting beckons us to pick up a brush. This device of drawing us into involvement, common to Zen arts from haiku to ink painting, is one of the great insights of Zen creativity, and it is something we in the West are only now learning to use effectively.

ZEN AND PERCEPTION

One of the major insights of Zen is that the world should be perceived directly, not as an array of embodied names. As noted, the Zen arts reinforce this attitude by deliberately thwarting verbal or analytical appreciation. We are forced to approach them with our logical faculties in abeyance. This insistence on direct perception is one of the greatest gifts of Zen. No other major system of thought champions this insight so clearly and forthrightly. Zen would have our perception of the world, indeed our very thoughts, be nonverbal. By experiencing nature directly, and by thinking in pure ideas rather than with "internalized speech," we can immeasurably enrich our existence. The dawn, the flower, the breeze are now experienced more exquisitely—in their full reality. Zen worked hard to debunk the mysterious power we mistakenly ascribe to names and concepts, since the Zen masters knew these serve only to separate us from life. Shutting off the constant babble in our head is difficult, but the richness of experience and imagery that emerges is astounding. It is as though a screen between us and our surroundings has suddenly dropped away, putting us in touch with the universe.

THE ZEN LIFE

The heart of Zen is practice, "sitting," physical discipline. For those wishing to experience Zen rather than merely speculate about it, there is no other way. Koans can be studied, but without the guidance of practice under a master, they are hardly more than an intellectual exercise. Only in formal meditation can there be the real beginning of understanding. Zen philosophy, and all that can be transmitted in words, is an abomination to those who really understand. There's no escaping the Taoist adage, "Those who speak do not know, those who know do not speak." Words can point the way, but the path must be traveled in silence.

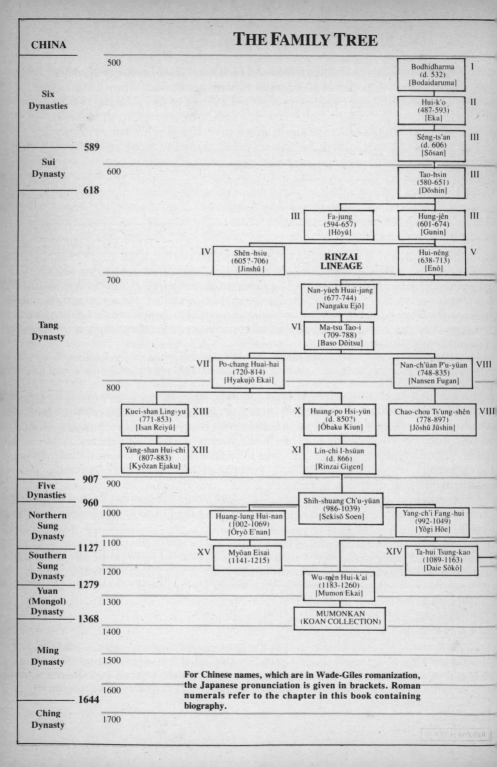

THE FAMILY TREE

CHINA

Six Dynasties

589

Sui Dynasty

618

Tang Dynasty

800

Five Dynasties — 907
960

Northern Sung Dynasty

1127

Southern Sung Dynasty

1279

Yuan (Mongol) Dynasty

1368

Ming Dynasty

1644

Ching Dynasty

Timeline markers: 500, 589, 600, 618, 700, 800, 900, 907, 960, 1000, 1100, 1127, 1200, 1279, 1300, 1368, 1400, 1500, 1600, 1644, 1700

I — Bodhidharma (d. 532) [Bodaidaruma]

II — Hui-k'o (487-593) [Eka]

III — Sêng-ts'an (d. 606) [Sōsan]

III — Tao-hsin (580-651) [Dōshin]

III — Fa-jung (594-657) [Hōyū]

III — Hung-jên (601-674) [Gunin]

IV — Shên-hsiu (605?-706) [Jinshū]

RINZAI LINEAGE

V — Hui-nêng (638-713) [Enō]

Nan-yüeh Huai-jang (677-744) [Nangaku Ejō]

VI — Ma-tsu Tao-i (709-788) [Baso Dōitsu]

VII — Po-chang Huai-hai (720-814) [Hyakujō Ekai]

VIII — Nan-ch'üan P'u-yüan (748-835) [Nansen Fugan]

XIII — Kuei-shan Ling-yu (771-853) [Isan Reiyū]

X — Huang-po Hsi-yün (d. 850?) [Ōbaku Kiun]

VIII — Chao-chou Ts'ung-shên (778-897) [Jōshū Jūshin]

XIII — Yang-shan Hui-chi (807-883) [Kyōzan Ejaku]

XI — Lin-chi I-hsüan (d. 866) [Rinzai Gigen]

Shih-shuang Ch'u-yüan (986-1039) [Sekisō Soen]

Huang-lung Hui-nan (1002-1069) [Ōryō E'nan]

Yang-ch'i Fang-hui (992-1049) [Yōgi Hōe]

XV — Myōan Eisai (1141-1215)

XIV — Ta-hui Tsung-kao (1089-1163) [Daie Sōkō]

Wu-mên Hui-k'ai (1183-1260) [Mumon Ekai]

MUMONKAN (KOAN COLLECTION)

For Chinese names, which are in Wade-Giles romanization, the Japanese pronunciation is given in brackets. Roman numerals refer to the chapter in this book containing biography.

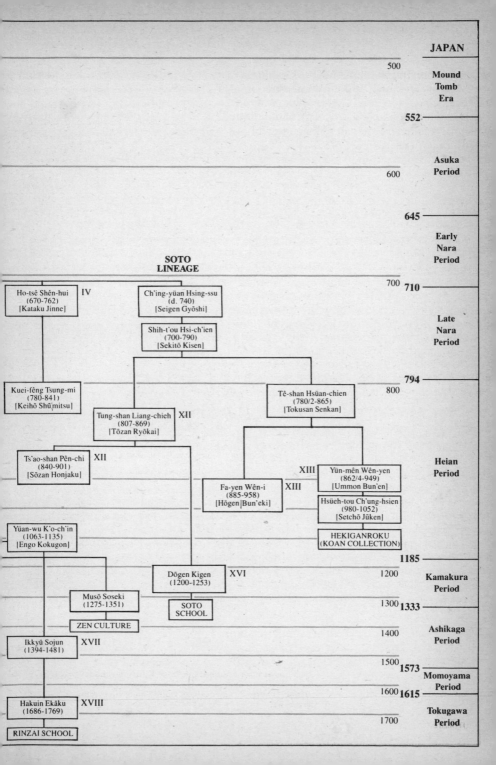

JAPAN

500

Mound
Tomb
Era

552

Asuka
Period

600

645

Early
Nara
Period

**SOTO
LINEAGE**

700 710

Ho-tsê Shên-hui
(670-762)
[Kataku Jinne]   IV

Ch'ing-yüan Hsing-ssu
(d. 740)
[Seigen Gyōshi]

Shih-t'ou Hsi-ch'ien
(700-790)
[Sekitō Kisen]

Late
Nara
Period

794

Kuei-fêng Tsung-mi
(780-841)
[Keihō Shūmitsu]

Tê-shan Hsüan-chien
(780/2-865)
[Tokusan Senkan]   800

Tung-shan Liang-chieh
(807-869)
[Tōzan Ryōkai]   XII

Ts'ao-shan Pên-chi
(840-901)
[Sōzan Honjaku]   XII

Yün-mên Wên-yen
(862/4-949)
[Ummon Bun'en]   XIII

Fa-yen Wên-i
(885-958)
[Hōgen Bun'eki]   XIII

Hsüeh-tou Ch'ung-hsien
(980-1052)
[Setchō Jūken]

Heian
Period

Yüan-wu K'o-ch'in
(1063-1135)
[Engo Kokugon]

HEKIGANROKU
(KOAN COLLECTION)

1185

Dōgen Kigen
(1200-1253)   XVI   1200

Kamakura
Period

Musō Soseki
(1275-1351)

SOTO
SCHOOL   1300 1333

ZEN CULTURE

Ashikaga
Period

1400

Ikkyū Sojun
(1394-1481)   XVII

1500 1573

Momoyama
Period

1600 1615

Hakuin Ekāku
(1686-1769)   XVIII

1700

Tokugawa
Period

RINZAI SCHOOL

NOTES

PREFACE TO ZEN

1. Chang Chung-yuan, *Tao: A New Way of Thinking* (New York: Perennial Library, 1977), p. 4.
2. Ibid., p. 6.
3. Ibid., p. 50.
4. Ibid., p. 145.
5. Ibid., p. 153.
6. Quoted in Max Kaltenmark, *Lao Tzu and Taoism* (Stanford, Calif.: Stanford University Press, 1969), p. 20.
7. Burton Watson, Introduction to *The Complete Works of Chuang Tzu* (New York: Columbia University Press, 1968), p. 7.
8. Arthur Waley, *Three Ways of Thought in Ancient China* (Garden City, N. Y.: Doubleday, undated reprint of 1939 edition), p. 15.
9. Gai-fu Feng and Jane English, trans., *Chuang Tsu* (New York: Vintage Books, 1974), p. 55.
10. Ibid. 309
11. Wm. Theodore de Bary, Wing-tsit Chan, and Burton Watson, *Sources of Chinese Tradition*, Vol. 1 (New York: Columbia University Press, 1960), p. 240.
12. Ibid., pp. 243–44.
13. Quoted by Fung Yu-lan, *A Short History of Chinese Philosophy* (New York: Macmillan Publishing Co., Inc., 1948), p. 230.
14. Quoted in ibid., p. 235.
15. D. Howard Smith, *Chinese Religions* (New York: Holt, Rinehart and Winston, 1968), p. 106.
16. Frederick J. Streng, *Emptiness: A Study in Religious Meaning* (Nashville: Abingdon Press, 1967), pp. 159–60.
17. Arthur F. Wright, *Buddhism in Chinese History* (Stanford: Stanford University Press, 1959), p. 63.
18. Walter Liebenthal, *Chao Lun: The Treatises of Seng-chao* (Hong Kong: Hong Kong University Press, 1968), p. 62.

19. Ibid., pp. 56–57.
20. Heinrich Dumoulin, *A History of Zen Buddhism* (Boston: Beacon Press, 1969), p. 60.
21. Quoted by Fung Yu-lan, *Short History of Chinese Philosophy*, p. 252.

1. BODHIDHARMA: FIRST PATRIARCH OF ZEN

1. Translated by D. T. Suzuki, *Essays in Zen Buddhism*, First Series (New York: Grove Press, 1961), p. 179. This is a translation of a passage from the *Records of the Transmission of the Lamp* compiled in 1004 by Tao-yuan. A simpler version of the story can be found in the original source document, the *Further Biographies of Eminent Priests (Hsu kao-seng chuan)*, prepared around the year 645 by Tao-hsuan, and translated in *Cat's Yawn*, published by the First Zen Institute of America, New York, 1947. The story is repeated also in the *Ch'uan fa-pao chi*, prepared ca. 700–10 by Tu Fei.

2. The fact that this episode does not appear in the earliest story of Bodhidharma's life makes one skeptical about its authenticity. It is known that Emperor Wu welcomed another famous Indian missionary, Paramartha, who landed in Canton in 546 (Smith, *Chinese Religions*, p. 120). This monk espoused the Idealistic school of Buddhism, which was at odds with the school of Ch'an. It seems possible that the story of Bodhidharma's meeting was constructed to counter the prestige that Wu's interest undoubtedly gave the Idealistic school.

3. The Buddhist concept of Merit might be likened to a spiritual savings account. Merit accrues on the record of one's good deeds and provides several forms of reward in this world and the next. The idea that good deeds do not engender Merit seems to have been pioneered by Tao-sheng (ca. 360–434), the Chinese originator of the idea of Sudden Enlightenment. "Emptiness" is, of course, the teaching of the Middle Path of Nagarjuna. The implication that Emperor Wu was startled by this concept is worth a raised eyebrow. *Sunyata* or "emptiness" was hardly unknown in the Buddhist schools of the time.

This whole story is suspect, being first found in the *Ch'uan fa-pao chi* of Tu Fei (ca. 700–10), but not in the earlier biography, the *Hsu kao-seng chuan (Further Biographies of Eminent Priests)*, compiled by Tao-hsuan around 645. There is, incidentally, another competing story of a monk named Bodhidharma in China. He was described as a Persian and was reported in Yang Hsuan-chih's *Buddhist Monasteries in Loyang (Lo-yang Ch'ieh-lan-chi)*, written in 547, to have been associated with the Yung-ning monastery, which would have been possible only between the years 516 and 528. This Persian figure apparently claimed to be 150 years in age, and he most probably came to China via the trading port of Canton used by Persians. This fact has been used by some to cast doubt on the more accepted story of a South Indian monk named Bodhidharma arriving at Canton between 520 and 525. Perhaps a legendary Persian was transformed into a legendary Indian by the Dhyana school, or perhaps it was a different individual.

4. This is the conclusion of the leading Zen scholar today, Philip Yampolsky, in *The Platform Sutra of the Sixth Patriarch* (New York: Columbia University Press, 1967), p. 10.

5. English translations of various versions of this essay may be found in *Cat's Yawn* by the First Zen Institute of America; in D. T. Suzuki, *Essays in Zen Buddhism*, First Series; and in John C. H. Wu, *The Golden Age of Zen* (Taipei: United Publishing Center, 1967). Concerning this essay, Philip Yampolsky (private communication) has noted, "Whereas a version exists in *The Transmission of the Lamp*, various texts have been found in the Tun-huang documents and elsewhere, so that a more complete version is available. It is considered authentic."

6. Suzuki, *Essays in Zen Buddhism*, First Series, p. 180.

7. Ibid., pp. 180–81.

8. This point is enlarged considerably in an essay attributed to Bodhidharma but most likely apocryphal, which is translated in D. T. Suzuki, *Essays in Zen Buddhism*, Third Series (New York: Samuel Weiser, Inc., 1971) pp. 24–29.

9. Suzuki, *Essays in Zen Buddhism*, First Series, p. 181.

10. Suzuki, Ibid.

11. Wu, *Golden Age of Zen*, pp. 49–50.

12. Ibid., p. 50.

13. Ibid., p. 50.

14. Suzuki translates the passage from the *Vajrasamadhi Sutra* in *Essays in Zen Buddhism*, First Series, pp. 183–84. Portions are as follows: "Said the Buddha: The two entrances are 'Entrance by Reason' and 'Entrance by Conduct.' 'Entrance by Reason' means to have a deep faith in that all sentient beings are identical in essence with the true nature which is neither unity nor multiplicity; only it is beclouded by external objects. The nature in itself neither departs nor comes. When a man in singleness of thought abides in *chueh-kuan*, he will clearly see into the Buddha-nature, of which we cannot say whether it exists or exists not, and in which there is neither selfhood nor otherness. . . ." Suzuki translates the term *chueh-kuan* as being "awakened" or "enlightened."

15. Hu Shih, "The Development of Zen Buddhism in China," *Chinese Social and Political Science Review*, 15,4 (January 1932), p. 483. Philip Yampolsky (private communication) has questioned this generalization of Hu Shih, noting, "There were few practicing 'Zen' Buddhists, but other Chinese Buddhists probably meditated seriously, although not exclusively."

16. Suzuki, *Essays in Zen Buddhism*, First Series, p. 186.

17. See Hu Shih, "Development of Zen Buddhism in China," p. 482: "But the whole system of *dhyana* practice, even in its concise form as presented in the translated manuals, was not fully understood by the Chinese Buddhists. . . . The best proof of this is the following quotation from Hui-chiao, the scholarly historian of Buddhism and author of the first series of *Buddhist Biographies* which was finished in 519. In his general summary of the biographies of practitioners of *dhyana*, Hui-chiao said: 'But the apparent utility of *dhyana* lies in the attainment of magic powers. . . .' "

18. Suzuki (*Essays in Zen Buddhism*, First Series, p. 191), points out, "Nagarjuna says in his famous commentary on the *Prajnaparamita sutra*, 'Moral conduct is the skin, meditation is the flesh, the higher understanding is the bone, and the mind subtle and good is the marrow.' " Since this commentary must have been common knowledge, the interest in Bodhidharma's alleged exchange with his disciples lies in his recasting of a common coinage.

19. From the *Ch'uan fa-pao chi* (ca. 700-10) of Tu Fei, as described by Yampolsky, *The Platform Sutra of the Sixth Patriarch*. This story happens to parallel closely the posthumous capers ascribed to certain famous religious Taoists of the age.

20. Dumoulin, *History of Zen Buddhism*, p. 72.

21. Hu Shih, "Development of Zen Buddhism in China," p. 52.

2. HUI-K'O: SECOND PATRIARCH OF ZEN

1. Translated in Suzuki, *Essays in Zen Buddhism*, First Series, p.190.

2. He is well documented in Tao-hsuan's *Hsu kao-seng chuan* or *Further Biographies of Eminent Priests* (A.D. 645). Selected portions of this biography are related in Yampolsky, *Platform Sutra of the Sixth Patriarch*; and Suzuki, *Essays in Zen Buddhism*, First Series, which form the basis for much of the historical information reported here. Other useful sources are Dumoulin, *History of Zen Buddhism*; and Chou Hsiang-kuang, *Dhyana Buddhism in China* (Allahabad, India: Indo-Chinese Literature Publications, 1960).

3. The *Further Biographies of Eminent Priests* by Tao-hsuan declares that bandits were responsible for severing his arm, but the 710 *Chuan fa-pao chi* of Tu Fei piously refutes this version, presumably since efforts were starting to get underway to construct a Zen lineage, and dramatic episodes of interaction were essential. This later work was also the first to report that Bodhidharma was poisoned and then later seen walking back to India.

4. As reported by Dumoulin (*History of Zen Buddhism*, p. 73), this story, which is typical of later Ch'an teaching methods, first appears some five hundred years after Bodhidharma's death, in the *Ching-te ch'uan-teng-lu* (1004).

5. Dumoulin, *History of Zen Buddhism*, p. 74.
6. D. T. Suzuki, *Studies in the Lankavatara Sutra* (London: Routledge & Kegan Paul, 1930) pp. 4–7.
7. Ibid, p. 59.
8. D. T. Suzuki, *Manual of Zen Buddhism* (New York: Grove Press, 1960), pp. 50–51.
9. D. T. Suzuki, *The Lankavatara Sutra* (London: Routledge & Kegan Paul, 1932), p. 79.
10. Ibid., p. 81.
11. Suzuki, *Essays in Zen Buddhism*, First Series, p. 193.
12. Ibid., p. 194.
13. Ibid., pp. 194–95.
14. Chou Hsiang-kuang, *Dhyana Buddhism in China*, p. 24.

3. SENG-TS'AN, TAO-HSIN, FA-JUNG, AND HUNG-JEN: FOUR EARLY MASTERS

1. As usual, the biography can be traced in three sources. The earliest, the *Hsu kao-seng chuan* of Tao-hsuan (645), apparently does not mention Seng-ts'an, or if it does so it gives him a different name. However, in the *Ch'uan fa-pao chi* of Tu Fei (710) he receives a perfunctory biography. The more embellished tale, giving exchanges and a copy of his supposed poem, is to be found in the later work, the *Ching-te ch'uan-teng-lu* (1004).
   Dumoulin *(History of Zen Buddhism)* provides a discussion of the earliest historical notices of Seng-ts'an. The 710 version of the history is translated in *Cat's Yawn* (p. 14) and the 1004 version is repeated in Suzuki, *Essays in Zen Buddhism*, First Series.
2. Suzuki, who recounts this last story in *Essays in Zen Buddhism*, First Series (p. 195), points out identical insights in the third chapter of the Vimalakirti Sutra.
3. Reportedly Hui-k'o also transmitted his copy of the Lankavatara to Seng-ts'an, declaring that after only four more generations the sutra would cease to have any significance (Yampolsky, *Platform Sutra of the Sixth Patriarch*, p. 11). As things turned out, this was more or less what happened, as the Lankavatara was replaced in the Ch'an schools by the more easily understood Diamond Sutra. The Lankavatara school was destined to be short-lived and to provide nothing more than a sacred relic for the dynamic Ch'an teachers who would follow.
4. Suzuki points out *(Essays in Zen Buddhism*, First Series, p. 196) that the Chinese word *hsin* can mean mind, heart, soul, and spirit, being all or any at a given time. He provides a full translation of the poem, as does R. H. Blyth in *Zen and Zen Classics*, Vol. 1 (Tokyo: Hokuseido Press, 1960).

5. Blyth, *Zen and Zen Classics*, Vol. 1, p. 100.
6. Ibid., p. 101.
7. Ibid., p. 103.
8. A detailed discussion of this era may be found in Woodbridge Bingham, *The Founding of the T'ang Dynasty* (New York: Octagon Books, 1970).
9. His biography may be found in C. P. Fitzgerald, *Son of Heaven* (New York: AMS Press Inc., 1971), reprint of 1933 Cambridge University Press edition.
10. See Dumoulin, *History of Zen Buddhism*, p. 78.
11. This story is translated in *Cat's Yawn*, p. 18.
12. Dumoulin, *History of Zen Buddhism*, pp. 78–79.
13. Suzuki, *Essays in Zen Buddhism*, Third Series, p. 28.
14. A lucid account of Fa-jung may be found in Chang Chung-yuan, trans., *Original Teachings of Ch'an Buddhism* (New York: Random House, 1969; paperback edition, Vintage, 1971), which is a beautiful translation of portions of *The Transmission of the Lamp (Ching-te ch'uan-teng-lu)*, the text from 1004. This text was a major source for the abbreviated biography given here.
15. Chang Chung-yuan, *Original Teachings of Ch'an Buddhism*, p. 19.
16. Ibid., p. 5.
17. A version of this exchange is given in Suzuki, *Essays in Zen Buddhism*, First Series, p. 202.
18. See Yampolsky, *Platform Sutra of the Sixth Patriarch*, p. 16.

4. SHEN-HSIU AND SHEN-HUI: "GRADUAL" AND "SUDDEN" MASTERS

1. For an excellent biography see C. P. Fitzgerald, *The Empress Wu* (Vancouver: University of British Columbia, 1968). Curiously, nowhere in this biography is there mention of her lionizing of the Ch'an master Shen-hsiu, something that figures largely in all Ch'an histories.
2. A biography of Shen-hsiu from Ch'an sources may be found in Yampolsky, *Platform Sutra of the Sixth Patriarch*. Further details may be found in Hu Shih, "Ch'an (Zen) Buddhism in China: Its History and Method," *Philosophy East and West*, 3, 1 (April 1953), pp. 3–24. See also Kenneth Ch'en, *Buddhism in China* (Princeton: Princeton University Press, 1964).
3. Suzuki, *Essays in Zen Buddhism*, First Series, p. 214.
4. Two books that give something of the intellectual atmosphere of T'ang China are biographies of its two leading poets: Arthur Waley, *The Poetry and Career of Li Po* (London: George Allen & Unwin, Ltd., 1950); and A. R. Davis, *Tu Fu* (New York: Twayne Publishers, Inc., 1971).

5. For a detailed biography of Shen-hui, see Yampolsky, *Platform Sutra of the Sixth Patriarch*.

6. The scholar who brought the significance of Shen-hui to the attention of the world was Hu Shih, whose landmark English-language papers on Zen are "Ch'an (Zen) Buddhism in China: Its History and Method" and "The Development of Zen Buddhism in China." These works draw upon the manuscripts discovered this century in the Tun-huang caves in the mountains of far northwest China. These manuscripts clarified many of the mysteries surrounding the early history of Ch'an, enabling scholars for the first time to distinguish between real and manufactured history—since some of the works were written before Ch'an historians began to embroider upon the known facts. A brief but useful account of the finding of these caves and the subsequent removal of many of the manuscripts to the British Museum in London and the Bibliothéque Nationale in Paris may be found in *Cat's Yawn*. The best discussion of the significance of these finds and of Hu Shih's lifelong interpretive work is provided by Yampolsky, *Platform Sutra of the Sixth Patriarch*.

   Regarding the circumstances of this sermon, Walter Liebenthal ("The Sermon of Shen-hui," *Asia Major*, N.S. 3, 2 [1952], p. 134) says, "There are only two opportunities to deliver addresses in the ritual of Buddhist monasteries, one during the *uposatha* ceremony held monthly when the *pratimoksa* rules are read to the members of the community and they are admonished to confess their sins, one during the initiation ceremony held once or twice a year. For the purpose of initiation special platforms are raised, one for monks and one for nuns, inside the compounds of some especially selected monasteries."

7. Quoted in Hilda Hookham, *A Short History of China* (New York: St. Martin's Press, Inc., 1972; paperback edition, New York: New American Library, 1972), p. 175.

8. Discussions of the adventures of An Lu-shan may be found in most general surveys of Chinese history, including Hookham, *Short History of China*, Wolfram Eberhard, *A History of China* (Berkeley: University of California Press, 1960); Kenneth Scott Latourette, *The Chinese: Their History and Culture* (New York: Macmillan, 1962); John A. Harrison, *The Chinese Empire* (New York: Harcourt Brace Jovanovich, Inc., 1972); and René Grousset, *The Rise and Splendour of the Chinese Empire* (Berkeley: University of California Press, 1962).

9. This is the interpretation of Hu Shih. For translations of the major works of Shen-hui, see Walter Liebenthal, "The Sermon of Shen-hui," pp. 132–55; and Wm. Theodore de Bary, ed., *Sources of Chinese Tradition*, Vol. 1., pp. 356–60. Also see Edward Conze, ed., *Buddhist Texts Through the Ages* (Oxford: Bruno Cassirer, 1954), excerpted in Wade Baskin, ed., *Classics in Chinese Philosophy* (Totowa, N. J.: Littlefield, Adams, 1974). A short translation is also provided in Suzuki, *Essays in Zen Buddhism*, Third Series, pp. 37 ff. The fullest translation of the works of Shen-hui found in the Tun-huang caves is

in Jacques Gernet, *Entretiens du Maître de Dhyana Chen-houei du Ho-tso* (Hanoi: Publications de l'ecole française d'Extreme-Orient, Vol. 31, 1949). An English translation of a portion of this text may be found in Wing-tsit Chan, *A Source Book in Chinese Philosophy* (Princeton: Princeton University Press, 1963).

10. Liebenthal, "Sermon of Shen-hui," pp. 136 ff.
11. Ibid., p. 144.
12. Ibid., pp. 146, 147, 149.
13. See Hu Shih, "Ch'an (Zen) Buddhism in China."
14. Hu Shih, "Development of Zen Buddhism in China," p. 493.
15. Hu Shih, "Ch'an (Zen) Buddhism in China," p. 11.
16. The differences between the Northern and Southern schools of Ch'an during the eighth century are explored in the works of Hu Shih, Philip Yampolsky, and Walter Liebenthal noted elsewhere in these notes. Other general surveys of Chinese religion and culture that have useful analyses of the question include Wing-tsit Chan, *Source Book in Chinese Philosophy*, pp. 425 ff., D. Howard Smith, *Chinese Religions*; and Fung Yu-lan, *Short History of Chinese Philosophy*.
17. A study of the last distinguished member of Shen-hui's school, the scholar Tsung-mi (780–841), may be found in Jeffrey Broughton, "Kuei-feng Tsung-mi: The Convergence of Ch'an and the Teachings" (Ph. D. dissertation, Columbia University, 1975).
18. D. T. Suzuki, "Zen: A Reply to Hu Shih," *Philosophy East and West*, 3, 1 (April 1953), pp. 25–46.

5. HUI-NENG: THE SIXTH PATRIARCH AND FATHER OF MODERN ZEN

1. A number of English translations of the Platform Sutra are in existence. Among the most authoritative must certainly be counted Yampolsky, *Platform Sutra of the Sixth Patriarch*; and Wing-tsit Chan, *The Platform Scripture* (New York: St. John's University Press, 1963). A widely circulated translation is in A. F. Price and Wong Mou-Lam, *The Diamond Sutra and the Sutra of Hui-Neng* (Berkeley, Calif.: Shambhala, 1969). Another well-known version is found in Charles Luk, *Ch'an and Zen Teaching: Third Series* (New York: Samuel Weiser, Inc., 1971). Two lesser-known translations are Paul F. Fung and George D. Fung, *The Sutra of the Sixth Patriarch on the Pristine Orthodox Dharma* (San Francisco: Buddha's Universal Church, 1964); and Hsuan Hua, *The Sixth Patriarch's Dharma Jewel Platform Sutra* (San Francisco: Buddhist Text Translation Society, 1971).
2. From the Diamond Sutra, contained in Dwight Goddard, ed., *A Buddhist Bible* (Boston: Beacon Press, 1970), p. 102. Another version may be found in Price and Wong, *Diamond Sutra and the Sutra of Hui-neng*. An extended commentary may be found in Charles Luk,

Ch'an and Zen Teaching, First Series, pp. 149–208. Later Ch'anists have maintained that Hung-jen taught *both* the Diamond Sutra and the Lankavatara Sutra, the respective scriptures of what came to be called Southern and Northern schools of Ch'an. However, most scholars today believe that his major emphasis was on the Lankavatara Sutra, not the Diamond Sutra as the legend of Hui-neng would have.

3. From Price and Wong, *Diamond Sutra and the Sutra of Hui-neng*, p. 15.

4. Ibid., p. 18.

5. The earliest version of the Platform Sutra is that found in the Tun-huang caves and translated by Yampolsky and Chan. This manuscript Yampolsky dates from the middle of the ninth century. A much later version, dated 1153, was found in a temple in Kyoto, Japan, in 1934. This is said to be a copy of a version dating from 967. The standard version up until this century was a much longer work which dates from 1291. As a general rule of thumb with the early Ch'an writings, the shorter the work, the better the chance it is early and authentic. For this reason, the shorter Tun-huang works are now believed to be the most authoritative and best account of the thoughts of the Sixth Patriarch.

6. Yampolsky, *Platform Sutra of the Sixth Patriarch*, p. 69.

7. The most obvious problem with attribution of the Platform Sutra to Hui-neng is that many of the sections of the sermon appear almost verbatim in The Sermon of Shen-hui, indicating that either one was a copy of the other or they had a common source (which could have been the simple setting down of a verbal tradition). It has been pointed out that Shen-hui, who praises Hui-neng to the skies in his sermon, never claims to be quoting the master. Instead, he pronounces as his own a number of passages that one day would be found in the work attributed to Hui-neng. The scholar Hu Shih has drawn the most obvious conclusion and has declared that Shen-hui and his school more or less created the legend of Hui-neng—lock, stock, and sutra. Others refuse to go this far, preferring instead to conclude that Shen-hui and Hui-neng are merely two representatives of the same school.

8. Yampolsky, *Platform Sutra of the Sixth Patriarch*, p. 157.

9. *Yampolsky*, Ibid., p. 140

10. Wu, *Golden Age of Zen*, p. 82.

11. See especially "Intimations of Immortality":

> Our birth is but a sleep and a forgetting:
> The Soul that rises with us, our life's Star,
> Hath had elsewhere its setting,
> and cometh from afar:
> Not in entire forgetfulness,
> And not in utter nakedness,
> But trailing clouds of glory do we come . . .

12. Yampolsky, *Platform Sutra of the Sixth Patriarch*, pp. 141–42.
13. Ibid., p. 117.
14. From Ibid., pp. 138–39. For interpretive comment see D. T. Suzuki, *The Zen Doctrine of No Mind* (New York: Samuel Weiser, 1972).
15. Yampolsky, *Platform Sutra of the Sixth Patriarch*, pp. 116-17.

6. MA-TSU: ORIGINATOR
OF "SHOCK" ENLIGHTENMENT

1. See Broughton, *Kuei-feng Tsung-mi: The Convergence of Ch'an and the Teachings*. It was also around this time that the idea of twenty-eight Indian Patriarchs of Zen, culminating in Bodhidharma, was finally ironed out and made part of the Zen tradition.
2. See Arthur Waley, *The Life and Times of Po Chü-i* (London: Allen & Unwin, 1949).
3. Hu Shih, "Development of Zen Buddhism in China," p. 497.
4. Hu-Shin, "Ch'an (Zen) Buddhism in China," p. 18.
5. For some of Huai-jang's attributed teachings, see Charles Luk, *The Transmission of the Mind Outside the Teaching* (New York: Grove Press, 1975), pp. 32–37. The reliability of this text should be questioned, however, if we accept Philip Yampolsky's essay in *Platform Sutra of the Sixth Patriarch*, p. 53: "Huai-jang (677–744) . . . is known as a disciple of Hui-neng. Information about him is based on sources composed much later than his death; no mention is made of him in any eighth-century work. . . ."
6. Jeffrey Broughton ("Kuei-feng Tsung-mi," p. 27) points out that Ma-tsu's master's technique for achieving "no-mind" was to chant a phrase until running out of breath, at which time the activities of the mind would seem to terminate—a reaction the more skeptical might call physiological. Breath control and breath exercises, it will be recalled, have always figured largely in Indian meditative practices.
7. Chang Chung-yuan, *Original Teachings of Ch'an Buddhism*, p. 148. The discussion of Ma-tsu in this volume supplied valuable background for the analysis provided here.
8. Hu Shih, "Development of Zen Buddhism in China," p. 498.
9. Chang Chung-yuan, *Original Teachings of Ch'an Buddhism*, p. 130.
10. Ibid., p. 149.
11. Ibid.
12. Ibid.
13. There are many translations of the Mumonkan. One of the more recent and scholarly is by Zenkai Shibayama, *Zen Comments on the Mumonkan* (New York: New American Library, 1975).
14. Chang Chung-yuan, *Original Teachings of Ch'an Buddhism*, p. 150.
15. Wu, *Golden Age of Zen*, p. 95.

16. The most recent and the most detailed translation of the Blue Cliff Record is by Thomas and J. C. Cleary, *The Blue Cliff Record*, 3 vols. (Berkeley, Calif.: Shambhala, 1977).
17. Chang Chung-yuan, *Original Teachings of Ch'an Buddhism*, p. 151.
18. Ibid., p.151.
19. This story is recounted in Wu, *Golden Age of Zen*, p. 100.
20. Ibid., p. 102.
21. Recounted in Ibid., p. 102.
22. See Chang Chung-yuan, *Original Teachings of Ch'an Buddhism*, pp. 150–52.
23. Ibid., p. 150.
24. See Luk, *Transmission of the Mind Outside the Teaching*, p. 46.

7. HUAI-HAI: FATHER OF MONASTIC CH'AN

1. This location is given by John Blofeld in *The Zen Teaching of Hui-Hai on Sudden Illumination* (London: Ryder & Co., 1962; paperback reprint, New York: Weiser, 1972), p. 29. Charles Luk (*Transmission of the Mind Outside the Teaching*, p. 50) says: "Huai-hai, the Dharma-successor of Ma Tsu, was also called Pai Chang [Po Ch'ang] after the mountain where he stayed at Hung Chou (now Nanchang, capital of Kiangsi province). Pai Chang means: *Pai*, one hundred, and *Chang*, a measure of ten feet, i.e., One-thousand-foot mountain." However, Luk identifies the birthplace of Huai-hai as Chang Lo in modern Fukien province, as does Chou Hsiang-kuang in *Dhyana Buddhism in China*.
2. This story is repeated in various places, including Wu, *Golden Age of Zen*; and Blofeld, *Zen Teaching of Hui Hai on Sudden Illumination*. This latter reference is as part of a document known as the Tsung-ching Record, being a recorded dialogue of the master taken down by a monk named Tsung-ching, who was a contemporary of Huai-hai.
3. This story is Case 53 of the Hekiganroku or Blue Cliff Record, a Sung Dynasty period collection of Ch'an stories and their interpretation. The best current translation is probably in Cleary and Cleary, *Blue Cliff Record*, Vol. 2, p. 357.
4. See Luk, *Transmission of the Mind Outside the Teaching*, p. 46.
5. Stories involving him may be found in the Mumonkan, Cases 2 and 40, and in the Hekiganroku or Blue Cliff Record, Cases 53, 70, 71, 72. The most complete accounting of anecdotes may be found in Blofeld, *Zen Teachings of Hui-Hai on Sudden Illumination*; and Thomas Cleary, *Sayings and Doings of Pai-chang* (Los Angeles: Center Publicatons, 1979).
6. Kenneth K. S. Ch'en, (*The Chinese Transformation of Buddhism* [Princeton: Princeton University Press, 1973], p. 95) says, "Besides the

Vinaya controlling the conduct of the Buddhist clergy, the basic code governing Buddhist and Taoist monks and nuns during the T'ang Dynasty was the *Tao-seng-ke* (Rules concerning Buddhist and Taoist clergy), formulated during the Chen-kuan era, probably 637. This *Tao-seng-ke* is no longer extant, however, but the Japanese work *Soni-ryo*, which governs the conduct of the community of monks and nuns in Japan, was based on it. Therefore a study of the *Soni-ryo* would give us a good idea of the contents of the *Tao-seng-ke*. . . . [Certain] provisions of the T'ang codes superseded the monastic code and called for penalties for offenses which went beyond those specified in the *Soni-ryo* or the Buddhist Vinaya."

7. For a scholarly discussion of the economic role of Buddhism in T'ang China, see D. C. Twitchett, "Monastic Estates in T'ang China," *Asia Major*, (1955–56), pp. 123–46. He explains that the T'ang government was always a trifle uneasy about the presence of un-taxed monastic establishments, and not without reason. Buddhism in T'ang China was big business. The large monasteries were beneficiaries of gifts and bequests from the aristocracy, as well as from the palace itself. (Eunuchs, along with palace ladies, were particularly generous.) Laymen often would bequeath their lands to a monastery, sometimes including in the will a curse on anyone who might later wish to take the land away from the church. These gifts were thought to ensure better fortunes in the world to come, while simultaneously resolving tax difficulties for the donor. For the monasteries themselves this wealth could only accumulate, since it never had to be divided among sons. After An Lu-shan's rebellion, a flavor of feudalism had penetrated Chinese society, and huge tracts came to be held by the Buddhist monasteries, to which entire estates were sometimes donated. As a result, the Buddhists had enormous economic power, although we may suspect the iconoclastic *dhyana* establishments in the south enjoyed little of it.

8. See Dumoulin, *History of Zen Buddhism*, pp. 102–03.

9. See Heinrich Dumoulin and Ruth Fuller Sasaki, *The Development of Chinese Zen* (New York: First Zen Institute of America, 1953), p.13. Interestingly, the Vinaya sect, founded by Tao-hsuan (596–667), was primarily concerned with the laws of monastic discipline. The familiarity of Ch'an teachers with the concerns of this sect may have contributed to the desire to create rules for their own assemblies.

10. Wu, *Golden Age of Zen*, p. 109.

11. See D. T. Suzuki, *The Zen Monk's Life* (New York: Olympia Press, 1972); Eshin Nishimura, *Unsui: A Diary of Zen Monastic Life* (Honolulu: University Press of Hawaii, 1973); Suzuki, *Essays in Zen Buddhism*, First Series, pp. 314–362; and Koji Sato, *The Zen Life* (New York: Weatherhill/Tankosha, 1977). A succinct summary of Zen monastic life is also provided by Sir Charles Eliot in *Japanese Buddhism* (London: Routledge & Kegan Paul, 1935), p. 406.

12. See Blofeld, *Zen Teaching of Hui Hai on Sudden Illumination*, p. 52.

13. Ibid., pp. 60–61.
14. Ibid., p. 48.
15. Ibid., p. 133.
16. Ibid., p. 77.
17. Ibid., p. 55.
18. Ibid., p. 56.
19. Ibid., p. 78.
20. Ibid., p. 54.

8. NAN-CH'UAN AND CHAO-CHOU: MASTERS OF THE IRRATIONAL

1. Chang Chung-yuan, *Original Teachings of Ch'an Buddhism*, p. 153.
2. Ibid., p. 178.
3. According to a biographical sketch of Nan-ch'uan given by Cleary and Cleary in *Blue Cliff Record*, p. 262.
4. See Chang Chung-yuan, *Original Teachings of Ch'an Buddhism*, p. 160. This was also incorporated in the Blue Cliff Record as Case 40 (Ibid., p. 292), where the Sung-era commentary is actually more obscure than what it attempts to explain.
5. See Chang Chung-yuan, *Original Teachings of Ch'an Buddhism*, p. 136.
6. Ibid., p. 136.
7. Blyth, *Zen and Zen Classics*, Vol. 3, p. 57.
8. Chang Chung-yuan, *Original Teachings of Ch'an Buddhism*, p. 159.
9. Ibid., p. 157. This anecdote is also Case 69 of the Blue Cliff Record.
10. Ibid., p. 161.
11. Ibid.
12. Ibid., p. 162.
13. Ibid., p. 164. Translation of a T'ang text, "The Sayings of Chao-chou," is provided by Yoel Hoffman, *Radical Zen* (Brookline, Mass.: Autumn Press, 1978).
14. Recounted by Garma C. C. Chang in *The Practice of Zen* (New York: Harper & Row, 1959), p. 24. This is also Case 14 of the Mumonkan and Cases 63 and 64 of the Blue Cliff Record.
15. Wu, *Golden Age of Zen*, p. 127. This is also Case 19 of the Mumonkan.
16. Chang Chung-yuan, *Original Teachings of Ch'an Buddhism*, p. 159.
17. Wu, *Golden Age of Zen*, p. 129.
18. Ibid., p. 133.
19. Chang Chung-yuan, *Original Teachings of Ch'an Buddhism*, p. 169.
20. Ibid., p. 140.
21. Wu, *Golden Age of Zen*, p. 136.
22. Chang Chung-yuan, *Original Teachings of Ch'an Buddhism*, p. 171.

23. This is Case 1 of the Mumonkan, here quoted from a very readable new translation by Katsuki Sekida, *Two Zen Classics: Mumonkan & Hekiganroku* (New York: Weatherhill, 1977), p. 27.
24. Wu, *Golden Age of Zen*, pp. 144–45.
25. Blyth, *Zen and Zen Classics*, Vol. 3, p. 77.
26. Wu, *Golden Age of Zen*, p. 145.
27. Ibid., p. 139.
28. Ibid., p. 146.
29. Ibid., p. 144.

9. P'ANG AND HAN-SHAN: LAYMAN AND POET

1. See Burton Watson, *Cold Mountain* (New York: Columbia University Press, 1970), p. 13. This concept of the Zen layman has long been a part of Zen practice in Japan, and for this reason both Layman P'ang and the poet Han-shan are favorite Ch'an figures with the Japanese. In fact, the eighteenth-century Japanese master Hakuin wrote a commentary on Han-shan.
2. See Ruth Fuller Sasaki, Yoshitaka Iriya, and Dana R. Frasier, *The Recorded Sayings of Layman P'ang* (New York: Weatherhill, 1971), p. 18.
3. See Chang Chung-yuan, *Original Teachings of Ch'an Buddhism*, p. 145. This story is famous and found in many sources.
4. As evidenced by a common saying of the time: "In Kiangsi the Master is Ma-tsu; in Hunan the Master is Shih-t'ou. People go back and forth between them all the time, and those who do not know these two great Masters are completely ignorant." Yampolsky, *Platform Sutra of the Sixth Patriarch*, p. 55.
5. Sasaki et al., *Recorded Sayings of Layman P'ang*, p. 46.
6. See Chang Chung-yuan, *Original Teachings of Ch'an Buddhism*, p. 145.
7. See Ibid., p. 175.
8. Sasaki et al., *Recorded Sayings of Layman P'ang*, p. 47.
9. Luk, *Transmission of the Mind Outside the Teaching*, p. 42.
10. Sasaki et al., *Recorded Sayings of Layman P'ang*, p. 58.
11. Ibid., p. 69.
12. Ibid., p. 71
13. Ibid., p.47.
14. Ibid., p. 88.
15. Ibid., pp. 54–55. The translators explain the last two verses as follows: "This is derived from the old Chinese proverb: 'To win by a fluke is to fall into a fluke' (and thus to lose by a fluke)." Concerning the meaning of this exchange, it would seem that water is here being used as a

metaphor for the undifferentiated Void, which subsumes the temporary individuality of its parts the way the sea is undifferentiated, yet contains waves. When Tan-hsia accepts this premise a little too automatically, P'ang is forced to show him (via a splash) that water (and by extension, physical manifestations of the components of the Void) can also assume a physical reality that impinges on daily life. Tan-hsia tries feebly to respond by returning the splash, but he clearly lost the exchange.

16. Ibid. p. 73.
17. See Chang Chung-yuan, *Original Teachings of Ch'an Buddhism,* p. 176. Also see Sasaki et al., *Recorded Sayings of Layman P'ang,* p. 75.
18. Chang Chung-yuan, *Original Teachings of Ch'an Buddhism,* p. 177.
19. Sasaki et al., *Recorded Sayings of Layman P'ang,* p. 42.
20. Arthur Waley, "27 Poems by Han-shan," *Encounter,* 3, 3 (September 1954), p. 3.
21. Watson, *Cold Mountain,* p. 50. Watson explains that the opening line about taking along books while hoeing in the field was "From the story of an impoverished scholar of the former Han Dynasty who was so fond of learning that he carried his copies of the Confucian classics along when he went to work in the fields." The last line is "An allusion to the perch, stranded in a carriage rut in the road, who asked the philosopher Chuang Tzu for a dipperful of water so that he could go on living."
22. Ibid., p. 56.
23. Waley, "27 Poems by Han-shan," p. 6.
24. From Wu Chi-yu, "A Study of Han Shan," *T'oung Pao,* 45, 4-5 (1957), p. 432.
25. Gary Snyder, "Han-shan," In Cyril Birch, ed., *Anthology of Chinese Literature,* (New York: Grove Press, 1965), p. 201.
26. See Ibid., pp. 194–96.
27. See Watson, *Cold Mountain,* p. 14. Watson says, "Zen commentators have therefore been forced to regard Han-shan's professions of loneliness, doubt, and discouragement not as revelations of his own feelings but as vicarious recitals of the ills of unenlightened men which he can still sympathize with, though he himself has transcended them. He thus becomes the traditional Bodhisattva figure—compassionate, in the world, but not of it." Watson rejects this interpretation.
28. Ibid., p. 67.
29. Ibid., p. 88.
30. Ibid., p. 78.
31. Ibid., p. 81.
32. Ibid., pp. 11–12.
33. Snyder, "Han-shan," p. 202.

10. HUANG-PO: MASTER OF
THE UNIVERSAL MIND

1. Chang Chung-yuan, *Original Teachings of Ch'an Buddhism*, p. 102.
2. This probably was during the last decade of the eighth century, since Ma-tsu died in 788.
3. This volume actually consists of two books, known as the *Chun-chou Record* (843) and the *Wan-ling Record* (849). They are translated and published together by John Blofeld as *The Zen Teaching of Huang Po*. (New York: Grove Press, 1958). This appears to have been the source for biographical and anecdotal material later included in *The Transmission of the Lamp*, portions of which are translated in Chang Chung-yuan, *Original Teachings of Ch'an Buddhism*. Another translation of biographical, didactic, and anecdotal material may be found in Charles Luk, *Transmission of the Mind Outside the Teaching*, whose source is unattributed but which possibly could be a translation of the 1602 work *Records of Pointing at The Moon*, a compilation of Ch'an materials.
4. Blofeld, *Zen Teaching of Huang Po*, p. 28.
5. Ibid., p. 27.
6. Chang Chung-yuan, *Original Teachings of Ch'an Buddhism*, p. 103.
7. Ibid.
8. Ibid., p. 90.
9. Ibid., p. 103.
10. Blofeld, *Zen Teaching of Huang Po*, p. 99.
11. This gesture of defeat is reported elsewhere to have been a triple prostration. Huang-po apparently claimed victory in these exchanges when he either kept silent or walked away.
12. Wan-ling is reported by Chang Chung-yuan to be the modern town of Hsuan-ch'eng in southern Anhwei province (*Original Teachings of Ch'an Buddhism*, p. 123). According to *The Transmission of the Lamp* the prime minister built a monastery and invited Huang-po to come lecture there, which the master did. The monastery was then named after a mountain where the master had once lived.
13. Ibid., p. 104.
14. Ibid.
15. Blofeld, *Zen Teaching of Huang Po*, p. 55.
16. Ibid., p. 130.
17. Ibid., pp. 81-82.
18. Ibid., p. 44
19. Chang Chung-yuan, *Original Teachings of Ch'an Buddhism*, p. 87.
20. Blofeld, *Zen Teaching of Huang Po*, p. 53.
21. Ibid., p. 39.
22. Ibid., p. 46.

23. Ibid., p. 37.
24. Ibid.
25. Ibid., p. 40.
26. Ibid., p. 61.
27. Ibid., p. 26.
28. Chang Chung-yuan, *Original Teachings of Ch'an Buddhism*, p. 85.
29. Blofeld, *Zen Teachings of Huang Po*, p. 50.
30. See Wu, *Golden Age of Zen*.
31. Chang Chung-yuan reports some disagreement over the actual date of Huang-po's death. It seems that he is reported to have died in 849 in *Records of Buddhas and Patriarchs in Various Dynasties*, whereas the year of his death is given as 855 in the *General Records of Buddhas and Patriarchs*.
32. Excerpts from the Han Yu treatise are provided in Edwin O. Reischauer, *Ennin's Travels in T'ang China* (New York: Ronald Press, 1955), pp. 221 ff. This recounting of a visit by a ninth-century Japanese monk to China reveals indirectly how lacking in influence the Ch'anists actually were. In a diary of many years Ch'an is mentioned only rarely, and then in tones of other than respect. He viewed the Ch'anists warily and described them as "extremely unruly men at heart" (p. 173). However, his trip in China was severely disturbed by the sudden eruption of the Great Persecution, making him so fearful that he actually destroyed the Buddhist art he had collected throughout the country.
33. See Hu Shih, "Ch'an (Zen) Buddhism in China."
34. See Ibid.
35. Kenneth Ch'en, in "The Economic Background of the Hui-Ch'ang Suppression of Buddhism," *Harvard Journal of Asiatic Studies*, 19 (1956), points out that the imperial decree required the turning in only of statues made from metals having economic value. Those made from clay, wood, and stone could remain in the temples. He uses this to support his contention that the main driving force behind the Great Persecution was the inordinate economic power of the Buddhist establishments.

11. LIN-CHI: FOUNDER OF RINZAI ZEN

1. A discussion of the five houses of Ch'an may be found in Dumoulin, *History of Zen Buddhism*, pp. 106–22; and Dumoulin and Sasaki, *Development of Chinese Zen*, pp. 17–32. Useful summaries of their teachings also may be found in Chou Hsiang-kuang, *Dhyana Buddhism in China*.
2. Accounts of Lin-chi's life are found in *The Record of Lin-chi, The Transmission of the Lamp, The Five Lamps Meeting at the Source*, and *Finger Pointing at the Moon*. The most reliable source is probably *The Record of Lin-chi*, since this was compiled by his follower(s). The

definitive translation of this work certainly must be that by Ruth F. Sasaki, *The Recorded Sayings of Ch'an Master Lin-chi Hui-chao of Chen Prefecture*, (Kyoto, Japan: Institute of Zen Studies, 1975) and recently re-issued by Heian International, Inc., South San Francisco, Calif. Another version, *The Zen Teachings of Rinzai*, translated by Irmgard Schloegl (Berkeley, Calif.: Shambhala, 1976), is less satisfactory. The Lin-chi excerpts from *The Transmission of the Lamp* may be found in Chang Chung-yuan, *Original Teachings of Ch'an Buddhism*. Excerpts from *The Five Lamps Meeting at the Source* and *Finger Pointing at the Moon* are provided in Charles Luk, *Ch'an and Zen Teaching*, Second Series (Berkeley: Shambhala, 1971). Translations of his sermons, sayings, etc. together with commentary may also be found in Wu, *Golden Age of Zen*; Chou Hsiang-kuang, *Dhyana Buddhism in China*; and Blyth, *Zen and Zen Classics, Vol. 3*.

3. R. H. Blyth is suspicious that Lin-chi's story was enhanced somewhat for dramatic purposes, claiming (*Zen and Zen Classics, Vol. 3*, p. 151), "As in the case of the Sixth Patriarch, [Lin-chi's] enlightenment is recounted 'dramatically,' that is to say minimizing his previous understanding of Zen in order to bring out the great change after enlightenment."

4. Sasaki, *Recorded Sayings of Lin-chi*, pp. 24–25.

5. Ibid., p. 25.

6. Chang Chung-yuan, *Original Teachings of Ch'an Buddhism*, pp. 117–18.

7. Wu, *Golden Age of Zen*, p. 194.

8. Chang Chung-yuan, *Original Teachings of Ch'an Buddhism*, p. 118.

9. Wu, *Golden Age of Zen*, p. 195.

10. Chang Chung-yuan, *Original Teachings of Ch'an Buddhism*, p. 119.

11. Sasaki, *Recorded Sayings of Lin-chi*, p. 43.

12. Ibid., p. 45.

13. Dumoulin, *History of Zen Buddhism*, p. 122.

14. Of Lin-chi's shout, R. H. Blyth says (*Zen and Zen Classics, Vol. 3*, p. 154): "[The shout] is a war-cry, but the fight is a sort of shadow-boxing. The universe shouts at us, we shout back. We shout at the universe, and the echo comes back in the same way. But the shouting and the echoing are continuous, and, spiritually speaking, simultaneous. Thus the [shout] is not an expression of anything; it has no (separable) meaning. It is pure energy, without cause or effect, rhyme or reason."

15. After Sasaki, *Recorded Sayings of Lin-chi*, p. 47.

16. See Wu, *Golden Age of Zen*, p. 201.

17. Chang Chung-yuan, *Original Teachings of Ch'an Buddhism*, pp. 121–22.

18. Sasaki, *Recorded Sayings of Lin-chi*, p. 4.

19. Ibid., p. 41.

20. Ibid., p. 48.

21. Ibid., p. 2.
22. Ibid., p. 70.
23. Ibid., p. 6.
24. Chang Chung-yuan, *Original Teachings of Ch'an Buddhism*, p. 98.
25. Wu, *Golden Age of Zen*, pp. 204–05.
26. Chang Chung-yuan, *Original Teachings of Ch'an Buddhism*, p. 99.
27. Dumoulin, *Development of Chinese Zen*, p. 22.
28. Chang Chung-yuan, *Original Teachings of Ch'an Buddhism*, p. 99.
29. Dumoulin, *Development of Chinese Zen*, p. 23.
30. See Chang Chung-yuan, *Original Teachings of Ch'an Buddhism*, p. 95.
31. Sasaki, *Recorded Sayings of Lin-chi*, pp. 27–28.
32. See Chang Chung-yuan, *Original Teachings of Ch'an Buddhism*, p. 95.
33. Heinrich Dumoulin (*Development of Chinese Zen*, p. 22) notes that this is merely playing off the well-known "four propositions" of Indian Buddhist logic: existence, nonexistence, both existence and nonexistence, and neither existence nor nonexistence.
34. Wu, *Golden Age of Zen*, p. 202.
35. Ibid., p. 203.
36. Sasaki, *Recorded Sayings of Lin-chi*. p. 29.
37. Ibid., p. 24.
38. Ibid., p. 38.

12. TUNG-SHAN AND TS'AO-SHAN: FOUNDERS OF SOTO ZEN

1. Philip Yampolsky, in *Platform Sutra of the Sixth Patriarch*, alleges that Hsing-ssu was resurrected from anonymity because Shih-t'ou (700–90) was in need of a connection to the Sixth Patriarch. The mysterious master Hsing-ssu comes into prominence well over a hundred years after his death; his actual life was not chronicled by any of his contemporaries. Neither, for that matter, was the life of his pupil Shih-t'ou, although the latter left a heritage of disciples and a burgeoning movement to perpetuate his memory.
2. Ibid., p. 55.
3. The stories attached to Shih-t'ou are varied and questioned by most authorities. For example, there is the story that he was enlightened by reading Seng-chau's *Chao-lun (The Book of Chao)* but that his philosophy came from Lao Tzu.
4. See Chang Chung-yuan, *Original Teachings of Ch'an Buddhism*, p. 58.
5. Wu, *Golden Age of Zen*, p. 171.
6. Chang Chung-yuan, *Original Teachings of Ch'an Buddhism*, p. 58.
7. Ibid., p. 60.
8. Ibid., pp. 61–62.
9. Ibid., pp. 64–65.
10. Ibid., p. 76.

11. This is elaborated by Luk, *Ch'an and Zen Teaching*, Second Series, p. 166.
12. Ibid., p. 174.
13. Extended discussions of this concept are provided by Chang Chung-yuan, *Original Teachings of Ch'an Buddhism*, pp. 41–57; and by Wu, *Golden Age of Zen*, pp. 177–82.
14. Wu, *Golden Age of Zen*, p. 179.
15. See Chang Chung-yuan, *Original Teachings of Ch'an Buddhism*, p. 49.
16. See Luk, *Chan and Zen Teaching*, Second Series, p. 139.
17. See Chang Chung-yuan, *Original Teachings of Ch'an Buddhism*, p. 50.
18. Ibid., p. 69.
19. When R. H. Blyth translates this poem in *Zen and Zen Classics*, Vol. 2, called the Hokyozammai in Japanese, he includes a grand dose of skepticism concerning its real authorship, since he believes the poem unworthy of the master (p. 152).
20. Ibid., p. 157.
21. See Chang Chung-yuan, *Original Teachings of Ch'an Buddhism*, p. 48.
22. Ibid., p. 70.
23. Ibid., p. 71.
24. Ibid., p. 72.
25. Dumoulin, *Development of Chinese Zen*, p. 26.
26. Eliot, *Japanese Buddhism*, p. 168.

13. KUEI-SHAN, YUN-MEN, AND FA-YEN: THREE MINOR HOUSES

1. Accounts of the lives and teachings of the masters of the Kuei-yang school can be found in a number of translations, including Chang Chung-yuan, *Original Teachings of Ch'an Buddhism*; and Luk, *Ch'an and Zen Teachings*, Second Series. Both provide translations from *The Transmission of the Lamp*. Other sources appear to be used in Wu, *Golden Age of Zen*, which includes a lively discussion of Kuei-shan and the Kuei-yang sect.
2. Wu, *Golden Age of Zen*, p. 159.
3. Charles Luk (*Ch'an and Zen Teaching*, Second Series, p. 58) makes a valiant try at explication when he says, "[Huai-hai] wanted him to perceive 'that which gave the order' and 'that which obeyed it.' . . . [Huai-hai] continued to perform his great function by pressing the student hard, insisting that the latter should perceive 'that' which arose from the seat, used the poker, raised a little fire, showed it to him and said, 'Is this not fire?' . . . This time the student could actually perceive the reply by means of his self-nature. . . . Hence his enlightenment."
4. See Ibid., p. 58. Ssu-ma seems to have had a good record in predicting monastic success, and he was much in demand. Although the reliance

on a fortuneteller seems somewhat out of character for a Ch'an master, we should remember that fortunetelling and future prediction in China are at least as old as the I Ching.

5. Chang Chung-yuan, *Original Teachings of Ch'an Buddhism*, p. 202.
6. Ibid., p. 204.
7. Luk, *Ch'an and Zen Teaching*, Second Series, p. 67.
8. Ibid., p. 78.
9. Wu, *Golden Age of Zen*, p. 167.
10. Ibid., p. 167.
11. John Wu (*Golden Age of Zen*, p. 165) says, "The style of the house of Kuei-yang has a charm all of its own. It is not as steep and sharp-edged as the houses of Lin-chi and Yun-men, nor as close-knit and resourceful as the house of Ts'ao-tung nor as speculative and broad as the house of Fa-yen, but it has greater *depth* than the others."
12. See Chang Chung-yuan, *Original Teachings of Ch'an Buddhism*, p. 269. Other translations of Yun-men anecdotes, as well as interpretations and appreciations, can be found in Luk, *Ch'an and Zen Teaching*, Second Series; Chou, *Dhyana Buddhism in China*; Wu, *Golden Age of Zen*; and Blyth, *Zen and Zen Classics*, Vol. 2.
13. He had six koans out of forty-eight in the Mumonkan and eighteen koans out of a hundred in the Hekiganroku. Perhaps his extensive representation in the second collection is attributable to the fact that its compiler, Ch'ung-hsien (980–1025), was one of the last surviving representatives of Yun-men's school.
14. Chang Chung-yuan, *Original Teachings of Ch'an Buddhism* p. 284.
15. Ibid., p. 286.
16. Ibid., p. 229.
17. Ibid., p. 228.
18. Ibid., p. 229.
19. Sekida, *Two Zen Classics: Mumonkan & Hekiganroku*, p. 349. This koan is from Hekiganroku, Case 77.
20. From the Mumonkan, Case 21. The Chinese term used was *kan-shin chueh*, which Chang Chung-yuan (*Original Teachings of Ch'an Buddhism*, p. 300) characterizes as follows: "This may be translated either of two ways: a piece of dried excrement or a bamboo stick used for cleaning as toilet tissue is today."
21. Blyth, *Zen and Zen Classics*, Vol. 2, p. 142.
22. Those with insatiable curiosity may consult Wu, *Golden Age of Zen*, pp. 244 ff.
23. Translations of his teachings from *The Transmission of the Lamp* are provided by Chang Chung-yuan in *Original Teachings of Ch'an Buddhism* and by Charles Luk in *Ch'an and Zen Teachings*, Second Series. A translation of a completely different source, which varies significantly on all the major anecdotes, is provided in John Wu, *Golden Age of Zen*. A translation, presumably from a Japanese source, of some of his teachings is supplied by R. H. Blyth in *Zen and Zen*

Classics, Vol. 2. Heinrich Dumoulin offers a brief assessment of his influence in his two books: *Development of Chinese Zen* and *History of Zen Buddhism*.

24. Chang Chung-yuan, *Original Teachings of Ch'an Buddhism*, p. 238. A completely different version may be found in Wu, *Golden Age of Zen*, pp. 232–33.
25. Chang Chung-yuan, *Original Teachings of Ch'an Buddhism*, p. 242.

14. TA-HUI: MASTER OF THE KOAN

1. See Dumoulin, *History of Zen Buddhism*, p. 128.
2. Isshu Miura and Ruth Fuller Sasaki, *Zen Dust* (New York: Harcourt, Brace & World, 1966), pp. 10-11.
3. Ibid., p. 10. This individual is identified as Nan-yuan Hui-yang (d. 930).
4. This is Case 1 in the Mumonkan, usually the first koan given to a beginning student.
5. This is Case 26 of the Mumonkan. The version given here is after the translation in Sekida, *Two Zen Classics: Mumonkan & Hekiganroku*, p. 89.
6. This is Case 54 of the Hekiganroku. The version given is after Ibid., p. 296, and Cleary and Cleary, *Blue Cliff Record*, p. 362.
7. Isshu and Sasaki, *Zen Dust*, p. 13.
8. There are a number of translations of the Mumonkan currently available in English. The most recent is Sekida, *Two Zen Classics: Mumonkan & Hekiganroku*; but perhaps the most authoritative is Zenkei Shibayama, *Zen Comments on the Mumonkan*, trans. Sumiko Kudo (New York: Harper & Row, 1974; paperback edition, New York: New American Library, 1975). Other translations are Nyogen Senzaki and Paul Reps, "The Gateless Gate," in Paul Reps, ed., *Zen Flesh, Zen Bones* (Rutland and Tokyo: Tuttle, 1957); Sohkau Ogata, "The Mu Mon Kwan," in *Zen for the West* (New York: Dial, 1959); and R. H. Blyth, *Zen and Zen Classics*, Vol. 4, "Mumonkan" (Tokyo: Hokuseido, 1966).
   Three translations of the Blue Cliff Record are currently available in English. There is the early and unsatisfactory version by R. D. M. Shaw (London: Michael Joseph, 1961). A readable version is provided in Sekida, *Two Zen Classics*, although this excludes some of the traditional commentary. The authoritative version is certainly that by Cleary and Cleary, *Blue Cliff Record*.
9. This is the case with the version provided in Sekida, *Two Zen Classics*.
10. See Dumoulin, *History of Zen Buddhism*, p. 128.
11. See L. Carrington Goodrich, *A Short History of the Chinese People* (New York: Harper & Row, 1943), p. 161.
12. The most comprehensive collection of Ta-hui's writings is translated in Christopher Cleary, *Swampland Flowers: The Letters and Lectures*

of Zen Master Ta Hui (New York: Grove Press, 1977). Excerpts are also translated by Suzuki, Essays in Zen Buddhism, Second Series. Biographical information may also be found in Isshu and Sasaki, Zen Dust.

13. Translated in Isshu and Sasaki, Zen Dust, p. 163.
14. A work known today as the Cheng-fa-yen-tsang. See Isshu and Sasaki, Zen Dust, p. 163.
15. See Ibid.
16. See Ibid.
17. Translated by Cleary, Swampland Flowers, pp. 129–30.
18. See Sekida, Two Zen Classics, p. 17.
19. Suzuki, Essays in Zen Buddhism, Second Series, p. 103.
20. Cleary, Swampland Flowers, p. 64.
21. Ibid., p. 57.
22. Ibid., p. 14.
23. But he destroyed them in vain. Around 1300 a monk managed to assemble most of the koans and commentary from scattered sources and put the book back into print. The problem continues to this day; there is now available a book of "answers" to a number of koans—Yoel Hoffman, The Sound of One Hand Clapping (New York: Basic Books, 1975). One reviewer of this book observed sadly, "Now if only getting the 'answer' were the same as getting the point."

15. EISAI: THE FIRST JAPANESE MASTER

1. This anecdote is in Martin Charles Collcutt, "The Zen Monastic Institution in Medieval Japan" (Ph.D. dissertation, Harvard University, 1975).
2. Although there were various attempts to introduce Ch'an into Japan prior to the twelfth century, nothing ever seemed to stick. Dumoulin (History of Zen Buddhism, pp. 138–39) summarized these efforts as follows: "The first certain information we possess regarding Zen in Japan goes back to the early period of her history. The outstanding Japanese Buddhist monk during that age, Dosho, was attracted to Zen through the influence of his Chinese teacher, Hsuan-tsang, under whom he studied the Yogacara philosophy (653). . . . Dosho thus came into immediate contact with the tradition of Bodhidharma and brought the Zen of the patriarchs to Japan. He built the first meditation hall, at a temple in Nara. . . .
"A century later, for the first time in history, a Chinese Zen master came to Japan. This was Tao-hsuan, who belonged to the northern sect of Chinese Zen in the third generation after Shen-hsiu. Responding to an invitation from Japanese Buddhist monks, he took up residence in Nara and contributed to the growth of Japanese culture during the Tempyo period (729–749). . . . The contemplative element in the

Tendai tradition, which held an important place from the beginning, was strengthened in both China and Japan by repeated contacts with Zen.

"A further step in the spread of Zen occurred in the following century when I-k'ung, a Chinese master of the Lin-chi sect, visited Japan. He came at the invitation of the Empress Tachibana Kachiko, wife of the Emperor Saga, during the early part of the Showa era (834–848), to teach Zen, first at the imperial court and later at the Danrinji temple in Kyoto, which the empress had built for him. However, these first efforts in the systematic propagation of Zen according to the Chinese pattern did not meet with lasting success. I-k'ung was unable to launch a vigorous movement. Disappointed, he returned to China, and for three centuries Zen was inactive in Japan."

Another opportunity for the Japanese to learn about Ch'an was missed by the famous Japanese pilgrim Ennin, who was in China to witness the Great Persecution of 845, but who paid almost no attention to Ch'an, which he regarded as the obsession of unruly ne'er-do-wells.

3. A number of books provide information concerning early Japanese history and the circumstances surrounding the introduction of Buddhism to Japan. General historical works of particular relevance include: John Whitney Hall, *Japan, from Prehistory to Modern Times* (New York: Delacorte, 1970); Mikiso Hane, *Japan, A Historical Survey* (New York: Scribner's, 1972); Edwin O. Reischauer, *Japan: Past and Present*, 3rd ed. (New York: Knopf, 1964); and George B. Sansom, *A History of Japan*, 3 vols. (Stanford, Calif.: Stanford University Press, 1958–63).

Studies of early Japanese Buddhism may be found in: Masaharu Anesaki, *History of Japanese Religion* (London: Kegan Paul, Trench, Trubner, 1930: reissue, Rutland, Vt.: Tuttle, 1963); William K. Bunce, *Religions in Japan* (Rutland, Vt.: Tuttle, 1955); Ch'en, *Buddhism in China*; Eliot, *Japanese Buddhism*; Shinsho Hanayama, *A History of Japanese Buddhism* (Tokyo: Bukkyo Dendo Kyokai, 1966); and E. Dale Saunders, *Buddhism in Japan* (Philadelphia: University of Pennsylvania Press, 1964).

4. In fact, the popularity of esoteric rituals was such that they were an important part of early Zen practice in Japan.

5. This world is well described by Ivan Morris in *The World of the Shining Prince: Court Life in Ancient Japan* (New York: Knopf, 1964). A discussion of the relation of this aesthetic life to the formation of Japanese Zen may be found in Thomas Hoover, *Zen Culture* (New York: Random House, 1977; paperback edition, New York: Vintage, 1978).

6. One of the most readable accounts of the rise of the Japanese military class may be found in Paul Varley, *Samurai* (New York: Delacorte, 1970; paperback edition, New York: Dell, 1972).

7. This theory is advanced eloquently in Collcutt, "Zen Monastic Institution in Medieval Japan." In later years the Ch'an sect in China

itself actually entered a phase of decadence, with the inclusion of esoteric rites and an ecumenical movement that advocated the chanting of the *nembutsu* by Ch'anists—some of whom claimed there was great similarity between the psychological aspects of this mechanical chant and those of the koan.

8. Accounts of Eisai's life may be found in Dumoulin, *History of Zen Buddhism;* and in Collcutt, "Zen Monastic Institution in Medieval Japan."

9. See Collcutt, "Zen Monastic Institution in Medieval Japan."

10. See Saunders, *Buddhism in Japan,* p. 221.

11. Translated in Wm. Theodore de Bary, ed. *Sources of Japanese Tradition,* Vol. 1 (New York: Columbia University Press, 1958), pp. 236–37.

12. Ibid., p. 237.

13. De Bary, *Sources of Japanese Tradition,* pp. 239–40.

14. Again the best discussion of this intrigue is provided by Collcutt, "Zen Monastic Institution in Medieval Japan."

15. Varley, *Samurai,* p. 45.

16. DOGEN: FATHER OF JAPANESE SOTO ZEN

1. Dumoulin, *History of Zen Buddhism,* p. 151. This statement may be faint praise, for Japan has never been especially noted for its religious thinkers. As philosophers, the Japanese have been great artists and poets. Perhaps no culture can do everything.

2. Biographical information on Dogen may be found in Hee-Jin Kim, *Dogen Kigen—Mystical Realist* (Tucson: University of Arizona Press, 1975); Yuho Yokoi, *Zen Master Dogen* (New York: Weatherhill, 1976); and Dumoulin, *History of Zen Buddhism.* Translations of his writings may be found in *Dogen Kigen—Mystical Realist* and *Zen Master Dogen* as well as in Jiyu Kennett, *Zen is Eternal Life* (Emeryville, Calif.: Dharma, 1976); Dogen, *Record of Things Heard from the Treasury of the Eye of the True Teaching* trans. by Thomas Cleary (Boulder, Colo.: Great Eastern Book Company, 1978); Francis Dojun Cook, *How to Raise an Ox* (Los Angeles: Center Publications, 1978); and Kosen Nishiyama and John Steven, *Shobogenzo: The Eye and Treasury of the True Law* (New York: Weatherhill, 1977).

3. Kim, *Dogen Kigen—Mystical Realist,* p. 25.

4. Yokoi, *Zen Master Dogen,* p. 28.

5. See Collcutt, "Zen Monastic Institution in Medieval Japan."

6. Kim, *Dogen Kigen—Mystical Realist,* p. 29.

7. Ibid., p. 35.

8. See Yokoi, *Zen Master Dogen,* p. 32.

9. Ibid., pp. 45–46.

10. Ibid., p. 46.

11. Kennett, *Zen Is Eternal Life,* pp. 141–42.

12. Ibid., p. 152.
13. Ibid., pp. 150–51.
14. Dogen's attitude toward women was revolutionary for his time. A sampling is provided in Kim, *Dogen Kigen—Mystical Realist,* pp. 54–55: "Some people, foolish in the extreme, also think of woman as nothing but the object of sensual pleasures, and see her this way without ever correcting their view. A Buddhist should not do so. If man detests woman as the sexual object, she must detest him for the same reason. Both man and woman become objects, thus being equally involved in defilement. . . . What charge is there against woman? What virtue is there in man? There are wicked men in the world; there are virtuous women in the world. The desire to hear Dharma and the search for enlightenment do not necessarily rely on the difference in sex."
15. Yokoi, *Zen Master Dogen,* pp. 35–36.
16. See Collcutt, "Zen Monastic Training in Medieval Japan," p. 59.
17. Translated in de Bary, *Sources of Japanese Tradition,* Vol. 1., p. 247.
18. See Collcutt, "Zen Monastic Institution in Medieval Japan," p. 62.
19. See Ibid., pp. 62 ff.
20. See Philip Yampolsky, trans., *The Zen Master Hakuin: Selected Writings,* (New York: Columbia University Press, 1971), p. 5.

17. IKKYU: ZEN ECCENTRIC

1. This view is advanced convincingly by Collcutt in "Zen Monastic Institution in Medieval Japan," p. 113 ff.
2. Ibid., p. 80.
3. This would seem to be one of the reasons for what became of a host of emigrating Ch'an teachers as sub-sects of the Yogi branch struggled for ascendency over each other.
4. Wu-an's strength of mind is illustrated by a story related in Collcutt, "Zen Monastic Institution in Medieval Japan," p. 84: "Wu-an is said to have shocked the religious sensibilities of many warriors and monks when, in what has been interpreted as a deliberate attempt to sever the connection between Zen and prayer in Japanese minds, he publicly refused to worship before the statue of Jizo in the Buddha Hill of Kencho-ji on the grounds that whereas Jizo was merely a Bodhisattva, he, Wu-an, was a Buddha."
5. Related in Ibid., p. 88.
6. Collcutt ("Zen Monastic Institution in Medieval Japan," p. 114) points out that the warrior interest in Zen and its Chinese cultural trappings should also be credited partly to their desire to stand up to the snobbery of the Kyoto aristocracy. By making themselves emissaries of a prestigious foreign civilization, the warrior class achieved a bit of cultural one-upmanship on the Kyoto snob set.

7. Collcutt ("Zen Monastic Institution in Medieval Japan," p. 106) reports that this conversion of temples to Zen was not always spontaneous. There is the story of one local governor who was called to Kamakura and in the course of a public assembly asked pointedly whether his family had yet built a Zen monastery in their home province. The terrified official declared he had built a monastery for a hundred Zen monks, and then raced home to start construction.

8. A discussion of the contribution of Zen to Japanese civilization may be found in Hoover, *Zen Culture*. An older survey is D. T. Suzuki, *Zen and Japanese Culture* (Princeton, N. J.: Princeton University Press, 1959).

9. Yampolsky, *Zen Master Hakuin*, p. 8.

10. Philip Yampolsky, "Muromachi Zen and the Gozan System," in John W. Hall and Toyoda Takeshi, eds., *Japan in the Muromachi Age* (Berkeley: University of California Press, 1977), p. 319.

11. One of the best political histories of this era is Sansom, *History of Japan*. For the history of Zen, the best work appears to be Martin Collcutt, *The Zen Monastic Institution in Medieval Japan* (Cambridge: Harvard University Press, in press), a revised version of the dissertation cited above.

12. English sources on Ikkyu are less common than might at first be supposed. The most exhaustive study and translation of original Ikkyu writings to date is certainly that of James Sanford, "Zen-Man Ikkyu" (Ph.D. dissertation, Harvard University, 1972). There is also a lively and characteristically insightful essay by Donald Keene, "The Portrait of Ikkyu," in *Archives of Asian Art*, Vol. 20 (1966–67), pp. 54–65. This essay has been collected in Donald Keene, *Landscapes and Portraits* (Palo Alto: Kodansha International, 1971). Another work of Ikkyu scholarship is Sonja Arntzen, "A Presentation of the Poet Ikkyu with Translations from the Kyounshu 'Mad Cloud Anthology'" (Unpublished thesis, University of British Columbia, Vancouver, 1966).

13. See Thomas Cleary, *The Original Face: An Anthology of Rinzai Zen* (New York: Grove Press, 1978), p. 13. An example of a Nasrudin-esque parable told about Ikkyu is the story of his approaching the house of a rich man one day to beg for food wearing his torn robes and straw sandals. The man drove him away, but when he returned the following day in the luxurious robe of a Buddhist prelate, he was invited in for a banquet. But when the food arrived Ikkyu removed his robe and offered the food to it.

14. Sanford, "Zen-Man Ikkyu," p. 48.

15. Ibid., p. 68.

16. Ibid. pp. 80–81.

17. Translated by Keene, *Landscapes and Portraits*, p. 235. Professor Keene (personal communication) has provided a revised and,

he believes, more fully accurate translation of this verse as follows:

> After ten days of living in this temple my mind's in turmoil;
> Red strings, very long, tug at my feet.
> If one day you get around to looking for me,
> Try the restaurants, the drinking places or the brothels.

He notes that the "red strings" of the second line refer to the ties of physical attachment to women that drew Ikkyu from the temple to the pleasure quarters.

18. Jon Covell and Yamada Sobin, *Zen at Daitoku-ji* (New York: Kodansha International, 1974), p. 36.
19. Sanford, "Zen-Man Ikkyu," p. 221.
20. Ibid., p. 226.
21. Ibid., p. 235.
22. Ibid., p. 225.
23. Ibid., pp. 253–54. A translation may also be found in Cleary, *Original Face*; and in R. H. Blyth and N. A. Waddell, "Ikkyu's Skeletons," *The Eastern Buddhist*, N.S. 7, 3 (May 1973), pp. 111–25. Also see Blyth, *Zen and Zen Classics*, Vol. 7.
24. Sanford claims ("Zen-Man Ikkyu," p. 341) that Ikkyu's prose is "almost totally unknown" in Japan.
25. Ibid., pp. 326–27.
26. Ibid., p. 172.
27. Jan Covell (*Zen at Daitoku-ji*, p. 38) says, "Ikkyu's own ink paintings are unpretentious and seemingly artless, always with the flung-ink technique. His calligraphy is ranked among history's greatest . . ."
28. Sanford, "Zen-Man Ikkyu," p. 342.

18. HAKUIN: JAPANESE MASTER OF THE KOAN

1. Yampolsky, *Zen Master Hakuin*, p. 116. This is undoubtedly the definitive work by and about Hakuin in English and has been used for all the quotations that follow. Another translation of some of Hakuin's works is R. D. M. Shaw, *The Embossed Teakettle* (London: George Allen & Unwin, 1963). A short translation of Hakuin's writings may be found in Cleary, *Original Face*. Perhaps the most incisive biographical and interpretive material may be found, respectively, in Dumoulin, *History of Zen Buddhism*; and Isshu and Sasaki, *Zen Dust*.
2. Yampolsky, *Zen Master Hakuin*, p. 117.
3. Ibid., p. 18.
4. Ibid., pp. 118–19.
5. Ibid., p. 119.
6. Ibid., p. 121.

7. Ibid., pp. 31–32.
8. Ibid., p. 33.
9. Ibid., p. 49.
10. Ibid., p. 33.
11. Ibid., pp. 52–53.
12. Ibid., p. 53.
13. Ibid., p. 58.
14. Ibid.
15. Ibid., p. 35.
16. Ibid., pp. 63–64.
17. The "great ball of doubt," known in Chinese as *i-t'uan*, was a classic Zen phrase and has been traced by Ruth Fuller Sasaki (*Zen Dust*, p. 247) back to a tenth-century Chinese monk, who claimed in a poem, "The ball of doubt within my heart/Was as big as a big wicker basket." Hakuin's analysis of the "great ball of doubt" is translated in *Zen Dust*, p. 43.
18. Hakuin's invention of his own koans, which were kept secret and never published, is a significant departure from the usual technique of simply taking situations from the classic literature, and demonstrates both his creativity and his intellectual independence. It also raises the question of whether they really were "koans" under the traditional definition of "public case" or whether they should be given a different name.
19. Yampolsky, *Zen Master Hakuin*, p. 164.
20. The koan system of Hakuin is discussed by Yampolsky in *Zen Master Hakuin*, p. 15; and by Sasaki, in *The Zen Koan*, pp. 27–30.
21. Yampolsky, *Zen Master Hakuin*, p. 32.
22. See D. T. Suzuki, *Sengai: The Zen Master* (Greenwich, Conn.: New York Graphic Society, 1971); Burton Watson, *Ryokan: Zen Monk-Poet of Japan* (New York: Columbia University Press, 1977); and John Stevens, *One Robe, One Bowl: The Zen Poetry of Ryokan* (New York: Weatherhill, 1977).

BIBLIOGRAPHY

Anesaki, Masaharu. *History of Japanese Religion*. London: Kegan Paul, Trench, Trubner, 1930 (reissue, Rutland, Vt.: Tuttle, 1963).

Arntzen, Sonja. "A Presentation of the Poet Ikkyu with Translations from the Kyounshu 'Mad Cloud Anthology.' " Master's thesis, University of British Columbia, Vancouver, 1966.

Baskin, Wade, ed. *Classics in Chinese Philosophy*. Totowa, N. J.: Littlefield, Adams, 1974.

Berry, Thomas. *Buddhism*. New York: Thomas Y. Crowell Co., 1975.

Bingham, Woodbridge. *The Founding of the T'ang Dynasty*. New York: Octagon, 1970.

Birch, Cyril. *Anthology of Chinese Literature*. New York: Grove, 1965.

Blofeld, John. *The Secret and Sublime: Taoist Mysteries and Magic*. New York: E. P. Dutton, 1973.

Blofeld, John, trans. *The Zen Teaching of Huang Po*. New York: Grove, 1958.

Blofeld, John. *The Zen Teaching of Hui Hai on Sudden Illumination*. London: Ryder, 1962; paperback reprint, New York: Weiser, 1972.

Bloodworth, Dennis. *The Chinese Looking Glass*. New York: Dell, 1966.

Blyth, R. H. *Zen and Zen Classics*. 7 Vols. Tokyo: Hokuseido, 1960-1970.

―――― and N. A. Waddell, "Ikkyu's Skeletons," *The Eastern Buddhist*, N. S. 7, 3.

Broughton, Jeffrey. "Kuei-Feng Tsung-Mi: The Convergence of Ch'an and the Teachings." Ph.D. dissertation, Columbia University, 1975.

Bunce, William K. *Religions in Japan*. Rutland: Tuttle, 1955.

Bynner, Witter. *The Jade Mountain*. New York: Vintage, 1957.

Chai, Ch'u, and Winberg Chai. *Confucianism*. New York: Barron's Educational Series, 1973.

―――― *The Humanist Way in Ancient China: Essential Works of Confucianism*. New York: Bantam, 1965.

Chan, Wing-tsit, trans. *The Platform Scripture*. New York: St. Johns University Press, 1963.

―――― *A Source Book in Chinese Philosophy*. Princeton: Princeton University Press, 1963.

———"Transformation of Buddhism in China," *Philosophy East and West,* VII (1957-58) pp. 107–16.

Chang, Garma C. C. *The Practice of Zen.* New York: Harper & Row, 1959; paperback edition, Perennial Library, 1970.

Chang, Chung-yuan. *Creativity and Taoism: A Study of Chinese Philosophy, Art, and Poetry.* New York: Harper & Row, 1970.

———*Tao: A New Way of Thinking.* New York: Harper & Row, 1975; paperback edition, Perennial Library, 1977.

———trans. *Original Teachings of Ch'an Buddhism (The Transmission of the Lamp).* New York: Random House, 1969; paperback edition, Vintage, 1971.

Chatterjee, H., ed. *Mula-Madhyamaka-Karika of Nagarjuna.* Calcutta: K. L. Mukhopadhyay, 1962.

Chau, Bhikshu Thich Minh. *Hsuan Tsang, The Pilgrim & Scholar.* Nha-trang, Vietnam: Vietnam Buddhist Institute, n.d.

Chen, C. M. *The Lighthouse in the Ocean of Ch'an.* Kalimpong: Buddhist Association of the United States, 1965.

Ch'en, Kenneth. *Buddhism in China.* Princeton: Princeton University Press, 1972.

———. *Buddhism: The Light of Asia.* New York: Barron's Educational Series, Inc., 1968

———. *The Chinese Transformation of Buddhism.* Princeton: Princeton University Press, 1973.

———. "The Economic Background of the Hui-ch'ang Suppression of Buddhism," *Harvard Journal of Asiatic Studies,* 19, (1956), pp. 67–105.

Chiang, Yee. *The Chinese Eye.* Bloomington: Indiana University Press, 1964.

Chou, Hsiang-kuang. *Dhyana Buddhism in China.* Allahabad, India: Indo-Chinese Literature Publications, 1960.

Cleary, Christopher, trans. *Swampland Flowers: The Letters and Lectures of Zen Master Ta Hui.* New York: Grove, 1977.

Cleary, Thomas, trans. *The Original Face.* New York: Grove, 1978.

———, *Sayings and Doings of Pai-chang.* Los Angeles: Center Publications, 1979.

———, and J. C. Cleary, trans. *The Blue Cliff Record.* 3 vols. Berkeley, Calif.: Shambhala, 1977.

Conze, Edward, ed. *Buddhist Texts Through the Ages.* Oxford: Bruno Cassirer, 1954.

Cook, Francis Dojun. *How to Raise an Ox.* Los Angeles: Center Publications, 1978.

Covell, Jon, and Yamada Sobin. *Zen at Daitoku-ji.* New York: Kodansha International, 1974.

Creel, Herrlee G. *What Is Taoism? And Other Studies in Chinese Cultural History.* Chicago: The University of Chicago Press, 1970.

Davis, A. R. *Tu Fu.* New York: Twayne, 1971.

Day, Clarence Burton. *The Philosophers of China*. New York: Philosophical Library, 1962; paperback edition, Secaucus, N. J.: Citadel, 1978.

de Bary, William Theodore. *The Buddhist Tradition in India, China and Japan*. New York: Random House, 1972.

de Bary, William Theodore, ed. *Sources of Japanese Tradition*. 2 vols. New York: Columbia University Press, 1958.

———, Wing-tsit Chan, and Burton Watson. *Sources of Chinese Tradition*, Vol. I. New York: Columbia University Press, 1960.

Dogen, *Record of Things Heard from the Treasury of the Eye of the True Teaching*. Trans. Thomas Cleary. Boulder, Colo.: Great Eastern Book Co., 1978.

Dogen, Trans. Jiyu Kennett. *Zen is Eternal Life*. Emeryville, Calif.: Dharma, 1976.

Dumoulin, Heinrich. *A History of Zen Buddhism*. New York: Random House, 1963; paperback edition, Boston: Beacon, 1969.

———, and Ruth Fuller Sasaki. *The Development of Chinese Zen*. New York: First Zen Institute of America, 1953.

Eberhard, Wolfram. *A History of China*. Berkeley: University of California Press, 1977.

Eliot, Sir Charles. *Japanese Buddhism*. New York: Barnes & Noble, 1969.

Feng, Gai-fu, and Jane English, trans. *Chuang Tsu*. New York: Vintage, 1974.

———. *Tao Te-Ching*. New York: Vintage, 1972.

First Zen Institute of America. *Cat's Yawn*. New York: 1947.

Fitzgerald, C. P. *China—A Short Cultural History*. New York: Praeger, 1961.

———. *The Empress Wu*. Vancouver: University of British Columbia, 1968.

———. *Son of Heaven: A Biography of Li Shih-min, Founder of the T'ang Dynasty*. Cambridge: University Press, 1933.

Frederic, Louis. *Daily Life in Japan at the Time of the Samurai*. Tokyo: Tuttle, 1972.

Fung, Paul F., and George D. Fung, trans. *The Sutra of the Sixth Patriarch on the Pristine Orthodox Dharma*. San Francisco: Buddha's Universal Church, 1964.

Fung Yu-lan. *A Short History of Chinese Philosophy*. New York: Macmillan, 1948; paperback edition, Free Press, 1966.

———. *The Spirit of Chinese Philosophy*. Boston: Beacon Press, 1962.

Gernet, Jacques. "Biographie du Matre Chen-houei de Ho-tso," *Journal Asiatique*, 249 (1951), pp. 29–60.

———. "Complement aux Entretiens du Maître de Dhyana Chen-houei (668–760)," *BEFEO*, 44, 2 (1954), pp. 453–66.

———. *Daily Life in China on the Eve of the Mongol Invasion*. Trans. H. M. Wright. New York: Macmillan, 1962.

———. "Entretiens du Maître de Dhyana Chen-bouei du Ho-tso," Hanoi, 1949. (Publications de l'école française d'Extreme-Orient, Vol. 31).

Giles, Herbert A. *A History of Chinese Literature*. New York: Grove, 1923.

Goddard, Dwight, ed. *A Buddhist Bible.* New York: Dutton, 1938; paperback edition, Boston: Beacon, 1970.

Goodrich, L. Carrington. *A Short History of the Chinese People,* 4th edn. New York: Harper & Row, 1963.

Graham, A. C. *Poems of the Late T'ang.* Baltimore: Penguin, 1965.

Grousset, René. *In The Footsteps of the Buddha.* New York: Grossman, 1971.

———. *The Rise and Splendour of the Chinese Empire.* Berkeley: University of California Press, 1962.

Hall, John Whitney. *Japan, From Prehistory to Modern Times.* New York: Delacorte, 1970.

———, and Toyoda Takeshi, eds. *Japan in The Muromachi Age.* Berkeley: University of California Press, 1977.

Hanayama, Shinsho. *A History of Japanese Buddhism.* Tokyo: Bukkyo Dendo Kyokai, 1966.

Harrison, John A. *The Chinese Empire.* New York: Harcourt Brace Jovanovich, 1972.

Hoffmann, Yoel. *Radical Zen.* Brookline, Mass.: Autumn Press, 1978.

———. *The Sound of One Hand Clapping.* New York: Basic Books, 1975.

Hookham, Hilda. *A Short History of China.* New York: St. Martin's Press, Inc., 1972; paperback edition, New York: New American Library, 1972.

Hoover, Thomas. *Zen Culture.* New York: Random House, 1977; paperback edition, Vintage, 1978.

Hsuan Hua. *The Sixth Patriarch's Dharma Jewel Platform Sutra.* San Francisco: Buddhist Text Translation Society, 1971.

Hu Shih. "Ch'an (Zen) Buddhism in China: Its History and Method," *Philosophy East and West,* 3, 1 (April 1953), pp. 3–24.

———. "The Development of Zen Buddhism in China," *Chinese Social and Political Science Review,* 15, 4 (January 1932), pp. 475–505.

Inada, Kenneth K. *Nagarjuna—A Translation of his Mulamadhyamaka-karika With An Introductory Essay.* Tokyo: Hokuseido, 1970.

Ishihara, Akira, and Howard S. Levy, *The Tao of Sex.* Tokyo: Shibundo, 1968.

Kaltenmark, Max. *Lao Tzu and Taoism.* Stanford, Calif.: Stanford University Press, 1969.

Kalupahana, David J. *Buddhist Philosophy: A Historical Analysis.* Honolulu: University Press of Hawaii, 1976.

Kato, Bunno, Yoshiro Tamura, and Kojiro Miyasaka, trans. *The Threefold Lotus Sutra.* New York: Weatherhill/Kosei, 1975.

Keene, Donald, "The Portrait of Ikkyu," *Landscapes and Portraits.* Palo Alto: Kodansha International, 1971.

Kim, Hee-jin. *Dogen Kigen: Mystical Realist.* Phoenix: University of Arizona Press, 1975.

Kodera, Takashi James. *Dogen's Formative Years in China.* London: Routledge & Kegan Paul, 1979.

Kubose, Gyomay M. *Zen Koans.* Chicago: Regnery, 1973.

Latourette, Kenneth Scott. *The Chinese: Their History and Culture.* New York: Macmillan, 1964.

Lau, D. C. *Lao Tzu—Tao Te Ching.* Baltimore: Penguin, 1963.

———. *Mencius.* Baltimore: Penguin, 1970.

Legge, James. *A Record of Buddhistic Kingdoms.* New York: Dover, 1965.

Levenson, Joseph R., and Franz Schurmann. *China: An Interpretive History.* Berkeley: University of California Press, 1969.

Liebenthal, Walter. *Chao Lun: The Treatises of Seng-chao.* Hong Kong: Hong Kong University Press, 1968.

———. "Chinese Buddhism During the 4th and 5th Centuries," *Monumenta Nipponica*, 11 (1955), pp. 44–83.

———. "The Sermon of Shen-hui," *Asia Major*, N. S. 3, 2 (1952), pp. 132–55.

Ling, Trevor. *The Buddha.* Baltimore: Penguin, 1973.

Luk, Charles. *Ch'an and Zen Teachings.* 3 vols. London: Rider, 1960-62.

———. *The Transmission of the Mind Outside the Teaching.* New York: Grove, 1975.

———. *The Vimalakirti Nirdesa Sutra.* Berkeley, Calif.: Shambhala, 1972.

McNaughton, William. *The Taoist Vision.* Ann Arbor: University of Michigan, 1971.

Miura, Isshu, and Ruth Fuller Sasaki. *Zen Dust.* New York: Harcourt, Brace & World, 1966.

Morris, Ivan. *The World of the Shining Prince: Court Life in Ancient Japan.* New York: Knopf, 1964.

Munro, Donald J. *The Concept of Man in Early China.* Stanford, Calif.: Stanford University Press, 1969.

Nishimura, Eshin. *Unsui: A Diary of Zen Monastic Life.* Honolulu: University Press of Hawaii, 1973.

Nishiyama, Kosen, and John Stevens. *Shobogenzo: The Eye and Treasury of the True Law.* New York: Weatherhill, 1977.

Ogata, Sohaku. *Zen for the West.* New York: Dial, 1959.

Pardue, Peter A. *Buddhism: A Historical Introduction to Buddhist Values and the Social and Political Forms they have Assumed in Asia.* New York: Macmillan, 1971.

Price, A. F., and Wong Mou-Lam, trans. *The Diamond Sutra and the Sutra of Hui Neng.* Berkeley, Calif.: Shambhala, 1969.

Pullyblank, Edwin. *The Background of the Rebellion of An Lu-shan.* London: 1955.

Ramanan, K. Venkata. *Nagarjuna's Philosophy.* New Delhi: Motilal Banarsidass, 1975.

Reichelt, Karl Ludvig. *Truth and Tradition in Chinese Buddhism.* New York: Paragon, 1968.

Reischauer, Edwin O. *Ennin's Travels in T'ang China.* New York: Ronald Press, 1955.

———. *Japan: Past and Present,* 3rd. ed. New York: Knopf. 1964.

Reps, Paul, ed. *Zen Flesh, Zen Bones.* Rutland and Tokyo: Tuttle, 1957.

Robinson, Richard H. *The Buddhist Religion*. (Revised Edition) Belmont, California: Dickenson Publishing Co., Inc., 1970.

————. Review of *Buddhism in Chinese History*, by Arthur F. Wright, *Journal of American Oriental Society*, 79, 4 (October-December, 1959), pp. 313–38.

Sanford, James. "Zen-Man Ikkyu." Ph.D. dissertation, Harvard University, 1972. (Obtainable only from James Sanford, Department of Religion, University of North Carolina, Chapel Hill, N. C. 27514.)

Sansom, George B. *A History of Japan*. 3 vols. Stanford, Calif.: Stanford University Press, 1958–63.

Sasaki, Ruth Fuller, trans. *The Recorded Sayings of Ch'an Master Lin-chi Hui-chao of Chen Prefecture*. Kyoto: Institute for Zen Studies, 1975.

————, Yoshitaka Iriya, and Dana R. Fraser. *The Recorded Sayings of Layman P'ang: A Ninth-Century Zen Classic*. New York: Weatherhill, 1971.

Sato, Koji. *The Zen Life*. New York: Weatherhill/Tankosha, 1977.

Saunders, E. Dale. *Buddhism in Japan*. Philadelphia: University of Pennsylvania Press, 1964.

Schloegl, Irmgard, trans. *The Zen Teachings of Rinzai*. Berkeley, Calif.: Shambhala, 1976.

Sekida, Katsuki, trans. *Two Zen Classics: Mumonkan & Hekiganroku*. New York: Weatherhill, 1977.

Shafer, Edward. "The Last Years of Ch'ang-an." *Oriens Extremus*, 2 (October 1963), pp. 133–79.

Shaw, R. D. M. *The Embossed Teakettle*. London: Allen & Unwin, 1963.

————, trans. *The Blue Cliff Records*. London: Michael Joseph, 1961.

Shibayama, Zenkei. *Zen Comments on the Mumonkan*. Trans. Sumiko Kudo. New York: Harper & Row, 1974.

Shoko, Watanabe. *Japanese Buddhism: A Critical Appraisal*. Tokyo: Japanese Cultural Society, 1970.

Smith, D. Howard. *Chinese Religions*. New York: Holt, Rinehart and Winston, 1968.

Snyder, Gary. "Han-shan," in Cyril Birch, ed., *Anthology of Chinese Literature*. New York: Grove, 1965.

Stevens, John. *One Robe One Bowl: The Zen Poetry of Ryokan*. New York: Weatherhill, 1977.

Streng, Frederick J. *Emptiness: A Study in Religious Meaning*. Nashville: Abingdon, 1967.

Suzuki, Daisetz T. *Essays in Zen Buddhism* (First Series). London: Rider, 1949; paperback edition, New York: Grove, 1961.

————. *Essays in Zen Buddhism* (Second Series). London: Rider, 1953; paperback edition, New York: Weiser, 1971.

————. *Essays in Zen Buddhism* (Third Series). London: Rider, 1953; paperback edition, New York: Weiser, 1971.

————. *The Lankavatara Sutra*. London: Routledge & Kegan Paul, 1968.

————. *Manual of Zen Buddhism*. New York: Grove, 1960.

————. *Sengai: The Zen Master*. Greenwich, Conn.: New York Graphic Society, 1971.

————. *Studies in the Lankavatara Sutra*. London: Routledge & Kegan Paul, 1930.

———. *Zen and Japanese Culture*. Princeton, N. J.: Princeton University Press, 1959.

———. *The Zen Doctrine of No Mind*. New York: Weiser, 1972.

———. *The Zen Monk's Life*. Kyoto: Eastern Buddhist Society, 1934; paperback edition, New York: Olympia, 1972.

Trevor, H. M., trans. *The Ox and His Herdsman, A Chinese Zen Text*. Tokyo: Hokuseido, 1969.

Twitchett, Denis. "Monastic Estates in T'ang China," *Asia Major*, 5 (1955–56), pp. 123–46.

Varley, H. Paul. *Imperial Restoration in Medieval Japan*. New York: Columbia University Press, 1971.

———. *The Onin War*. New York: Columbia University Press, 1967.

———. *Samurai*. New York: Delacorte, 1970; paperback edition, New York: Dell, 1972.

Walcy, Arthur. *The Analects of Confucius*. New York: Vintage, 1938.

———. *The Book of Songs*. New York: Grove, 1937.

———. *The Life and Times of Po Chü-I*. London: Allen & Unwin, 1949.

———. *The Poetry and Career of Li Po*. London: Allen & Unwin, 1950.

———. *Three Ways of Thought in Ancient China*. New York: Doubleday, undated reprint of 1939 edition.

———. *Translations from the Chinese*. New York: Vintage, 1968.

———. "27 Poems by Han-shan." *Encounter*, 3, 3 (September 1954), p. 3.

———. *The Way and Its Power: A Study of the Tao Te Ching and Its Place in Chinese Thought*. New York: Grove Press, 1958.

Waltham, Clae. *Chuang-Tzu: Genius of the Absurd*. New York: Ace, 1971.

Watson, Burton. *Chinese Lyricism*. New York: Columbia University Press, 1971.

———. *Cold Mountain*. New York: Columbia University Press, 1970.

———. *Ryokan: Zen Monk-Poet of Japan*. New York: Columbia University Press, 1977.

———, trans. *The Complete Works of Chuang Tzu*. New York: Columbia University Press, 1968.

Weber, Max. *The Religion of China*. New York: Free Press, 1951.

Welch, Holmes. *Taoism: The Parting of the Way*. Boston: Beacon Press, 1957.

Wilhelm, Richard, trans. *The Secret of the Golden Flower*. New York: Harcourt, Brace, 1931.

Wright, Arthur F. "Buddhism and Chinese Culture: Phases of Interaction," *Journal of Asian Studies*, 18 (1957–58) pp. 17–42.

———. *Buddhism in Chinese History*. Stanford: Stanford University Press, 1959.

Wu, John C. H. *The Golden Age of Zen*. Taipei, Taiwan: Committee on Compilation of the Chinese Library, 1967.

Wu, Chi-yu. "A Study of Han Shan." *T'oung Pao*, 4-5 (1957).

Yamada, Koun. *Gateless Gate*. Los Angeles: Center Publications, 1979.

Yampolsky, Philip B. *The Platform Sutra of the Sixth Patriarch*. New York: Columbia University Press, 1967.

———, trans. *The Zen Master Hakuin: Selected Writings*. New York: Columbia University Press, 1971.

Yokol, Yuho. *Zen Master Dogen*. New York: Weatherhill, 1976.

INDEX

Numbers in italics refer to illustrations

Ⓟ